TOURISM SUPPLY CHAIN MANAGEMENT

Fierce global competition in the tourism industry is now focused on integral parts of supply chains rather than on individual firms. The highly competitive environment has forced tourism firms to look for ways to enhance their competitive advantage. Tourism products are often viewed by consumers as a value–added chain of different service components and identifying ways to effectively manage the inter-related tourism business operations will enable tourism firms to better meet customer needs and accomplish business goals, thus maintaining competitive advantage over their equally efficient rivals.

This significant and timely volume is the first to apply supply chain management theories and practices in the context of tourism. By doing so the book offers insight into the relationships between tourism enterprises, how coordination across organisations can be effectively achieved and how business performance can be improved. It provides comprehensive and systematic coverage of modern supply chain management concepts and methodologies applied to the tourism and hospitality industries. The text covers key issues and principles, including marketing and product development, demand forecasting, supplier selection and management, distribution channels, capacity management, customer relationship management, tourism supply chain competition and coordination, and eTourism.

The book combines essential theory and comparative international examples based on primary research to show challenges and opportunities of effective tourism supply chain management. This text is essential for final year undergraduate and postgraduate students studying tourism management, tourism planning and tourism economics.

Haiyan Song is Chair Professor of Tourism in the School of Hotel and Tourism Management, The Hong Kong Polytechnic University.

Routledge Advances in Tourism

Edited by Stephen Page, London Metropolitan University, UK

TOURISM SUPPLY CHAIN MANAGEMENT

Haiyan Song

Routledge
Taylor & Francis Group

LONDON AND NEW YORK

First edition published 2012
by Routledge
2 Park Square, Milton Park, Abingdon, OX14 4RN

Simultaneously published in the USA and Canada
by Routledge
711 Third Avenue, New York, NY 10017

Routledge is an imprint of the Taylor & Francis Group, an informa business

British Library Cataloguing in Publication Data
A catalogue record for this book is available from the British Library

Library of Congress Cataloging in Publication Data
Song, Haiyan.
    Tourism supply chain management/Haiyan Song.
        p. cm.
    Includes bibliographical references and index.
    1. Tourism—Management. 2. Hospitality industry—Management.
    3. Business logistics. I. Title.
    G155.A1S594 2011
    910.68'7—dc22   2011009567

ISBN: 978–0–415–58155–4 (hbk)
ISBN: 978–0–415–58156–1 (pbk)
ISBN: 978–0–203–80439–1 (ebk)

Typeset in Bembo and Stone Sans by
Florence Production Ltd, Stoodleigh, Devon

Printed and bound in Great Britain by the MPG Books Group

CONTENTS

FIGURES

TABLES

PREFACE

I am pleased to see *Tourism Supply Chain Management* finally published. From inception to publication, this project has lasted for almost two years. The reason it has taken so long to complete is that I was Associate Director of the School of Hotel and Tourism Management at The Hong Kong Polytechnic University when the project started, and my administrative responsibilities made it very difficult to find chunks of time to concentrate on writing. Fortunately, I have been able to off-load most of my administrative duties over the past six months to allow greater concentration on the book. With the help of several individuals, I was able to complete the book just after Chinese New Year in the Year of the Rabbit. According to Chinese tradition, the Year of the Rabbit confers good luck and happiness. I am certainly very happy that this book is finally being printed.

Tourism supply chain management (TSCM) is an important area for study. In practice, hotels, airlines, retail shops and destination governments are practising supply chain management with great success. Published research on the topic, however, is limited. The gap that exists between academic research and practice in TSCM is an unnecessary one. Two years ago, I had a discussion with Professor Stephen Page, the editor of the *Routledge Advances in Tourism* series, about my plan to write a book on TSCM to fill this gap. He encouraged me to come up with a book proposal, which was subsequently read by several reviewers who provided very positive feedback and recommended publication of the book. I am very grateful for Professor Page's enthusiastic support. Without his encouragement, this book would not even have been started. I would also like to take this opportunity to thank a few others who helped me in preparing the book. First, I would like to thank Alina Zhang, Yang Shu, Chen Wanli and Li Wenli for their invaluable assistance in preparing the initial draft. Second, I would also like to thank Stephen Witt and Candy Li, who proofread the entire manuscript. The financial support from the School of Hotel and Tourism Management at The Hong Kong

Polytechnic University is also kindly acknowledged. Last, and most importantly, this book is dedicated to Jing, Carol and Scott in gratitude for their unconditional love and support for my work.

As this book represents a first attempt to bring together TSCM theories and practices, I have to admit that its coverage is incomplete, with further work needed in such areas as tourism supply chain (TSC) configuration and network design, TSCM outsourcing, the measurement issues surrounding TSC performance and TSC financial flows. It is my hope that this book will stimulate future research in these areas.

Haiyan Song
12 February 2011
Hong Kong

LIST OF ABBREVIATIONS

ADLM	autoregressive distributed lag model
ADR	average daily rate
AIC	Akaike information criterion
AIDS	almost ideal demand system
ANN	artificial neural networks
AR	autoregressive
ARIMA	autoregressive integrated moving average
ARMA	autoregressive moving average
ATPCO	Airline Tariff Publishing Company
B2B	business to business
B2C	business to customer
CNTA	China National Tourism Administration
CRM	customer relationship management
CRS	computer reservation system
CSM	customer service management
CVRM	customer value requirement map
EDI	electronic data interchange
ES	environmental scanning
ETL	extract–transport–load
FAQs	frequently asked questions
FB	food and beverage
FIT	foreign independent traveller
GDS	global distribution system
GIS	geographical information system
GSM	global system for mobile communication
GT	game theory
HA	accommodation providers

HIS	hotel information system
HKDL	Hong Kong Disneyland
HKOP	Hong Kong Ocean Park
HRM	human resource management
HTTP	hypertext transfer protocol
ICT	information communication technologies
IIS	internet information server
IT	information technology
IVS	individual visit scheme
LTO	local tourism organisation
MA	moving average
NTO	national tourism organisation
OAG	Official Airline Guide
ODBC	open database connectivity
OLS	ordinary least squares
OWC	office web component
PDA	personal digital assistant
PMS	property management system
RDBMS	relational database management system
RevMax	revenue maximisation
RTO	regional tourism organisation
SARIMA	seasonal autoregressive integrated moving average
SCM	supply chain management
SIC	Schwarz information criterion
SITA	Société Internationale Télécomminications Aéronautiques
SMTE	small- and medium-sized tourism enterprises
SOAP	simple object access protocol
TO	tour operators
TP	theme park
TS	tourist satisfaction
TSC	tourism supply chain
TSCM	tourism supply chain management
TVP	time-varying parameter
UNWTO	United Nations World Tourism Organisation
VAR	vector autoregressive
VMI	vendor management inventory
VTC	virtual travel community
WAP	wireless application protocol
WDW	Walt Disney World
XML	extensible markup language

1

INTRODUCTION TO TOURISM SUPPLY CHAIN MANAGEMENT[1]

Learning objectives

After reading this chapter you will be able to:

1 Understand the basic background of Tourism Supply Chain Management (TSCM) Issues.
2 Familiarise with the current status and future directions of TSCM research.
3 Understand some of the basic concepts and theoretical framework of TSCM.

This chapter highlights the background of supply chain management (SCM) research and practice within the context of tourism. SCM in the manufacturing industry has attracted widespread research interests over the past two decades while SCM studies in the tourism industry are very limited. Stakeholders in the tourism industry interact with each other to resolve their divergent business objectives with different operating scopes. The potential benefit of considering not only individual enterprises but also the tourism value chain becomes evident. The chapter examines the characteristics of tourism products and identifies and explores core issues and concepts in tourism supply chains (TSCs) and tourism supply chain management (TSCM). While the literature on TSCM or its equivalents emerges recently, the progress is variable with most research being focused on distribution and marketing activities, without fully considering the whole range of different suppliers involved in the provision and consumption of tourism products.

This chapter provides a systematic review of current tourism studies from the TSCM perspective and develops a framework for TSCM research which should be of great value, not only to those who wish to extend their research into this new and exciting area, but also to tourism and hospitality decision makers. The chapter also identifies key research questions in TSCM worthy of future theoretical and empirical explorations.

1.1 Background

During the last two decades, the tourism industry has evolved and modernised considerably. The highly competitive environment of the tourism industry has forced tourism firms to look for ways to enhance their competitive advantage. For example, there has been considerable growth in the implementation of new information technologies and the development of new commercial formats such as eTourism. In addition to these technological measures, one of the strategies that tourism firms could adopt to increase their competitiveness is effective tourism supply chain management. Although academics have debated whether or not tourism can be viewed as an industry, the term *tourism industry* is used throughout this book as it is commonly used by both researchers and practitioners in the tourism field.

Adversarial relationships are the norm in the tourism industry (Sinclair and Stabler, 1997), but TSCM entails a new perspective. TSCM can be referred to as a set of approaches utilised to efficiently manage the operations of the tourism supply chain within a specific tourism destination to meet tourist needs from the targeted source markets and accomplish the business objectives of different enterprises within the TSC. This TSCM philosophy requires moving away from arms-length relationships towards coordination across organisations throughout a TSC.

Tourism products are often viewed by consumers as a value-added chain of different service components, forming a service network. Therefore, identifying ways to manage this network is vital, especially for large tourism firms that are keen to maintain a competitive advantage over their equally efficient rivals. Many tourism researchers have used a systematic approach from the marketing perspective to investigate tourism distribution channels, including Buhalis (2000), Middleton and Clarke (2001), Pearce and Schott (2005), Stuart *et al.* (2005) and Pearce *et al.* (2007).

The supply side of the tourism industry, however, has been largely neglected (Sinclair and Stabler, 1997). Whereas distribution channels involve promotional and marketing activities, supply networks involve inter-firm relationships and product development. The lack of attention to supply networks is not unique to tourism. Most service industries also emphasise marketing over supply (Smith, 1994). This situation is in contrast to that of the manufacturing industry, in which product development and the actions of interrelated firms have generated a considerable number of published studies.

Despite the focus on distribution channels, the improvement of the distribution side seems to be insufficient to benefit the single tourism enterprise or the tourism industry as a whole. There is a need to analyse the entire industry from an integrative perspective, that is, as a tourism supply chain. Until very recently, studies of TSCs or their equivalents, such as the tourism value chains or tourism industry chains, have been limited. Examples include Kaukal *et al.* (2000), Page (2003), Tapper and Font (2004), Alford (2005) and Yilmaz and Bititci (2006).

Supply chain management is a concept that originated from and flourished in the manufacturing industry. Comparatively little research attention has been paid to SCM in the tourism industry. The paucity of research is surprising considering the amount of SCM research in other service industries, such as the retail industry. Retail researchers and practitioners have investigated SCM strategies to counter the increasing uncertainty and complexity of the marketplace and increase efficiency by reducing inventories along the entire supply chain (Ellram *et al.*, 1989; Fernie, 1995; Tan, 2001; Gimenez and Ventura, 2003; Hugos and Thomas, 2006). Researchers have also discussed inventory management policies, such as vendor management inventory (VMI) solutions, which were popularised by Wal-Mart and Procter & Gamble (Waller *et al.*, 1999), the application of information technologies (Kämäräinen and Punakivi, 2002; Prater *et al.*, 2005), information sharing and supply chain coordination (Clark *et al.*, 2001; Hill and Scudder, 2002; Han *et al.*, 2002; Hornibrook and Fearne, 2002), supply chain relationships (Fearne, 2000; Duffy and Fearne, 2004) and collaborative forecasting (Småros, 2007).

It is believed that SCM practices that are successful in other industries should be useful in the tourism industry. The key is to determine the SCM issues that are beneficial to the tourism industry, bearing in mind its specific nature and characteristics. Because of the complex interactions among numerous stakeholders in the tourism industry, who have divergent objectives and scopes, the potential benefits of adopting best practices of TSCM would be huge.

An examination of the existing studies shows that there is an emergent literature on TSCM or its equivalents in recent years, especially from the perspective of tourism distribution channels. However, consensus has not yet been reached on how best to characterise a TSC and the limited literature cannot provide guidance for tourism and hospitality researchers and managers. The need for clearly defined conceptions and conceptual frameworks becomes apparent to advance the field. In the process of developing a common framework, we examine and consolidate published studies on tourism management related to the diverse issues mentioned above. The contributions from the various studies exist in isolation, but they have many of the critical elements necessary for successful TSCM.

1.2 Supply chain management in tourism

Overview of supply chain management

The fierce global competition in the twenty-first century is focused on supply chains rather than on individual companies. From a macro perspective, a supply chain is a network of enterprises which are engaged in different functions ranging from the supply of raw materials through to the production and delivery of the end-product to the target customers. From a micro perspective of a firm, a supply chain is a network of nodes which perform functions such as procurement of raw materials, fabrication of parts, assembly of components and subassemblies, final assembly of end products and delivery of finished products to regional distribution centres/customers. A supply chain is characterised by a forward flow of goods and a backward flow of information. It is comprised of seven main business processes: customer relationship management, customer service management, demand management, order fulfilment, manufacturing flow management, procurement, product development and commercialisation (Cooper et al., 1997).

Although there is no systematic way of defining the scope of a *firm-specific* supply chain problem, there is a simple guideline proposed by Simchi-Levi et al. (2003). This guideline is based on the three levels of decision hierarchy: (1) strategic level; (2) tactical level; (3) operational level. The classes of supply chain problems encountered in strategic level involve decisions concerning long-term issues such as demand planning, strategic alliances, new product development, outsourcing, supplier selection, pricing and network configuration decisions. Although most supply chain problems are strategic by nature, there are also some tactical problems which involve medium-term decisions such as inventory control, production/distribution coordination, material handling and equipment selection. The problems which fall into the operational level concern weekly or daily events such as vehicle scheduling, routing, workforce allocation and process planning.

The concept of supply chain management has been used extensively for manufactured products to improve the efficiency across the value chain of, for example, logistics and planning activities and materials and information control, internally within a company or externally between companies (Christopher, 1992; Cooper et al., 1997; Fisher, 1997). Since being coined by Houlihan in 1985 (Houlihan, 1985), the term supply chain management has been advocated for the last two decades. Despite the popularity of the term both in academia and practice, there is no commonly accepted definition. The most popular definition of supply chain management is given by Simchi-Levi et al. (2003) as:

> a set of approaches utilized to efficiently integrate suppliers, manufacturers, warehouses, and stores, so that merchandise is produced and distributed at the right quantities, to the right locations, and at the right time, in order to minimize system-wide costs while satisfying service level requirements.

The key concern in SCM philosophy is to recognise the interdependency in the supply chain and thereby generate strategies that support the efficient integration of the various links. Thus, SCM takes a system approach to viewing the supply chain as a whole (Simchi-Levi et al., 2003) and emphasises the need for the integration of various links of the chain (Cooper et al., 1997; Lambert et al., 1998). Various subject areas, such as strategic, inter-organisational issues (Cox, 1997; Harland et al., 1999), vertical integration (Thorelli, 1986; Hakansson and Snehota, 1995), supplier relationship (Helper, 1991; Hines, 1994; Narus and Anderson, 1995) and purchasing and supply (Morgan and Monczka, 1996; Farmer, 1997), have contributed to the explosion of SCM literature. There also exists a number of surveys of SCM literature published in academic journals (see, for example, Min and Zhou (2002), Tan (2001) and Ganeshan *et al.* (1999)).

Concept of tourism supply chain

From the myriad of research on SCM, it can be seen that much of the literature focuses on the manufacturing industry with little attention being paid to the service sector. From the perspective of the tourism industry, this lack of attention is somewhat surprising. As early as 1975, the United Nations World Tourism Organization (UNWTO) published a report on the distribution channels of the tourism industry (UNWTO, 1975). The term *distribution channel* is a supply chain in a different guise. It could be narrowly defined as a supply chain that focuses mainly on the distribution and marketing activities in the chain.

The attention from the academic community on supply chains in tourism does not increase in pace with the rapid development of tourism industry in recent decades. Nevertheless, there have appeared several studies on supply chains in tourism, including UNWTO (1994), Sinclair and Stabler (1997), Buhalis and Laws (2001) and Page (2003). Sinclair and Stabler (1997) emphasise the importance of the supply side of tourism industry. *Tourism Distribution Channels: Practices, Issues and Transformations*, a key text edited by Buhalis and Laws (2001), consists of twenty-three chapters written by various contributors and many of these chapters are related to the distribution networks in the tourism industry. Page (2003) notably points out that the provision of tourism products and services involves a wide range of interrelated tourism suppliers and plots a structure of a tourism supply chain. The supply chains in tourism have not been extensively examined and have only gained increasing attention recently. Exceptions include Scavarda *et al.* (2001), Tapper and Font (2004), Alford (2005) and Yilmaz and Bititci (2006). However, the research does not go beyond descriptive studies.

Although literature of tourism supply chains is scarce, some authors have alluded to or touched on the concept or its equivalents, such as the tourism value chains or tourism industry chains. Kaukal *et al.* (2000) note that a typical tourism value chain consists of four components: tourism supplier, tour operator, travel agent and customer, and they are in a single-link chain. Alford (2005) presents a visual presentation of the tourism supply chain produced by Business and Cost Analysis Working Group in order to analyse pressure points where costs can be stripped out. Yilmaz and Bititci (2006) develop a tourism value chain concept to manage the tourism product as an end-to-end seamless product. In their report, Tapper and Font (2004) define a TSC as a chain that:

> comprises the suppliers of all the goods and services that go into the delivery of tourism products to consumers.

According to Porter (1980), every industry has an underlying structure, or a set of fundamental economic and technical characteristics, that gives rise to its operational and competitive characteristics. That is, every supply chain varies according to the type of products supplied. Thus, identifying the features of the tourism industry and its products is of great importance when describing a TSC. For instance, tourism products are normally rooted in a specific territory and provided to tourists from a specific source market, so they often vary according to destinations and source markets. Based on the existing definitions of TSCs in the literature and taking into consideration the characteristics of the tourism industry, the following definition of a TSC is advanced.

> A tourism supply chain (TSC) can be defined as a network of tourism organizations supplying different components of tourism products/services such as flights and accommodation for the distribution and marketing of the final tourism products at a specific tourism destination, and involves a wide range of participants in both the private and public sectors.

Supply chain management in tourism

To understand the key challenges faced by the successful management of TSC, the characteristics of tourism products and the tourism industry are of central importance. As part of the services sector of the global economy, tourism possesses a number of distinguished characteristics that are different from the manufacturing and primary sectors. Six characteristics of tourism can be observed, as follows.

First, tourism is a *coordination-intensive* industry where different products/services (transportation, accommodation, etc.) are bundled together to form a final tourism product. Second, as service cannot be stored for future use, tourism as a product is *perishable*. Third, tourists need to travel to the destinations where tourism products are produced to consume these products. Tourism products cannot normally be examined prior to their purchase, which means that the sale of tourism products is very much dependent upon the presentation and interpretation of the products. Therefore, the tourism industry is a very *information-intensive* or information-dependent industry (Ujma, 2001). Fourth, tourism products are *complex* in nature. Normally, they are heterogeneous and compound, consisting of many different service components such as accommodation, transportation, sightseeing, dining and shopping. Finally, the tourism industry often faces higher *demand uncertainty* and more complex *dynamics* than its counterparts because of intensive competition among service providers. Many factors contribute to market uncertainty in terms of the demand for tourism products. For example, effective advertising can attract more tourists whereas negative word-of-mouth effect can lead to a fall in demand. The economic conditions in tourist-generating countries and regions often serve as a push factor, influencing the demand for tourism products in a particular destination.

Based on these characteristics of the tourism industry, the following seven key management TSCM issues are identified: demand management, two-party relationships, supply management, inventory management, product development, TSC

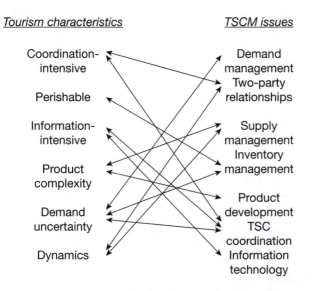

Tourism characteristics   *TSCM issues*

FIGURE 1.1 Tourism characteristics and related TSCM issues

coordination and information technology. These key TSCM issues are discussed in greater detail in the following sections.

1.3 Critical issues in TSCM

To facilitate a better understanding of both the critical elements and activities associated with TSCM research, a framework that provides a coherent view of these essentials is provided in Figure 1.2. The development and justification of the framework is presented in greater detail in section 1.4. Critical issues in TSCM are carefully analysed as they contribute to the core of TSCM research.

Demand management

Demand management is a vital part of SCM that links the processes within the chain. Generally speaking, demand management includes demand forecasting, marketing and sales planning based on the projected demand and service/ production capacity.

Demand management is crucial in successfully implementing TSCM. From a strategic point of view, tourism investment decision making, especially investment in destination infrastructures such as airports, highways and rail-links, relies on demand estimation as it requires long-term financial commitment, and the sunk costs can be very high if investment projects fail to fulfil their designed capacities. In addition, government macroeconomic policies largely depend on the relative importance of individual sectors within a destination. From the operational point of view, the activities of supply chain members such as airlines, tour operators, hotels, cruise ship lines and recreation facility providers are directly driven by tourism demand. The success of many businesses depends largely or entirely on the state of tourism demand and market failure is quite often due to the failure of the firms to meet the market demand. Because of the key role of demand as a determinant of business profitability, estimates of expected future demand constitute a very important element in all TSC planning activities.

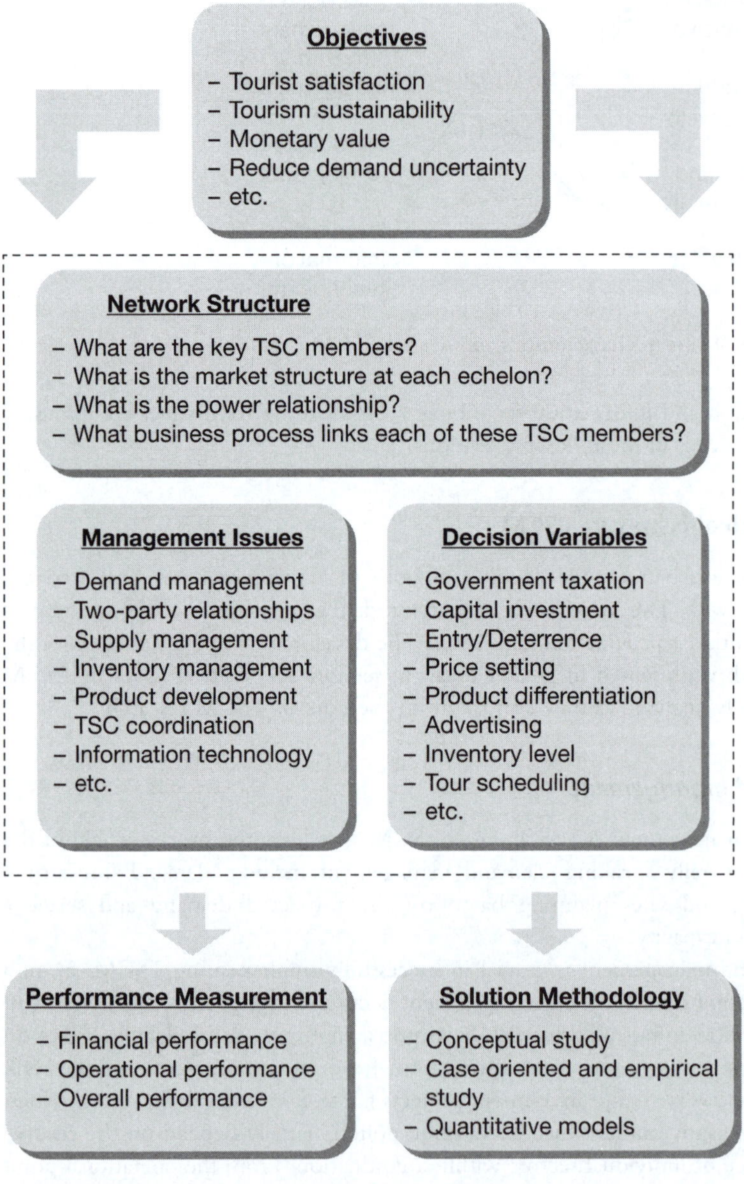

Objectives
- Tourist satisfaction
- Tourism sustainability
- Monetary value
- Reduce demand uncertainty
- etc.

Network Structure
- What are the key TSC members?
- What is the market structure at each echelon?
- What is the power relationship?
- What business process links each of these TSC members?

Management Issues
- Demand management
- Two-party relationships
- Supply management
- Inventory management
- Product development
- TSC coordination
- Information technology
- etc.

Decision Variables
- Government taxation
- Capital investment
- Entry/Deterrence
- Price setting
- Product differentiation
- Advertising
- Inventory level
- Tour scheduling
- etc.

Performance Measurement
- Financial performance
- Operational performance
- Overall performance

Solution Methodology
- Conceptual study
- Case oriented and empirical study
- Quantitative models

FIGURE 1.2 Theoretical framework for TSCM research

As an important area in the tourism-related literature, tourism demand forecasting has attracted considerable research interest. According to a comprehensive review by Li *et al.* (2005b), about 420 studies on this topic were published during the 1960–2002 period. Most studies of tourism demand forecasting are based on statistical methods, especially econometric and time-series approaches (for detailed reviews of the tourism demand forecasting literature, see, for example, Witt and Witt (1995), Li *et al.* (2005b), Song and Li (2008)). Although many advanced quantitative demand forecasting models have been developed in the literature, tourism practitioners usually have little interest in scholarly journals, so they are either unfamiliar with modern forecasting methods that have been presented in the literature or simply do not have the time to be involved in the design and development of such advanced models to generate more accurate forecasts. Hence, a new kind of forecasting mechanism that can facilitate the mutual transfer of information and knowledge between the experts in tourism forecasting and practitioners in the tourism industry is highly desirable.

For a TSC to be managed effectively, demand management clearly has to have at least some kind of centralised position in the entire chain. In recent years, collaborative supply chain forecasting has become popular. The value of collaborative forecasting lies in the broad exchange of information to improve forecasting accuracy when the supply chain members collaborate through joint knowledge of sales promotions, pricing strategies, marketing and production information. Although there is a wide body of literature concerning collaborative forecasting within supply chains for physical goods, it has not yet been considered in the tourism literature. The study of Song *et al.* (2008) is the only exception.

Two-party relationships

The term *supply chain* implies two-party relationships in which all tourism organisations have relationships with other entities such as suppliers, distributors, competitors, partners, governments and other firms carrying out complementary activities, to better accomplish their operations and fulfil customer needs. For this reason, the effective management of two-party relationships within a TSC is a crucial issue in TSCM.

Relationships in a supply chain are categorised into two groups according to their direction – vertical relationships and horizontal relationships. Vertical relationships exist among heterogeneous players who do not have overlap capability. An example is a travel agency's relationship with its suppliers. In contrast, horizontal relationships concern homogeneous players in the same echelon of the supply chain who usually have overlapping capabilities. An example is the relationship between two hotels supplying similar hotel accommodation. According to the market structure of each echelon within the supply chain as well as the power and dependency between each player and the number of players, the relationships can be classified into four types: many-to-many, one-to-many, many-to-one and one-to-one relationships. Additionally, the relationships in a supply chain can take a variety of forms, such as arm's length, strategic alliance, vertical integration, cooperation, coordination and competition.

Effective supply chain management, therefore, relies greatly on the success of relationship management. As mentioned, a TSC is a complex network involving a wide range of sectors, each of which has its own market structure. Tourism organisations need to consider not only their market structure but also that of others. In addition, a very important phenomenon in the tourism industry is its dynamic structure, which allows the players to change business partners from time to time to maximise their profitability and competitiveness. For example, the relationships between governments and tourism firms, and between tourists and the environment, evolve over time. The involvement of various players together with the evolving TSC relationships makes relationship management in a TSC even more difficult. However, a good understanding of the relationships in a TSC is helpful and critical to achieving efficient and effective TSCM.

In tourism research, significant efforts have been directed to understanding the relationships in the industry. Existing studies cover topics including integration in TSCs (Theuvsen, 2004; Lafferty and Fossen, 2001), competition issues related to hotels (Chung, 2000; García and Tugores, 2006; Mazzeo, 2002), tour operators (Baum and Mudambi, 1994; Taylor, 1996; Caccomo and Solonandrasana, 2001), attractions (Wie, 2004, 2005; Candela and Cellini, 2006), relationships between the local government and tourism organisations (Piga, 1999, 2003a, 2003b; Accinelli *et al.*, 2006a), tour operators and destinations (Baloglu and Mangaloglu, 2001; Carey *et al.*, 1997; Curtin and Busby, 1999; Klemm and Parkinson, 2001), tourism organisations and tourists (Taylor, 1998; Han *et al.*, 2004); and the evolutionary relationships between tourists and residents (Accinelli *et al.*, 2006b; Bimonte and Punzo, 2007). A review of the literature shows that attention has tended to concentrate on competitive interactions between tourism firms, which may reflect the current position in many tourism markets. Tour operators often have market power to directly interact with tourists and therefore play a key role in the development of sustainable TSCs in the destinations. Theuvsen (2004) points out that coordination among enterprises could benefit the tourism industry.

Supply management

Supply management emphasises the buyer–supplier relationship in a supply chain (Leenders *et al.*, 2002). Because suppliers have a profound impact on the costs and quality of the buying firms in supply chains, supply management has been of great interest to SCM researchers. Topics of supply management include long-term relations, supplier selection, supplier base reduction, supplier involvement and supplier certification (Chen and Paulraj, 2004). Although there are a few tourism studies that have addressed supply management issues, these studies are scattered and lack a clear focus. Existing studies of supply management in the tourism industry fall into three broad categories: (1) the relationships between suppliers (hotels, resorts, attractions and airlines) and travel agencies/tour operators; (2) the relationships between wholesale and retail travel agencies; and (3) supplier selection problems.

Research into supply management in tourism has focused on the relationship between tour operators and hotels (March, 1997; García-Falcón and Medina-Muñoz, 1999; Buhalis, 2000; Karamustafa, 2000; Medina-Muñoz and García-Falcón, 2000; Medina-Muñoz et al., 2002, 2003; Tse, 2003; Bastakis et al., 2004). March (1997) finds that Australian travel suppliers are extremely dependent upon travel buyers. García-Falcón and Medina-Muñoz (1999) examine the diversity in and major characteristics of the relationships between hotels and travel agencies in the United States through an empirical survey. The results show that having good relationships with travel agents is an important element for the success of hotels. Karamustafa (2000) notes that hotels in Turkey depend heavily on package tour operators and that the success of hoteliers relies on the willingness of tour operators to work with the local lodging industry. Buhalis (2000) studies conflict in the relationships between hotels and tour operators in the context of Mediterranean summer seaside resorts through in-depth interviews. He finds that Mediterranean hotels consider the market power of tour operators from North European countries very challenging. Medina-Muñoz and García-Falcón (2000) are the first to try to identify the determinants of successful relationships between hotels and travel agencies and the most cost-effective way for a hotel to extend its sales and market-ing efforts. Their empirical results show that trust, commitment, coordination, communication quality, information exchange, participation, use of constructive resolution techniques and similar relative dependence are the key factors that affect successful relationships between hotels and travel agencies. Tse (2003) investigates the relationship between travel agents and hotels when the latter take distribution back into their own hands by setting up websites allowing online bookings. The possible responses of agents are analysed and suggestions for improving the quality of the buyer–supplier relationship are put forward. Medina-Muñoz et al. (2003) look at the control that German and British tour operators exercise over the accommodation companies with whom they do business and the characteristics of the two types of companies that influence the control. The study helps tour operators to gain suitable control over accommodation companies and identifies possible actions to be taken by accommodation providers in improving their relationship with tour operators.

Other studies discuss the relationships between airlines and travel agencies (Alamdari, 2002; Appelman and Go, 2001) and wholesale and retail travel agencies (Tsaur et al., 2006). Alamdari (2002) explores the interactions between airlines and travel agents by analysing the distribution strategies of major carriers in the United States, Europe and Asia. Appelman and Go (2001) describe the beginning of the transformation of the relationships between worldwide airlines and travel agencies engaged in international travel. Tsaur et al. (2006) examine a relational behaviour model between wholesale and retail travel agencies in Taiwan. Several influencing factors of the relationship are identified through surveys.

Selecting suppliers for specific services is critical for most tourism organisations as tourists often view a tourism product as a seamless service. Supply performance can therefore have direct financial and operational impacts on the business.

Recognising this, some tourism researchers investigate supplier selection issues (see, for example, Cobanoglu *et al.*, 2003; March, 2000; Pearce, 2007). Cobanoglu *et al.* (2003) survey 612 Turkish business travellers to determine the importance they place on hotel selection attributes. March (2000) examines the purchasing attitudes of tour operators regarding three types of tourism products: hotels, coach companies and restaurants. He surveys twenty-six inbound tour operators in Asia who deal with inbound tourists to Australia. Pearce (2007) investigates supplier selection in the New Zealand inbound tourism market, especially the factors that lead tour operators to change their suppliers.

Inventory management

Supply chains are classified into two categories: push supply chains and pull supply chains. In push supply chains, the production of a product is authorised based on the demand forecasts ahead of the customer purchases. Demand is forecast based on historical sales data. The demand for products by end users can be met through inventory. In contrast, in pull supply chains the final assembly of the product components is triggered by customer purchasing orders. Good inventories are minimised in pull supply chains. Flexible capacities are required to meet variations in demand. The type of supply chain is determined by the nature of the product produced and the production process. A TSC can be categorised as a push system because the production of tourism products is normally based on demand forecasts. Therefore, inventory plays a key role in a TSC.

Because tourism products are perishable and have relatively high fixed costs that are paid in advance to build up a fixed level of capacity, the variable costs incurred during the production process are relatively low. This makes it difficult for tourism managers to balance supply and demand in the short run by varying production capacity. Additionally, many tourism products are often produced well before the existence of the demand (in the push system) and the demand is usually realised by inventory. That is, demand uncertainty and variation can be treated by inventories, which represent financial expenditures. Therefore, developing effective inventory management strategies is crucial for achieving efficient TSCM.

In a TSC, hotels and airlines often collaborate with a number of tour operators whose offices are located in various destinations. The agreements on inventory allocations from hotels and airlines to different tour operators are usually assigned on a regular basis. In the tourism literature, inventory management problems, such as overbooking and revenue/yield management, have been addressed in the context of the hotel sector (Rothstein, 1974; Liberman and Yechiali, 1978; Lambert *et al.*, 1989; Holder, 1991; Bitran and Mondschein, 1995; Baker and Collier, 1999) and airline sector (Rothstein, 1971, 1985; Shlifer and Vardi, 1975; Belobaba, 1987, 1989; Smith *et al.*, 1992). Overbooking is a practice used to overcome cancellations or no-shows (Rothstein, 1974). Revenue management is a profit maximisation method that 'can help a firm sell the right inventory unit to the right type of customer, at the right time and for the right price' (Kimes, 1989). Weatherford and Bodily (1992) provide a review of research related to the above topics. Studies of TSC inventory issues, however, have not been found.

Product development

SCM aims to satisfy customer needs at the right time with the right products. Therefore, product development plays a critical role in the supply chain. Effective product development can speed time to market, improve the quality of products, reduce production costs and smooth out demand variation. Product development, however, is not an easy task. It is a complex process that requires joint efforts from different players within the supply chain. It also requires a good understanding of customer needs and involves a careful analysis of product components and elements to identify potential products that suit continuously changing consumer tastes.

Although there is a wide body of literature concerning product development in the manufacturing industry, it is a relatively neglected area of research within the tourism context. This lack of attention may be due to the composite nature of tourism products (Smith, 1994). In fact, discussion on tourism product formulations began with Medlik and Middleton (1973). However, with very few exceptions, notably the studies of Smith (1994), Bramwell (1998) and Agarwal et al. (2000), there has been very little analysis of tourism product development, in contrast to the significant efforts made in tourism marketing research.

However, as in all service industries, satisfying customer needs with the appropriate products is of the utmost importance. If tourists are satisfied with a travel product, then they will purchase the product again and there is a better chance that they will recommend it to others (see, for example, Kozak, 2001b; Tian-Cole amd Crompton, 2003). Therefore, the issue of tourism product development is worth further investigation.

TSC coordination

Tourism is a coordination-intensive industry in which different service products (transportation, accommodation, excursions, etc.) are bundled together to form a final tourism product. Coordination is a pattern of decision making and com-munication among a set of interrelated players who perform tasks to achieve goals such as maximising their utilities or the overall profit of the supply chain (Malone, 1987). It requires that each actor within a supply chain perform its task by considering the impact of its actions on the other players. Researchers generally agree that through coordination, redundant activities and repetitive efforts can be reduced to achieve a sustainable and competitive supply chain. For example, many studies of manufacturing supply chains (e.g., Jeuland and Shugan, 1983; Parlar and Wang, 1994; Weng, 1995; Corbett and de Groote, 2000; Chen et al., 2001) show that coordination can result in improved performance and greater profitability for the entire supply chain and its participants.

To maintain a competitive advantage over equally efficient rivals, many large tourism firms have already adopted supply chain coordination strategies (Sinclair and Stabler, 1997; Buhalis and Laws, 2001). Supply chain coordination can take a variety of forms, ranging from full or partial integration of business processes to contractual arrangements between individual firms, either horizontally or vertically. In the context of TSC, coordination occurs between service providers such as hotels and airlines, and tour operators and travel agencies, within the same echelon and/or among different echelons. For example, major European tour operators are highly vertically integrated with airlines, hotels and other travel intermediaries (Theuvsen, 2004). The existing research on TSC coordination reveals that much of the effort has been directed towards full integration. For instance, Gomez and Sinclair (1991) examine the vertical integration and contractual relationships between tourism enterprises in different sectors of TSCs in the UK and Spain through interviews with participants of the major firms in the TSCs. Lafferty and Fossen (2001) discuss both horizontal integration within service sectors and vertical integration between them, particularly in relation to airlines and hotels. Theuvsen (2004) conducts an empirical analysis of the vertical integration of European travel operators and points out that coordination among the operators could greatly benefit the tourism industry.

Unlike their counterparts in manufacturing supply chains, TSC players are heterogeneous organisations that often have conflicting objectives. In this case, full vertical integration is the most apparent and efficient way to achieve coordination. Nevertheless, as Simchi-Levi et al. (2003) point out, achieving full integration in supply chains is never easy. In addition, full integration in TSCs is normally associated with increased fixed costs and reduced flexibility in meeting market changes (Gomez and Sinclair, 1991; Sinclair and Stabler, 1997). Coordination in the form of contractual arrangements between individual firms in a TSC provides a new research opportunity.

Information technology

The salient feature of tourism products is that they usually cannot be examined prior to purchase. Tourists have to travel to the destinations where the tourism products are produced, which means tourists' purchase decisions depend upon the presentation and interpretation of these products. Thus, information is 'the life-blood of the travel industry' (Sheldon, 1994) which holds together activities within the TSC in terms of both inter-firm links and tourism product distributions. It is hardly surprising that since its emergence, information technology (IT) has played a significant role in the tourism industry. Developments such as computer reservation systems (CRSs), global distribution systems (GDSs), the world wide web and the internet have transformed the ways in which tourists travel and tourism firms operate (Bennett, 1993; Buhalis, 2003; Buhalis and Main, 1998; Connolly et al., 1998; Emmer et al., 1993; Klein, 2002; Lu and Lu, 2004; O'Connor, 1999; Prideaux, 2001). Buhalis (1998) provides a framework for the utilisation of IT in tourism by adopting a strategic perspective. Bahaire and Elliott-White (1999) examine the progress that tourism organisations have made towards the application of geographical information systems (GISs) and their integration with sustainable development policies in the UK. Frew (2000) explores the interaction of IT with tourism and provides a research framework to characterise the utilisation of IT in the tourism industry. O'Connor and Murphy (2004) review recent research on information technology in the hospitality industry. More recently, Buhalis and Law (2008) comprehensively review and analyse the published studies in the context of internet applications to tourism over the past twenty years.

In addition to transforming business operations, IT can also enhance the coordination of activities regionally, nationally and globally, thereby creating new opportunities for tourism businesses and enhancing their competitive advantage (Porter and Millar, 1985). As the key driving force for moving material management to supply chain management, IT is found to be an effective means of promoting collaboration between supply chain members and enhancing supply chain efficiency through providing real-time information regarding product availability, inventory levels, shipment status and production requirements (Radstaak and Ketelaar, 1998). It allows upstream TSC suppliers, that is, airlines and hotels, to monitor, manage and control their capacities through communicating with intermediaries, that is, tour operators and travel agencies and tourists. For example, authorised tour operators can access a hotel chain's intranet to see the room rates and availability for their customers. The transparency and communication achieved through IT reduce unit operating costs and enhance firm competitiveness, efficiency, flexibility and cooperation throughout the entire TSC.

Although the literature has been dominated by investigations into how to effectively apply IT to tourism organisations, there is gradually growing interest in the importance and necessity of IT usage in TSCs. Go and Williams (1993) discuss the changes in the tourism channel system in terms of demand and supply and the ways in which IT can affect and market tourism distribution channels. O'Connor et al. (2001) examine the effect of changes in IT on tourism distribution channels and highlight the key areas of concern for tourism suppliers. The impacts of the internet (Wynee et al., 2001) and computer reservation systems (Duliba et al., 2001; Alamdari, 2002) on tourism distribution channels have also been discussed. Recent research on IT emphasises its vast potential to facilitate collaborative planning and forecasting among supply chain partners by sharing information on demand forecasts and production schedules and to dictate supply chain activities (Karoway, 1997). However, to the best of our knowledge, little research has been done in the tourism context except for that of Song et al. (2008).

1.4 Theoretical framework

TSCM is a novel management topic in the tourism industry. Figure 1.2 depicts a theoretical framework for TSCM research. This framework is developed to guide research efforts and provide insights for managerial practice. The theoretical support for the framework is offered below. Because of space limitations, detailed analysis of the relevant literature is omitted. Instead, a brief taxonomy of the literature is given in Table 1.1.

TABLE 1.1 Review of the TSCM literature

Study	Network structure (Region)	Main study area (TSC decision)	Methodology
Accinelli et al. (2006a)	Local government and tourism organisations	Two-party relationship (tourism industry investments)	Quantitative
Accinelli et al. (2006b)	Tourists and residents	Two-party relationship	Conceptual
Alamdari (2002)	Airlines and travel agencies (Asia–Pacific)	Supply management	Empirical
Alford (2005)	The entire TSC (Europe)	Performance measurement	Empirical
Appelman and Go (2001)	Airlines and travel agencies	Supply management	Empirical
Baloglu and Mangaloglu (2001)	Tour operators and the destinations (USA)	Two-party relationship	Empirical
Bastakis et al. (2004)	Hotels and travel agencies (Eastern Mediterranean)	Supply management	Empirical
Baum and Mudambi (1994)	Tour operators (UK)	Two-party relationship (pricing strategy of tour operators)	Quantitative
Bimonte and Punzo (2007)	Tourists and residents	Two-party relationship	Conceptual
Buhalis (2000)	Hotels and tour operators (Mediterranean region)	Supply management	Empirical
Caccomo and Solonandrasana (2001)	Tour operators	Two-party relationship	Quantitative
Campo and Yagüe (2009)	Tour operator, travel, and tourists	Two-party relationship (discounted pricing)	Empirical
Candela and Cellini (2006)	Excursions	Two-party relationship (the amount of investment made by tourism destinations)	Quantitative
Carey et al. (1997)	Tour operators and the destinations (UK)	Two-party relationship	Conceptual
Chung (2000)	Accommodation suppliers	Two-party relationship (pricing strategy of hotel rooms)	Quantitative
Cobanoglu et al. (2003)	Hotels and tourists (Turkey)	Supply management (supplier selection)	Empirical

continued . . .

TABLE 1.1 Review of the TSCM literature . . . *continued*

Study	Network structure (Region)	Main study area (TSC decision)	Methodology
Curtin and Busby (1999)	Tour operators and the destinations (UK)	Two-party relationship	Empirical
Duliba *et al.* (2001)	Airlines and travel agencies	Information technology	Case study
García and Tugores (2006)	Accommodation suppliers	Two-party relationship (choice of quality and prices in hotel services)	Quantitative
García-Falcón and Medina-Muñoz (1999)	Hotels and travel agencies (USA)	Two-party relationship	Empirical
Go and Williams (1993)	The entire TSC	Information technology	Conceptual
Gomez and Sinclair (1991)	Travel agencies and tour operators (UK)	TSC integration	Case study
Hadjinicola and Panayi (1997)	One hotel and multiple tour operators	Supply management (supplier selection)	Quantitative
Han *et al.* (2004)	Tourism organisations and tourists	Two-party relationship (tourist activity planning decisions)	Quantitative
Karamustafa (2000)	Hotels and travel agencies (Turkey)	Supply management	Empirical
Klemm and Parkinson (2001)	Tour operators and the destinations (UK)	Two-party relationship	Conceptual
Lafferty and Fossen (2001)	Hotels and airlines	TSC coordination	Case study
March (1997)	Hotels and travel agencies (Australia)	Supply management	Empirical
March (2000)	Hotels, coach companies, restaurants, and tour operators (Australia)	Supply management (supplier selection)	Empirical
Mazzeo (2002)	Accommodation suppliers (USA)	Two-party relationship (entry and product-type decisions of motels)	Quantitative
Medina-Muñoz and García-Falcón (2000)	Hotels and travel agencies (USA)	Supply management	Empirical
Medina-Muñoz *et al.* (2002, 2003)	Hotels and travel agencies (Europe)	Supply management	Empirical
O'Connor *et al.* (2001)	Airlines/hotels and tour operators	Information technology	Conceptual

continued . . .

TABLE 1.1 Review of the TSCM literature . . . *continued*

Study	Network structure (Region)	Main study area (TSC decision)	Methodology
Page (2003)	The entire TSC	Overall management of TSC	Conceptual
Pearce (2007)	Suppliers of travel products and tour operators (New Zealand)	Supply management (supplier selection)	Empirical
Pearce *et al.* (2007)	Tour operators and travel agencies (New Zealand)	Supply management	Case study
Piga (2003a, 2003b, 1999)	Local government and tourism organisations	Two-party relationship (tourism development tax)	Quantitative
Scavarda *et al.* (2001)	The entire TSC	Performance measurement	
Tapper and Font (2004)	The entire TSC	Overall management of TSC	Conceptual
Taylor (1996)	Tour operators	Two-party relationship	Quantitative
Taylor (1998)	Tourism organisations and tourists (UK)	Two-party relationship (pricing behaviour in package tour industry)	Quantitative
Theuvsen (2004)	Tour operators (Europe)	TSC coordination	Conceptual
Tsaur *et al.* (2006)	Tour operators and travel agencies (Taiwan)	Supply management	Empirical
Tse (2003)	Hotels and travel agencies	Supply management	Conceptual
Wie (2004, 2005)	Excursions	Two-party relationship (capacity investment in the cruise line)	Quantitative
Wynne *et al.* (2001)	Travel agencies and tour operators (South Africa)	Information technology	Conceptual
Yilmaz and Bititci (2006)	The entire TSC	Performance measurement	Conceptual

Note: The items in parentheses are given only when they are available from the study being considered.

Objectives of TSCM

Goal setting is the first step of TSCM. To set goals, the major driving forces (objectives) behind TSC linkages need to be identified. These drivers can include, but are not limited to, tourist satisfaction, tourism sustainability, monetary value, demand uncertainty and inventory reduction.

The ultimate goal of a TSC is tourist satisfaction, or more generally, customer satisfaction. Tourist satisfaction is the degree to which tourists are satisfied with the tourism products and services received and can be examined from two perspectives. One is the overall satisfaction with the tourism product and the other is the level of satisfaction with individual service attributes of a specific tourism service encountered. However, tourists normally see a tourism product as a combination of a number of different service components; therefore, the service attributes of a tourism product/service, such as those defined by the SERVQUAL model (Parasuraman *et al.*, 1988), are all linked and depend upon one another. If the service attributes of a particular tourism product component such as the airline service fails to satisfy tourists, the overall tourist satisfaction level is negatively affected.

The tourism industry relies heavily on environmental resources, which are freely available and potentially subject to degradation through excessive use. An associated research area is the increasingly important status accorded to the sustainable development of tourism. The central problem is to find an equilibrium point between the use and preservation of resources to maintain sustainable tourism development in the destination.

Monetary value is defined as the ratio of tourist revenue to the total cost incurred in the development of the tourism product. It can be enhanced either through increases in sales revenue, market share and labour productivity or through reduction in expenditures and operational costs. Because such value directly reflects the cost efficiency and profitability of a supply chain, it is the most widely used objective of supply chain management. Monetary value is of special importance for a TSC. As noted, tourism products tend to be perishable and have relatively high fixed costs that are paid in advance to build up a fixed level of capacity. Therefore, increasing monetary value through revenue generation and cost reduction is a key problem of TSCM.

Uncertainty about future demand is one of the most significant characteristics of the tourism industry (Gomez and Sinclair, 1991). It is beyond dispute that demand uncertainty can bring significant monetary loss for the business entities that are involved in a TSC if it is not managed properly. Demand uncertainty is also related to inventory problems in a TSC. As the global economy grows and more and more options exist for tourists, the uncertainty and complexity of the tourism marketplace will increase. Under conditions of increased uncertainty and the lack of alternatives, organisations in the TSC are more likely to resort to collective action to stabilise their environment.

Network structure

Understanding the network configuration of a TSC is a prerequisite for successfully analysing and managing the TSC.

Most of the studies listed in Table 1.1 propose a TSC structure. Among them, the one developed by Page (2003) is the most representative. On the basis of Page's work, we propose a more general TSC network within a destination (see Figure 1.3).

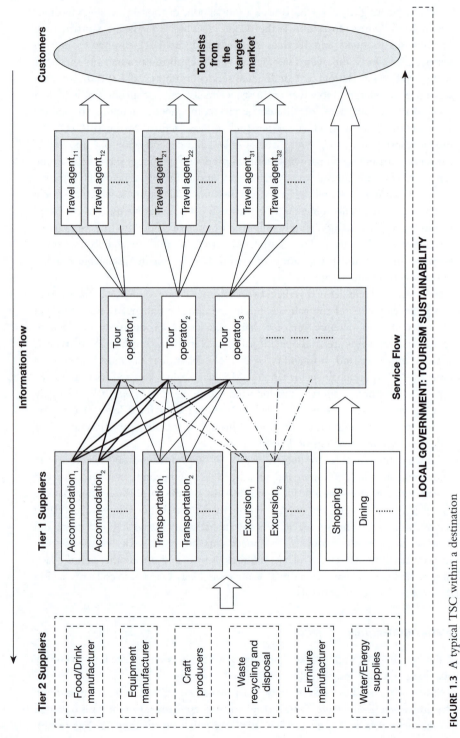

FIGURE 1.3 A typical TSC within a destination

Source: adapted from Zhang *et al.* (2009)

The downstream end includes tourists from the target market. Travel agents are the retail branches of tourism products dealing with tourists and tour operators. Travel agents and tour operators can be the same or separate business entities. Tour operators have enormous influence over all the activities involved in the TSC. They buy individual travel services (such as transport and accommodation) from their suppliers (such as carriers and hotels) and assemble them into holiday packages, which are sold to the public directly or through travel agents (Ujma, 2001). Tour operators can oversee the entire holiday experience so that they normally have first-hand knowledge of the behaviour of tourists during their holiday in the destinations.

The first tier of the upstream end of a TSC involves direct suppliers that directly supply tourism services to intermediaries. Typical direct suppliers include theme parks, shopping centres, hotels, bars and restaurants, handicraft shops and transportation operators. A more complex TSC may also include second-tier suppliers that supply services or products to first-tier suppliers. As noted, non-business entities are also involved in the TSC, one of which is the natural environment or scenery. Another typical player in the TSC is the local government or business association that facilitates public and private sector collaboration through policy intervention.

In addition to the identification of the TSC members, other issues, such as what the power relationships and the business links are among them, should also be considered when analysing the TSC structure.

Decision variables

TSCM decisions span a large spectrum of an organisation's activities and can be strategic, tactical, or operational.

- Strategic decisions have a long-lasting effect on the organisation. They include decisions regarding the tourism taxation policies of the local government, capital investment in the tourism industry, capacity building of tourism facilities and the entry or deterrence of potential tourism businesses.
- Tactical decisions consist of medium-term (quarterly or annual) actions of tourism organisations such as purchasing and production decisions, pricing strategies, product differentiation, advertising and inventory policies.
- Operational decisions mainly concern weekly or daily endeavours of tourism organisations in tour scheduling, route planning and issuing quotations on tour products.

Performance measurement

Effective performance measurement is essential for TSCM. Not only does it influence the activities throughout the chain, it also evaluates the efforts made by TSC members. Given the inherent complexity of a TSC, selecting appropriate performance measures for TSC analysis is particularly critical. Despite the wealth of literature on performance measurement of manufacturing supply chains, little attention has been paid to it in the tourism industry. Most of the relevant literature focuses mainly on the hotel sector (Yilmaz and Bititci, 2006). In their conceptual study, Yilmaz and Bititci (2006) compare the performance measures of the manufacturing and tourism industries from a TSC perspective and propose a general framework for TSC performance measurement.

Performance measures that have been used in supply chain analysis can be categorised as follows.

TABLE 1.2 Supply chain performance measures

Financial Performance	Operational Performance	Overall Supply Chain Performance
– Total cost – Distribution cost – Manufacturing cost – Inventory cost – Return on investment (ROI) – Total revenue – Profit	– Customer response time – Manufacturing lead time – Product quality – Product availability	– Customer satisfaction – Supply chain flexibility

It is clear that the overall performance measurement of the supply chain system involves not just financial or operational measurement. Given the complexity of assessing a system's flexibility, various frameworks have been proposed (Chen and Paulraj, 2004). As in other service industries, customer satisfaction (tourist satisfaction (TS)) is one of the most important performance measures for the TSC. Tourism researchers have been interested in measuring both overall TS with a particular destination (e.g., Alegre and Cladera, 2006; Kozak, 2001a; Yu and Goulden, 2006) and TS with specific service sectors, such as accommodation (Saleh and Ryan, 1992), restaurants (Chadee and Mattsson, 1996), attractions (Dorfman, 1979), travel agencies (LeBlanc, 1992), package tours (Pizam and Milman, 1993) and retail shops (Reisinger and Turner, 2002).

Methodology

The solution methodologies that can be used to address TSCM problems can be divided into the following areas:

1. Conceptual studies – research that analyses TSCs in an attempt to define, describe and develop methods for TSCM, including frameworks, taxonomies and literature reviews.
2. Case-oriented empirical studies – research that works with specific firms and uses the data collected by the researchers or from other qualified sources to analyse TSC issues.

3. Quantitative studies – research that attempts to develop methods for TSCM using quantifiable models (including optimisation, simulation, stochastic models and heuristics).

Most of the research in the area of TSCM uses the first and second methodologies listed above, whereas quantitative studies are very limited. However, in the existing studies of SCM in other industries, quantitative methods are those most widely used (see Min and Zhou (2002) and Ganeshan *et al.* (1999) for comprehensive reviews of the research methodologies in the SCM research). The lack of quantitative studies in the TSCM research may be due to the inherent complexity of TSCs and difficulty in establishing quantifiable standards. It is worth mentioning one quantitative method, namely, game theory (GT), which is able to account for the complexity of TSCM problems. GT has been widely used to understand the decision making in economic and social situations in which the outcomes depend upon the decisions of two or more decision makers. Many researchers have used GT to study supply chain problems. Cachon and Netessine (2004) provide a comprehensive overview of the application of GT to SCM problems. Research on TSCM using GT has begun to appear recently in the tourism literature and includes the studies of Chung (2000), Wie (2004, 2005), Yang *et al.* (2008), Yang *et al.* (2009) and Song *et al.* (2009).

1.5 Summary

This chapter provided an introduction to some of the basic concepts and theories of TSCM based on a review of the existing literature on TSCM, which has emerged as an important area for future tourism study attracting increasing attention from both the academic and practitioner communities. Based on the characteristics of the tourism industry, seven key TSCM issues are identified: demand management, two-party relationships, supply management, inventory management, product development, TSC coordination and information technology. The subsequent chapters of the book will further elaborate these TSCM issues in a more detailed manner.

Discussion questions

1. Why is the supply chain management concept relevant to tourism business operations?
2. How can we define a tourism supply chain?
3. What do we mean by tourism supply chain management?
4. What are the critical issues in tourism supply chain management?
5. What are the key components of a TSCM framework?

Note

1 Parts of this chapter were published in Zhang *et al.* (2009).

2

DEMAND MANAGEMENT AND FORECASTING

Learning objectives

After reading this chapter you will be able to:

1. Understand the importance of TSC forecasting.
2. Feel familiar with the concepts of tourism demand planning and management.
3. Understand how to carry out collaborative forecasting in the context of TSCM.
4. Feel comfortable with different forecasting methods.
5. Know the basic requirements of forecasting system design.

2.1 Introduction

Because demand plays a key role in determining the profitability of tourism businesses, managing and forecasting the demand for tourism products/services constitutes very important elements of all tourism planning activities. From the strategic point of view, tourism investment decisions, especially those concerning investments in infrastructure and tourism resorts, which require a long-term financial commitment, are heavily dependent on demand forecasts. The sunk costs can be very high if the investment projects fail to generate demand that matches their design capacities. From the operational point of view, the activities of tourism businesses such as airlines, tour operators, hotels, cruise lines and recreation facility providers are driven by tourism demand. As a result, the forecasting of such demand has attracted substantial attention from both academics and practitioners (Song and Turner, 2006).

Most of this attention to date has been directed towards the development of advanced quantitative forecasting methods. Such methods can undoubtedly facilitate the generation of more accurate forecasts, although the traditional stand-alone demand forecasting approach can be improved upon to assist in the planning activities of TSCs. A tourism product is often configured from a variety of service providers (accommodation, transport and attraction providers) that form a TSC. The fragmented nature of tourism products/services implies that individual suppliers often rely on cooperation with one another, which creates a need for collaboration in tourism demand forecasting. For example, the hotels in a given destination may be very interested in the passenger number forecasts produced by airlines, as they can help them to generate their own occupancy predictions.

Unlike traditional forecasting methods, the collaborative forecasting approach breaks down the units of analysis and involves reliance on supply chain partners to provide specific and timely information. It is based on cooperation and information sharing amongst the links in the chain. Accordingly, collaborative forecasting for a TSC requires that a variety of individuals from various echelons of the chain work together. With the aim of applying the collaborative forecasting concept to the forecasting function of a TSC, this chapter examines the concept of demand management in the context of TSCM, followed by an introduction to the current situation of tourism demand forecasting and then discusses both the potential benefits and challenges of collaborative forecasting in this arena. Practical solutions for the establishment of collaborative forecasting in a TSC are presented, and the methodology and design of a collaborative TSC forecasting system are described in detail.

2.2 Tourism demand management

Many studies of tourism demand modelling and forecasting have been published over the years, with particular attention paid to the performance of different forecasting models. Little attention has been paid to the role played by forecasting and demand management in the TSC context. In practice, the individual members of a TSC often try to generate demand forecasts for their own products/services, failing to realise that it is unnecessary for every supply chain member to do so. To address the issue of which party should be responsible for supply chain forecasts, we first need to understand the difference between independent forecasts and derived forecasts.

Independent forecasts versus derived forecasts

Independent forecasts predict the number of final tourism products/services demanded by the end-user customers of a TSC at a given location and within a specific period of time. Final products/services refer to the total purchases of tourism products/services by tourists, for example, the total number of tourists who purchase the same package tour or cruise holiday. It is these total purchases that determine the true tourism demand – the independent demand – that flows through the TSC. Hence, only travel agents and tour operators actually experience true demand. All subsequent suppliers in the TSC, including airlines, accommodation providers, tourist attractions and retail shops, experience primarily the demands that are generated by the purchasers of package holidays. This type of demand is known as derived demand, that is, the demand derived from the suppliers that directly provide the final tourism products/services to the end-user customers in the TSC.

In the case of package holidays, the demand for hotel rooms, airline seats and attraction admission is regarded as derived demand, which can be estimated on the basis of independent demand, as measured by package holiday purchases via a travel agent/tour operator. In reality, tourism product suppliers may work with different travel agents/tour operators to utilise their capacities fully; hence, the derived demand for a particular supplier is the sum of the independent demands from all companies that directly provide final products/services to end-users. In an ideal TSC, there will be only one supplier that is directly affected by independent demand, with the remainder interested only in derived demand. As a result, depending on whether they are concerned with independent or derived demand, different suppliers tend to adopt different forecasting methods. In practice, tourism product providers such as airlines, hotels, and theme parks prefer to develop their own demand forecasting methods or procedures when, in fact, they do not even need to engage in forecasting! It is thus very important that the final product/service provider shares its forecasts with the other suppliers in the TSC to allow the effective utilisation of resources in the provision of tourism products/services. The following example illustrates this point.

Suppose that a TSC provides a package holiday that includes travelling to a destination and visiting and dining at a theme park in that destination. The suppliers contributing this package holiday include a travel agent, tour operator, the theme park and a restaurant within the theme park. If there is no coordination or information sharing amongst these suppliers, then it is likely that each will produce its own demand forecasts. Suppose that the retail travel agent predicts that 500 of these package holidays will be sold to tourists in the next few months. Given that forecasting errors have been observed to be about 10 per cent in the past, this travel agent will order 550 package holidays from the tour operator. Without knowing the travel agent's forecast, the tour operator will generate its own forecast of 550 package holidays that need to be arranged on the basis of the agent's historic order data. Again assuming a forecasting error rate of around 10 per cent, the tour operator will order 605 admission tickets from the theme park, and the restaurant will predict its demand to be 605 customers based on the order data it receives from the theme park. Adding another 10 per cent forecasting error (safety stock) leads to a prediction that 670 guests will visit the restaurant. As a result of these calculations, the derived demands for the tour operator, theme park and restaurant are inflated by 10, 21 and 34 per cent, respectively.

Demand planning and management

If the individual suppliers within the TSC do not generate their own forecasts, but instead adopt those generated by the retail travel agent, then 550 package holidays or tourists will be used as the system forecast. As a result, all of the suppliers can plan their business operations on the basis of this forecast. Doing so reduces the system-wide forecasting error rate by 21.8 per cent.

This practice is known as tourism demand planning, which is the coordinated flow of derived demand through the suppliers in the TSC. Although tourism demand planning is important for each supply chain member, the motivation and incentives for each to participate in such planning vary greatly. For example, a restaurant has much less incentive to participate, although demand planning reduces its forecast errors the most. In fact, the very suppliers that most need to implement demand planning generally have the least economic motivation to cooperate in it. Tourism demand management, which refers to the creation of a coordinated tourism demand flow across the TSC and its markets, is closely related to tourism demand planning, and its definition has the following implications.

First, it is important for a TSC partner to share its promotional/marketing information internally and with the other suppliers in the TSC. For example, the sales department of a theme park should communicate its marketing efforts with the operations department, as the park's carrying capacity may be unable to absorb the demand created by the sales department, thus leading to an advertisement for the park's competitors. In other words, the theme park creates demand for its competitors because it is unable to meet the increased demand for its product due to capacity constraints. If TSC partners do not share their market creation information with one another, then the market demand created by chain members may benefit competing TSCs.

Second, tourism demand management may sometimes lead to decreased demand. This may sound counterintuitive, but demand for a tourism product often exists at a level that the TSC cannot realistically fulfil. Many tourism enterprises, such as hotels, tour operators and theme parks, often pay a bonus for each product sold or account opened by their sales personnel without considering capacity constraints. Good demand management thus requires that all TSC partners assess the profit contributions of various products/services and then retain demand for the most profitable and reduce or eliminate that for the most unprofitable.

Finally, although collaborative forecasts can reduce forecasting errors and the costs of unnecessary inventory, the rewards may not always be consistent with the need to obtain collaboration from all TSC partners. One of the most important aspects of tourism demand management is thus the management of TSC relationships. Effective TSC relationship management is achieved by coordinating the various TSC partners with a view to matching rewards with performance (TSC coordination is further discussed in Chapter 3).

2.3 Collaborative TSC forecasting

Although collaborative forecasting is crucial for the success of TSCs, little attention has been paid to this topic by either academics or practitioners, which is partly due to the lack of development or employment of supply chain management (SCM) strategies in the tourism industry. This section therefore addresses the benefits and challenges of collaborative TSC forecasting.

As a tourism product is normally produced by a wide range of tourism businesses, and because of the multiplier effect, the impacts of economic conditions on a destination and its source markets tend to be far-reaching, thus rendering the tourism industry highly vulnerable to the influence of these conditions. Travel is a luxury product, and individuals thus tend to cut back on holidays when economic conditions are bad. Unpredictable economic shocks such as the current global financial turmoil and economic recessions can cause significant demand uncertainty in the tourism arena. In addition, many other factors also contribute to market uncertainty in terms of the demand for tourism products. For example, effective advertising can increase the number of tourist arrivals, whereas negative word-of-mouth publicity can lead to a fall in demand.

The most common method of dealing with such uncertainty is the building up of inventories. Tourism products/services, however, cannot normally be stored for future use; this characteristic is often referred to as 'perishability' (Lovelock, 1980). Further, unlike the manufacturing industry, tourism service providers are normally unable to increase supply rapidly in accordance with an increase in demand. Uncertainty about demand levels can therefore precipitate losses for tourism businesses due to insufficient capacity to meet demand or excess capacity as a result of over-investment. Given that capacity is a fixed component, the only viable option for managers is to follow strategies that assist them in obtaining more accurate predictions, that allow them to match supply and demand more closely. Tourism practitioners, however, usually have little interest in scholarly journals, and thus they are either unfamiliar with the modern forecasting methods presented in these journals or simply do not have the time to design and develop such methods. A forecasting mechanism that can facilitate the mutual transfer of information and knowledge between tourism forecasting experts and practitioners would thus be highly desirable.

Most tourism demand forecasting studies have been based on statistical methods and rely on the availability and quality of historical data (Song and Li, 2008). Current knowledge of special events or information on the marketing activities of TSC partners is often difficult to obtain, rendering the inclusion of such knowledge/information in forecasting models almost impossible. Collaborative TSC forecasting can be expected to produce two main benefits: reduced reliance on historical records and enhanced information sharing amongst TSC partners. The focus of collaborative TSC forecasting is therefore not merely on the improvement of forecast accuracy, but also on breaking down the forecasting responsibilities of individual TSC members and smoothing the information flows amongst them to benefit the entire TSC.

The achievement of collaborative TSC forecasting is no easy task, however. It requires that a variety of participants from various echelons of the chain work together. The first challenge is establishing a trusting relationship amongst TSC partners. The second is designing the forecasting process and identifying the steps required for the effective implementation of that process. The third challenge comprises the technical aspects involved, such as the establishment of forecasting support systems to facilitate the forecasting process and information sharing amongst the players within the TSC. The first challenge is itself a complex problem that lies outside the scope of this book, and hence this chapter will endeavour to propose solutions only for the latter two.

2.4 Forecasting methods

Collaborative forecasts can be generated using different forecasting methods. In the literature, tourism demand forecasting methods are categorised into different groups based on a variety of features (see Figure 2.1). First, they can be simply grouped into two broad categories: quantitative methods and qualitative methods. Quantitative forecasts rely largely on statistical models, whereas qualitative forecasts are made on the basis of expert views. Practitioners employ both methods in tourism demand forecasting, depending on the availability of historic demand data. Quantitative methods can be further divided into single-equation models and system-of-equation models. The former generate forecasts based on a single model for each of the products/services demanded, whilst the latter forecast a number of products/services using a number of models simultaneously. Single-equation methods can be further divided into univariate and multivariate models. The shaded boxes in Figure 2.1 are examples of different models, which are explained in further detail in the following subsections.

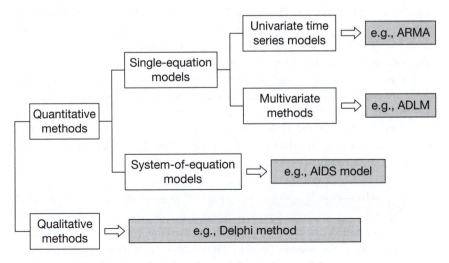

FIGURE 2.1 Classification of tourism demand forecasting models

Quantitative forecasting

According to Song and Li (2008), the most frequently used forecasting methods in tourism are quantitative methods, a few of which are briefly discussed in the following.

Univariate time series models

Univariate time series techniques forecast tourism demand based only on historic demand trends. The naïve model, exponential smoothing method, autoregressive (AR) model and the Box–Jenkins procedure (Box and Jenkins, 1970) are the most commonly used univariate time series models.

The naïve (no-change) model is the simplest forecasting model. It treats the observation at period $(t-1)$ as the forecast of period t. When seasonal data are examined, the forecast at period t is the observation at period $(t-4)$ for quarterly data and that at period $(t-12)$ for monthly data. Another naïve model, the constant-growth-rate model, is also widely applied. It treats the growth rate (or seasonal growth rate for seasonal data) at period $(t-1)$ (at period $(t-4)$ for quarterly data and $(t-12)$ for monthly data) as the forecast of the growth rate (or seasonal growth rate) at period t. Researchers often adopt the results of the naïve model as a benchmark for forecasting tourism demand.

The moving average (MA) model is a simple forecasting method in which forecasts are represented as the simple average of the latest n observations. The expression is specified as

$$\hat{y}_t = \frac{1}{n} \sum_{i=t-n}^{t-1} y_i \, ,$$ (2.1)

where $\hat{y}_t$ is a forecast of tourism demand at time t, y_t stands for the actual observations and n represents the rank of the moving average. During implementation, greater weights can be assigned to recent observations and lesser weights to distant observations when considering the rationality.

The exponential smoothing approach, another time series method, incorporates the exponential weighted average technique to smooth the series under study. The most widely used models in this approach include the single and double exponential smoothing models and the Holter–Winters (Winters, 1960) no seasonal, additive and multiplicative exponential smoothing models. The Holter–Winters multiplicative model is represented as follows.

$$\hat{y}_{t+k} = \left(\alpha_t + b_t k \right) c_{t-s+k} \, ,$$ (2.2)

where $\hat{y}_{t+k}$ is the forecast at $(t+k)$, α_t stands for the intercept, b_t denotes the slope, and c_t represents the seasonal factor. These three parameters are respectively specified as follows.

$$a_t = \alpha \frac{y_t}{c_{t-s}} + (1-\alpha)(a_{t-1} + b_{t-1}) \ . \tag{2.3}$$

$$b_t = \beta(a_t - a_{t-1}) + (1-\beta)b_{t-1} \ . \tag{2.4}$$

$$c_t = \gamma \frac{y_t}{a_t} + (1-\gamma)c_{t-s} \ . \tag{2.5}$$

α, β and γ are three smoothing coefficients that satisfy the condition $0 \leq \alpha$, β, $\gamma \leq 1$, whereas s is the length of the seasonal cycle, with $s = 12$ for monthly data and $s = 4$ for quarterly data. The foregoing equations demonstrate that these three parameters are obtained from smoothing. The seasonal parameter makes this method suitable for forecasting series that include both time trends and seasonal variations. Because of the characteristics of the smoothing technique, however, this approach is more suitable when only a few observations are available.

The AR model treats dependent variables as a function of its lagged values and random error, and is a special case of the autoregressive moving average (ARMA) model. More details of the AR approach can be found in the following detailed discussion of the ARMA model.

The ARMA model includes the AR, MA and ARMA models, but the general model takes the following form.

$$y_t = \sum_{i=1}^{p} \phi_i y_{t-i} + u_t + \sum_{i=1}^{q} \theta_i u_{t-i} \ . \tag{2.6}$$

The first part of the right-hand side of the equation is an AR term with lag length p. The second part denotes the MA term with lag lengths q, ϕ_i and θ_i as the coefficients to be estimated. The AR(p) and MA(q) models are both specific forms of the ARMA model, with $q = 0$ in the former and $p = 0$ in the latter.

The autoregressive integrated moving average (ARIMA) and seasonal ARIMA (SARIMA) models are generalisations of the ARMA model and used for series that have only one unit root or one unit root plus a seasonal trend, respectively. As tourism demand series are usually non-stationary, and one unit root can be found in most series, the ARIMA model has proved to be a reliable approach in the modelling and forecasting of monthly or quarterly tourism demand, as demonstrated by Goh and Law (2002).

Time series techniques have two obvious advantages: no significant obstacle to data collection exists, and they are easy to understand and use. However, they cannot be used to explore the impact of other factors on tourism demand and thus do not permit price elasticity.

Recent empirical studies have improved time series approaches by including explanatory variables in univariate time series models. For example, Akal (2004) incorporates explanatory variables into the ARMA model to forecast international tourism revenues for Turkey, with the results showing this model to outperform simple econometric techniques. In an empirical study of Australia's domestic tourism sector, Athanasopoulos and Hyndman (2008) find the exponential smoothing model combined with exogenous variables to capture time series dynamics well and to outperform regression models. Smeral and Wüger (2005) also find that more accurate forecasts can be generated when more explanatory variables are included in the forecasting model.

Multivariate econometric models

In contrast to univariate time series techniques, multivariate econometric models take into consideration influencing factors when modelling and forecasting tourism demand. The factors that affect tourism demand include the own price of tourism goods and services, substitute prices, tourist income, transport costs, marketing expenditure, seasonality and one-off events.

Policymakers in tourist destinations, especially those in which tourism is the major source of foreign exchange, have made great efforts to understand the key determinants of demand for their tourism products and services with the aim of formulating and implementing the most effective policies and strategies. Consequently, many econometric studies of tourism demand have been conducted, making significant contributions to the tourism demand literature (Li et al., 2005a; Song and Li, 2008; Witt and Witt, 1995).

Econometric techniques have undergone significant advances in the past two decades, with new developments in this arena playing an important role in our understanding of tourist consumption behaviour and the demand for tourism goods and services. Li et al. (2005a) review eighty-four studies of tourism demand published since the 1990s and find the majority of them to adopt econometric methods. For example, Song and Witt (2003) employ the general-to-specific approach, autoregressive distributed lag model (ADLM) to forecast inbound tourism to South Korea from four major origin countries, and the vector autoregressive (VAR) model to generate ex ante forecasts of tourist flows to Macau from eight major origin countries and regions (Song and Witt, 2006). The following section briefly introduces the main multivariate econometric approaches employed in tourism demand analysis.

Traditional static regression model. The traditional static regression model usually employs the ordinary least squares (OLS) method to estimate the relationship between the independent and dependent variables, but does not normally allow the inclusion of lagged variables. The application of this technique in the modelling and forecasting of tourism demand has been criticised by Engle and Granger (1987), who suggest that traditional OLS estimation may lead to the spurious regression problem when the variables considered are non-stationary. In such cases, the results of statistical tests based on regression models with non-stationary variables are unreliable and even misleading; therefore, the inferences drawn from these models tend to be suspect. The incorporation of the cointegration technique into the model in the late 1980s was effective in preventing the spurious regression problem (Song and Li, 2008).

The variables considered in tourism demand analysis, including tourist expenditure, visitor arrivals, consumer income and exchange rates, are usually non-stationary. The predominant use of traditional regression approaches in tourism forecasting studies started to change in the mid-1990s, as more researchers began to apply modern econometric techniques to model and forecast tourism demand.

Error-correction model. Engle and Granger (1987) point out that if the linear combination of two non-stationary variables in an economic system is a stationary series, then a cointegration relationship exists between them. In the case of more than two variables, multiple cointegrating relationships can be identified using the same principle. Engle and Granger (1987) prove that, if the variables under consideration are cointegrated, then a corresponding error-correction model can be established that takes into account the short-run dynamics. Thus, long-run cointegrating and short-run error-correction models can eliminate the spurious regression problem associated with traditional static models. Both types of models have been widely applied in a variety of tourism contexts (Song *et al.*, 2009).

ADLM. Known as the general-to-specific approach, the ADLM is a dynamic econometric modelling technique that was first proposed by Hendry (1986). This method involves a general functional form that contains both the current and lagged values of the variables. Stepwise reduction is then applied for model estimation. The following equation represents the general ADLM.

$$ y_t = \alpha + \sum_{i=1}^{p} \phi_i y_{t-i} + \sum_{i=0}^{q} \beta_i X_{t-i} + \epsilon_t , \qquad (2.7) $$

where y_t denotes tourism demand, X_t denotes a vector of exogenous independent variables with a lag length of q, and α, ϕ_i and β_i are the coefficients or coefficient vectors that require estimation.

Before the introduction of the ADLM, a large number of tourism demand modelling and forecasting studies adopted the specific-to-general approach (Song and Witt, 2003). In this approach, a relatively simple model based on demand theory must satisfy certain criteria, including a high R-squared value, statistically significant variables, and a lack of autocorrelation and heteroscedasticity in the error term. If some of these criteria are not satisfied, then the model is re-estimated by including new explanatory variables in a stepwise fashion, changing the functional form or using a different estimation method. This process continues until all of the criteria are satisfied.

Song and Witt (2003) identify a number of problems in the specific-to-general modelling process. First, this approach tends to result in a complicated final model specification that involves too many variables, and different researchers may obtain different models with the same dataset. Second, the model is unable to capture the dynamic characteristic of demand behaviour, which can lead to poor forecasting performance. Third, the aforementioned spurious regression problem may exist, and thus the final model is unable to reflect the real relationship between the dependent and independent variables.

However, the general-to-specific modelling approach, which was originally proposed by Davidson *et al.* (1978) and Hendry (1986), overcomes the limitations associated with the specific-to-general approach, as it features a clear model specification, estimation and selection strategy (Song and Witt, 2003). In recent years, the general-to-specific modelling approach has frequently been applied to tourism demand forecasting (e.g., Song and Witt, 2003; Song *et al.*, 2003; Song *et al.*, 2003). The modelling process in this approach follows four steps (Song and Witt, 2003, p. 68): first, a general ADLM is specified based on economic theory and the properties of the data; second, restriction tests are carried out based on the assumptions imposed by specific models on the coefficients in the general ADLM; third, diagnostic testing is performed on the specific models that are found to be superior to the general ADLM according to the results of the restriction tests; and, finally, the best models for policy evaluation and forecasting purposes are selected based on the results of both the diagnostic tests and the models' consistency with economic theory.

Following these steps, the resulting final specific model should be simple in structure and possess desirable statistical properties, such as an absence of auto-correlation, heteroscedasticity, multicollinearity and non-normality. In addition, all of the variables in the final model should be statistically significant.

VAR model. The econometric models discussed thus far are limited to cases in which tourism demand y_t is determined by a set of independent variables, $x_1, x_2, \ldots, x_i$. These independent variables are assumed to be exogenous and not to be influenced by the dependent variable (tourism demand), assumptions that do not always hold in economics. The VAR model (Sims, 1980) addresses this problem. It treats all variables, including tourism demand and its determinants, as endogenous, except for such deterministic variables as trend, intercept and dummy variables. Endogenous variables are those that are influenced by other variables within the economic system. The traditional regression model, error-correction model and ADLM assume that all variables except tourism demand are exogenous. Lagged variables are included in the VAR model to capture the dynamic nature of the dataset, although the lag length must be chosen carefully: too many lags result in over-parameterisation, whereas too few result in a loss of forecasting information. The general criteria adopted for a determination of lag length are the Akaike information criterion (AIC) and the Schwarz information criterion (SIC). The VAR model has been widely employed in macroeconomic modelling and forecasting since it was first introduced in 1980. Song and Witt (2006) and Witt *et al.* (2003) successfully apply this technique to generate employment and tourism flows, and De Mello and Nell (2005) examine the demand for French, Spanish and Portuguese tourism by UK residents.

One of the advantages of the VAR model is that it permits impulse response analysis to be carried out for policy simulation. This kind of analysis focuses on the impact of unitary changes in the error terms (shocks) on the dependent variables, which enables policy development and evaluation. Song and Witt (2006) discuss impulse response analysis in greater detail.

Although multivariate econometric models have been widely used by governments and tourism-related businesses in strategy and policy formulation, they cannot be employed to analyse the interdependence amongst budget allocations to different consumer goods and services by tourists (Eadington and Redman, 1991). For example, a decrease in hotel room rates may stimulate tourist spending on shopping and entertainment. However, the multivariate approach is unable to capture adequately the influence of a price change in one tourism product (or that in a particular destination) on the demand for other tourism products (or destinations) because it lacks an explicit foundation in consumer demand theory. Hence, the demand elasticity, especially the cross-price elasticity that is derived using the multivariate econometric approach, does not reflect real substitution effects and, consequently, may lead to unreliable policy recommendations. Another of the approach's limitations is that it does not allow tests of homogeneity and symmetry to be adequately performed according to demand theory.

System-of-equations demand models. System-of-equations demand models belong to the multivariate econometric group, but have several unique features. For example, they are explicitly derived on the basis of consumer demand theory, thus usually allowing theoretical assumptions to be formally tested and imposed. Such models are also capable of analysing the interdependence of tourist expenditures on a bundle of tourism products, meaning the cross–elasticities amongst them can also be examined. A review of the existing literature shows the almost ideal demand system (AIDS) model to be the most commonly employed system–of-equations model in tourism research and in demand analysis of other consumer products. In the tourism demand analysis arena, Li *et al.* (2004) employ long-run static and short-run error-correction AIDS models to examine tourism demand amongst UK residents for five European destinations. Li *et al.* (2005a) and Li *et al.* (2006) combine the time-varying parameter (TVP) technique with the AIDS model to analyse outbound tourism market share in the UK.

AIDS model. The basic AIDS model was proposed by Deaton and Muellbauer (1980). This model is able to analyse the interrelationships amongst budget allocations to different tourism goods and services. A group of equations (one for each tourism product) is estimated simultaneously, which allows examination of the way in which consumers choose bundles of tourism goods and services to maximise their utility given budget constraints. Although a number of system modelling approaches are available, the AIDS model is one of the most commonly employed in analysing consumer spending behaviour, as it has a number of advantages over the others. For example, it features a flexible functional form and imposes no prior restrictions on elasticities. Goods can be either normal or inferior, and pairs of goods can either substitute for or complement each other.

The AIDS model has been adopted in tourism research for more than twenty years. Fujii *et al.* (1985), for example, employ the long-run linear AIDS model in analysis of tourist expenditure categories including food and drink, lodging, recreation and entertainment, local transport, clothing, and other expenditures. The income, own-price and cross-price elasticities of demand are first estimated on the basis of visitors' expenditures in a tourist destination. Wu *et al.* (2011) recently examined the demand for different tourism products/services by tourists visiting Hong Kong from different source markets.

Other quantitative models

In addition to univariate time series and multivariate econometric approaches, methods developed for application in different fields of research have also been applied to analysis of tourism demand, including the artificial neural networks (ANN) model, which grew out of research into artificial intelligence in the early 1960s and has undergone rapid development since the 1980s. This approach is widely applied today as a control and forecasting tool in a variety of areas. It attempts to mimic the fault tolerance and capacity of biological neural systems by modelling the low-level structure of the brain. A well-defined neural network comprises three basic components: one input, one output and one or more hidden layers.

In the context of tourism demand analysis, the independent variables, that is, the factors that determine tourism demand, constitute the input layer of the ANN model. The output layer denotes the demand for tourism, which is the dependent variable. The hidden layer is the core of the model in which the non-linear modelling process is performed. During this process, different weights are assigned to each independent variable, and thus each node of the hidden layer is a weighted value of the input variables. Another set of weights is then allocated to make the dependent variable at the output layer a weighted value of the nodes at the hidden layer. Finally, the training process is repeated until a set of optimal weights is obtained. These weights can limit the discrepancy between the computed output and the observed values of the dependent variables within a threshold value. Empirical studies indicate that the ANN model performs well relative to other tourism demand models (Kon and Turner, 2005; Law and Au, 1999; Uysal and Roubi, 1999).

Nevertheless, the model does have limitations. First, a large amount of data is required for the learning process. In addition, although the model can generate accurate forecasts, the relationships amongst the different variables remain unknown. As a result, the impact of the independent variables on the dependent variable cannot be analysed. Moreover, own- and cross-price elasticities cannot be calculated, as the manipulation in the hidden layer is a black-box process.

Au and Law (2000, 2002) borrow the rough set approach from the field of artificial intelligence in computer science to examine sightseeing expenditure and tourism dining patterns in Hong Kong, and report it to exhibit superior forecasting performance.

State space models incorporating the TVP technique have recently been employed in tourism demand analysis. In standard statistical models, all influencing factors are assumed to be observable. Using historic data, these models obtain forecasts through parameters that are estimated on the basis of regression analysis or time series methods. However, some of the variables that affect the real state of the system are unobservable in practice. Models that contain unobservable variables are called unobservable component models. In contrast to standard regression methods, state space models are able to estimate different state vectors for analysis and forecasting by building a relationship between the observable variables and the unobservable inner structures of the system. An efficient recursive algorithm called the Kalman filter (Kalman, 1960) is employed to estimate these models.

Qualitative forecasting

Qualitative methods are also referred to as judgmental forecasts, as they involve judgmental input into the forecasts made by experts. Qualitative forecasts can be produced as point forecasts (e.g., the room occupancy rate is forecast to be 90 per cent in July), directional forecasts (e.g., there is to be an increase, decrease or no change in hotel room rates) or probabilistic forecasts (e.g., it is probable that the room occupancy rate will increase). One major advantage that probabilistic forecasts have over point forecasts is that they reflect the level of uncertainty associated with forecasts. Business forecasters often have access to historical information on the variables to be forecast (time series information), making it relatively easy for them to extrapolate historic demand data and produce point forecasts or to suggest the possible direction of the forecast variables on the basis of their beliefs about the future demand trend.

Studies of point forecasts are often divided into two groups: those with and those without the aid of domain knowledge. The quality of these forecasts is determined by whether the forecasters have any domain knowledge, which refers to their ability to identify the trend, seasonality, noise and instability of the data. The accuracy of point forecasts is also affected by the forecasting experience of the experts involved and whether contextual information is available to them. Lawrence *et al.* (2006) report that contextual information appears to be the key determinant of qualitative forecasts' superiority over statistical forecasts.

Another format for the provision of qualitative forecasts is the subjective estimation of probabilities, which can subsequently be employed to guide managerial decisions, either through informal or formal decision analysis (Goodwin and Wright, 1994; Webby and O'Connor, 1996). Probability forecasts and prediction intervals offer two effective means of accounting for the uncertainties associated with point forecasts. Probability forecasting has been applied in a variety of areas, including portfolio analysis and economic, weather, and technological forecasting. A TSC can also benefit from probability forecasting, as tourism suppliers are sometimes interested in future demand forecasts with a certain degree of confidence to allow them to deploy the resources needed to better prepare for a rise/decline in demand.

Qualitative forecasts can be obtained from a jury of opinions and in-depth interviews, as well as through the Delphi approach, the most frequently employed method of producing such forecasts. By administering a series of questionnaires, the Delphi approach combines the knowledge and experience of a select group of experts who understand the demand conditions of the product/service under consideration with the aim of forming a consensus of opinion about the likely level of demand for that product/service in a given time period. Expert panel members are normally selected from different functional departments of a TSC partner or from different TSC partners if the exercise concerns demand forecasts for the entire supply chain. The number of panel members can range from twelve to twenty-four. The advantages of using the Delphi approach to generate qualitative forecasts are respondent anonymity (which reduces the dominant members' effect), iteration and the attainment of controlled feedback from respondents (Frechtling, 2001, p. 217).

The most important elements of the Delphi approach are the recording of experts' forecasts and the subsequent processing (averaging) of these forecasts for re-submission to the panel members. This process normally continues for two to four rounds until consensus is reached. In the initial round of forecasting, it is likely that panel members' forecasts will be widely divergent. In subsequent rounds, however, the distribution of responses tends to converge towards the mean or median values. Once the forecasts over the forecasting periods have been agreed by the entire panel, they can be used as the final forecasts for decision-making purposes.

The Delphi forecasting process is illustrated in Figure 2.2, from which it can be seen that the method involves two stages. In the first stage, the individual responsible for generating the forecasts needs to convey the research question to panel members clearly. It is thus recommended that a background paper on tourism demand, market conditions and the forecasting objectives be incorporated into the first round of the questionnaire survey. Doing so will help the panel members to better understand the rationale for the forecasting exercise. This stage also requires a decision concerning the composition of the expert panel. The number of experts on the panel is determined by the scale of the forecast project. For small-scale projects, ten to twelve panel members are sufficient, whilst larger projects may require much larger panels.

In the second stage, the project co-coordinator needs to compile the questionnaire, which should be designed in a way that renders it suitable for obtaining forecasts for all of the demand variables under consideration. The questioning process is similar for all rounds of the Delphi survey. The first round, which includes a description of the study's intentions and purpose, is the critical stage. Before the questions are disseminated to the panellists, they need to be pre-tested by one or two experts to avoid ambiguity. After any necessary revisions, the questionnaires can then be sent to the select experts by email or post. Follow-up emails or letters may be necessary if the responses returned do not reach the number required. The same process is repeated until consensus is reached. According to

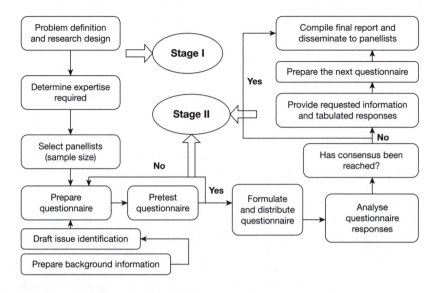

FIGURE 2.2 Delphi research design

Source: adapted from Kaynak and Macaulay (1984, p. 94)

Frechtling (2001), a simple rule for deciding how many rounds of the questionnaire survey are needed is this: the survey should continue until the interquartile range of forecasts is no more than ten per cent higher or lower than the mean. Three iterations are sufficient in most instances (Rowe and Wright, 2001, p. 131). The final step of the forecasting survey is to verify the forecasting results, compile the final report and disseminate it to all of the panellists. To obtain the final forecasts, the experts' estimates are equally weighed in the aggregation process, that is, the forecasts provided in the report should represent the average of the equally weighted estimates of all panel members' forecasts. Although different weighting schemes could be used, they would tend to render the forecasting procedure much more complicated in practice. Further, varying the weighting scheme would not necessarily generate more accurate forecasts.

For a systematic review of tourism demand forecasting models, see Song and Li (2008).

2.5 Collaborative forecasting system design

As previously noted, collaborative forecasting requires that a variety of participants from various echelons of the TSC work together. To facilitate such cooperation, the TSC's forecasters need to share information during their forecasting processes. An effective channel for such information sharing is the web-based forecasting system depicted in Figure 2.3.

Over the past decade, the web has become a ubiquitous and cost-effective communication medium for gathering and sharing information, and web-based technologies have evolved very rapidly. Although many web-based applications have been developed for various design and decision-making purposes, research on web-based forecasting systems is scarce. It is beyond dispute that web-based technologies can benefit TSC collaborative forecasting, as they not only facilitate information sharing and communication, but also bring considerable convenience to the practitioners engaged in collaborative forecasting at different locations. Apart from the improved collaboration amongst stakeholders it affords, the system is implemented as a web-based, distributed computing system as opposed to a standalone system for the following reasons.

- Ease of use – Users are familiar with web browsers, making it very easy for them to feel comfortable with the application of user interfaces. In addition, the web-based system is platform-independent, providing ease of access from anywhere.
- Easy to update – The web-based system is easily upgradeable with no costs or burden to clients. Forecasting models are normally updated on an ongoing basis as new data and models become available.
- Cheap solution – Use of the web-based system constitutes a cheaper solution than the purchase of expensive forecasting packages, and it requires no special or expensive software or hardware. As the user can cease the application's use at any time, he or she is not trapped into an investment.
- Platform independence – The web-based system can be developed independently of the type or nature of clients' computing environment, which allows more time to be spent on advancing the system's underlying methodology as opposed to its redundant implementation.

Two key points need to be considered in the design of a web-based TSC forecasting system. First, the forecasting process will benefit from the advanced tourism demand forecasting methods developed in the tourism literature. Second, collaborative forecasts need to be set up and generated by combining the inputs of various TSC members. Taking these two points into consideration, a collaborative TSC forecasting system is proposed here.

The collaborative forecasting process begins with the baseline statistical forecasts generated by certain of the aforementioned quantitative methods, which can be embedded in the proposed web-based forecasting system. Then, a variety of TSC members are invited to access the system on a regular basis to contribute their knowledge by making forecasts based on their individual views concerning the baseline forecasts. Finally, the system generates collaborative forecasts by combining both the baseline forecasts and the adjusted forecasts generated by the TSC members. The problems that require tackling include determining which forecasting techniques to employ in the creation of the baseline forecasts and deciding how to bring together the various pieces of information provided by the collaborative forecasting members. The two following sub-sections propose practical solutions to these problems.

Creation of baseline forecasts

As previously noted, most studies of tourism demand forecasting have been based on econometric and/or time-series techniques. The most significant difference between these two approaches is that the latter cannot be used for strategy/policy evaluation purposes, whilst the former allow estimated model parameters to be employed for business strategy evaluations. The established quantitative relationship between tourism demand and its determinants within econometric models enables 'what-if' scenario analyses of tourism demand forecasts, which can be very useful for judgemental inputs during collaborative forecasting. For these reasons, econometric approaches are preferred for baseline forecast generation. However, these models may not be feasible if data on the explanatory variables are unavailable either over time or across different TSC partners. If this is the case, then univariate time series models should be used.

Achieving collaborative forecasting through the Delphi approach

Producing collaborative forecasts by integrating the opinions of the members of a forecasting group involves qualitative forecasting techniques. Only a limited number of studies on qualitative forecasting have been published, with the Delphi approach attracting the most attention in the tourism literature (Witt and Witt, 1995). As discussed, the Delphi approach produces forecasts through individual opinions and group consensus. Its most important features include anonymity, iteration, controlled feedback and the statistical aggregation of group responses (Rowe and Wright, 1999).

In the Delphi-type approach, baseline forecasts are circulated amongst the forecasting group, and changes are then suggested by group members. The primary advantage of this method is that it allows contributions from group members who may be geographically dispersed. Most importantly, the Delphi approach produces more accurate results than traditional group meetings (Rowe and Wright, 1999). To summarise, the desirable features of the Delphi approach are that: responses are anonymous; the respondents come from the subject area; there is more than one round, that is, members are asked for their opinions on each question more than once; and controlled feedback is provided, that is, respondents are informed of the group's responses in the preceding round (Armstrong, 1985).

A detailed Delphi process can be designed as follows. It is regularly initiated by the administrator and incorporates at least two rounds per Delphi survey. In the first round, the collaborative forecasting system presents baseline forecasts produced by the econometric models, and members are encouraged to give their own estimates of future demand. The supporting reasoning for any changes must be clearly stated.

After the forecast has cycled through the entire team, the administrator generates revised forecasts by averaging the group's inputs. The reasons that the experts give for any adjustments are also summarised and provided anonymously to the group to inform the next round of adjustment. In the second round, the system provides the revised forecasts and comments obtained in the first round, and members are asked whether they agree with them. If they do all agree, then the Delphi process ends here; if they do not, then members provide their own forecasts and the reasons for them, and the administrator then averages these forecasts to arrive at average forecasts based on the second-round adjustments. If discrepancies still exist after the second round, then the process continues for as many rounds as are necessary to reach consensus.

Designing a web-based collaborative forecasting system

To facilitate the forecasting process described in the foregoing section, the web-based collaborative forecasting system illustrated in Figure 2.3 can be adopted.

As is the case with many web applications, this system can be built on a three-tier architecture. The first/client tier contains the user interface in the form of a 'thin client' web browser (typically Microsoft Internet Explorer or Netscape Navigator). TSC forecasting group members can simultaneously and independently access the web-based system through this tier. The forecasters and their computers are not actually part of the system initially. They become a part of it only when they visit the web server and interact with the system directly by inputting data and engaging in forecasting, analysis and decision-making.

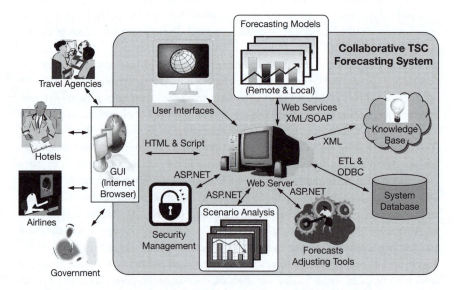

FIGURE 2.3 System architecture for a collaborative TSC forecasting system

The second tier of the system is the core of the architecture and serves as the engine of the forecasting system. It provides the procedures used by the forecasting group members and controls the communication of information between tiers. More specifically, the system engine contains a collection of software procedures written in ASP.NET and hosted on a Microsoft internet information server (IIS). Communication between the user interface and the engine is accomplished through the hypertext transfer protocol (HTTP). The procedures within the system engine comprise five main components: security management, user interface, forecasting models, scenario analysis and forecast adjustment tools.

The security management component is responsible for authentication and permission with regard to users' level of service, the entry of a user to the system and customisation of the application environment. It supports the following basic types of users: the administrator, forecasting group members and experts. The system's user interfaces are provided in the application tier in web page format. They are responsible for the interaction between the system and its users, acting on users' preferences and commands and controlling the input/output data and the form of display. In this component, office web components (OWCs) are employed to display data graphically (as in Microsoft Office).

The forecasting models component is responsible for generating the baseline forecasts and the forecasts required by the forecasting group members to support their decisions. This component is designed to be both modular (all models can be plugged, unplugged and re-plugged without affecting the other parts of the system) and flexible (the models' prediction capabilities are monitored over time to detect any deterioration and maintained accordingly). To accomplish these goals, we recommend the use of web services to design and implement every forecasting model as a distributed software component. A web service is a middleware system that can be developed in any kind of programming language and accessed by different kinds of software applications in both near and remote locations. These systems access web services via ubiquitous web protocols and data formats such as HTTP, extensible markup language (XML) and the simple object access protocol (SOAP), without worrying about how each such service is internally implemented. Web services can be accessed via software applications written in any language, using any component model and running on any operating system. The system server will employ XML and SOAP to communicate with the forecasting models in near and remote locations, which can be developed using the Visual Basic.NET and C# programming languages.

Scenario analysis is another key component of the forecasting system. Generally speaking, scenarios are plausible predictions that are produced by integrating statistical forecasting models and different user requests. Scenario analysis is an important and systematic way of examining the impacts of alternative values of the influencing factors on future demand. The system's scenario analysis component allows members to create their own scenarios by manipulating the values of the determinant variables of tourism demand in the forecasting models on the basis of their own knowledge. In addition to this component, the system also provides additional ways for members to add their own pieces of information to the system or make adjustments through the system's forecast adjustment tools. These two components are developed using ASP.NET and hosted on the web server.

The third/data tier is the system database in which forecast-related data are stored. It is a local or remote computer running a relational database management system (RDBMS) such as an SQL server or Oracle. The server retrieves data from the database via open database connectivity (ODBC) and extract–transport–load (ETL) procedures. The knowledge base comprises the collection of information and knowledge that members have accumulated from previous collaborative forecasting exercises using the system. It also contains the criteria that monitor the accuracy of the individual forecasting models and determine their adaptability. This knowledge base can serve as a forecasting support module or to provide system expertise in the collaborative forecasting process.

2.6 Summary

The tourism industry has evolved and modernised considerably in the past two decades, which have also witnessed growth in the implementation of new technologies such as computer reservation systems (CRSs), global distribution systems (GDSs), electronic data interchange (EDI), web-based technologies and new commercial formats such as eTourism. The most significant characteristics of the tourism industry are its large-scale service operations and the vast number of small businesses involved (Middleton and Clarke, 2001). Its highly competitive environment has prompted companies to look for competitive advantage. One route to gaining such advantage is the SCM approach, which considers the supply chain as a whole.

TSCM is increasingly evolving into one of the most critical factors affecting the development of the tourism industry today, and it is thus also attracting ever-greater attention from both academics and practitioners. The forecasting of tourism demand is particularly important for the policymakers and practitioners involved in TSCM. Success for many businesses is largely dependent on the level of such demand, and market failure quite often results from tourism firms' failure to meet market demand. However, although significant progress has been made in the development of advanced tourism demand forecasting methods, to date no standard such method is available for TSCs.

Recognising the important role played by TSCs and tourism demand forecasting, this chapter describes collaborative forecasting in the TSC context, highlights the importance of such forecasting and develops a collaborative forecasting system that involves multiple stakeholders. Unlike the traditional stand-alone tourism demand forecasting process, in which individual tourism firms make demand predictions based on their own or publicly available information, collaborative forecasting breaks down the barriers to information sharing amongst firms and involves supply chain partners in the provision of specific and timely information on future demand for their respective products/services.

Following an exploration of the current tourism demand forecasting situation, this chapter has considered the benefits and challenges of collaborative TSC forecasting and proposed practical solutions for the establishment of a system for such forecasting within TSCs. The proposed system, which is designed to facilitate the collaborative forecasting process, has been put forward with the aim of encouraging supply chain members to enhance knowledge sharing and take advantage of available modern tourism demand forecasting methods. The establishment of such a system will improve the performance and coordination of different tourism service providers within a TSC.

Discussion questions

1. Why is tourism demand management important in TSCM?
2. What do we mean by collaborative forecasting and how is it achieved?
3. What are the advantages and disadvantages of qualitative and quantitative forecasting? Can they be used jointly?
4. What are the differences between univariate time series models and multivariate econometric models?
5. How is the web-based tourism demand forecasting system useful in TSCM?

3

TOURISM SUPPLY CHAIN COORDINATION

Learning objectives

After reading this chapter you will be able to:

1. Understand why TSC coordination is important.
2. Understand the conflicting objectives of tourism businesses within a TSC.
3. Understand coordination mechanisms and capacity exchange in situations of demand uncertainty.
4. Describe information sharing in TSCs and the technologies used in information sharing.
5. Assess the effectiveness of information sharing amongst competitors.

This chapter discusses the importance of coordination in a TSC to improve service quality and performance and reduce operating costs. The mechanisms of TSC coordination and information sharing amongst TSC members are also presented.

3.1 Difficulties with TSC coordination

TSC coordination is a pattern of decision making and communication amongst tourism businesses applied to perform tasks to achieve supply chain goals, such as reducing overall supply chain costs, improving service quality, shortening response time and building good business relationships.

As a self-interested entity, an individual tourism business in a TSC may exhibit behaviour that prevents or hinders other TSC members from achieving their goals.

This situation is called conflict. Conflict of objectives amongst TSC members impedes communication and causes difficulties with TSC coordination. Bastakis *et al.* (2004) illustrate this with an example from the Greek island of Corfu, where small- and medium-sized tourism enterprises (SMTEs) are the main accommodation providers serving tourists. These SMTEs consider the large integrated tour operators as their distribution channels in the European tourism market. However, fierce price wars forced the large tour operators to sacrifice their profit margins to increase their market share. This price-cutting strategy inevitably led the tour operators to offer much lower room rates to the SMTEs, and the SMTEs responded by providing only very basic services to tourists coming from the tour operators so that they too could maintain their profit margins. Corfu thus became less attractive to European tourists, which further pushed the price of accommodation down.

Lack of information-sharing amongst TSC members is another obstacle to TSC coordination. Individual TSC members may possess certain market demand information that they consider to be confidential and do not want to share with other members of the same supply chain. For example, tour operators sometimes promote their products with price discounts or the provision of additional services to increase their market share. If they choose not to share information about their promotional activities with the upstream members of the supply chain, then the upstream partners may misunderstand the resulting temporary demand increase as a real increase and expand their capacity accordingly to satisfy the temporary demand spike. Hoteliers may make additional investment in developing new properties, and restaurants may increase their orders from food suppliers. If the tour operators stop their promotions, then the upstream members will suffer large losses due to their misinterpretation of the signals sent by the downstream members of the TSC. This will leave a large number of hotel rooms and larger restaurant inventories unoccupied, which could reduce the cash flow of both hotels and restaurants.

Another example is the overbooking of hotels due to a lack of information sharing amongst TSC members. A common method used by hotels to sell rooms is to allocate certain numbers of rooms to tour operators. If the hotels do not have sufficient knowledge about the market demand for their rooms, then they will sign allotment agreements with more tour operators to counter the demand uncertainty. The rooms allocated to the tour operators often exceed the actual room capacity, and the subsequent overbooking of hotels can lead to a scheduling problem for tour operators.

Information may be delayed or distorted in the process of being transferred from one TSC member to another. The upstream suppliers in a TSC acquire demand information from the number of orders received from high street travel agents or online booking agents. However, it takes time for these agents to process the bookings and compile the demand information, which means that when the information reaches the upstream suppliers in the form of orders it may already be too late for suppliers to plan effectively for the demand level. Information distortion occurs due to human errors in information processing and interpretation.

3.2 Conflicting objectives

One of the main objectives of a TSC is to maximise the overall profitability of the entire chain. A conflict of objectives amongst TSC members indicates that each member is trying to optimise its own objectives, but in so doing may fail to consider the negative impacts of its self-interested actions on other TSC members or indeed the entire chain. If this happens, then the total TSC profit tends to be less than could have been achieved by optimising the global TSC objectives. Song *et al.* (2009) provide a simple numerical example to illustrate this point. They consider a TSC that consists of a theme park – Hong Kong Disneyland (HKDL) – and one tour operator. HKDL sells some of its admission tickets through the tour operator, and the tour operator bundles the HKDL tickets with other services such as shopping and sightseeing and then sells the package to tourists. Tourists have different preferences for the package holiday offered by the tour operator. This preference is indexed by θ, which is a random variable that follows a uniform distribution that is normalised to $[0, 1]$. A tourist's utility is defined as a function of his or her perceived experience s and the package price p to give $u = v + \theta s - p$, in which v is the basic utility of the package holiday and is homogeneous amongst all tourists. If the utility is lower than zero ($v + \theta s - p < 0$), then tourists will stay at home or engage in other forms of tourism activity, resulting in the non-purchase of the package holiday. Tourists buy the package holiday only if $\theta \in [\hat{\theta}, 1]$, where $\hat{\theta} = (p - v)/s$. Thus, the demand for the package holiday is $D = 1 - \hat{\theta} = 1 - (p - v)/s$.

In this case, HKDL and the tour operator play a sequential game in which the former first sets the price of admission tickets, and the latter then decides on the details of the package holiday based on the cost of admission to HKDL and other relevant costs. In this game, HKDL and the tour operator have the same objective: to maximise its own profit. The profit of HKDL is $\pi_{TP}(w) = D(w - c)$, where w is the wholesale price of the admission ticket and c is the unit cost of operation for HKDL. The profit of the tour operator is $\pi_{TO}(p) = D(p - w)$, where p is the price of the package holiday. For simplicity, the tour operator's unit cost is assumed to be zero.

The game is solved by backward induction. The problem for the tour operator is to determine the optimal price of the package holiday to maximise its profit given the wholesale price of admission to HKDL, that is,

$$\text{Max } \pi_{TO}(p) = D(p - w) . \tag{3.1}$$

The first condition of π_{TO} with respect to p gives the optimal price of the package holiday: $p = (s + v + w)/2$. Substituting the price back into equation (3.1) – HKDL's profit – yields the following optimisation problem for HKDL.

$$\text{Max } \pi_{TP}(w) = \frac{(w - c)\,(s + v - w)}{2s} . \tag{3.2}$$

Solving equation (3.2) gives the optimal wholesale price and profit of HKDL as $w^{NC} = (s + v + c)/2$ and $\pi_{TP}^{NC} = (s + v - c)^2/8s$, respectively, where the superscript

NC denotes no coordination between HKDL and the tour operator. Thus, the optimal price and profit of the tour operator are $p^{NC} = (3s + 3v + c)/4$ and $\pi_{TO}^{NC} = (s + v - c)^2/16s$, respectively. The total profit of the TSC in this game is thus $\pi_{TSC}^{NC} = 3(s + v - c)^2/16s$.

When HKDL and the tour operator are considered as a single decision-making entity that has the single objective of maximising the overall profit of the TSC and seeks integrated optimisation, then

$$\text{Max } \pi_{TSC}(p) = D(p - c) . \tag{3.3}$$

It is then easy to obtain the optimal price of the package holiday and the profit of the TSC as $p^C = (s + v + c)/2$ and $\pi_{TSC}^C = (s + v - c)^2/4s$, respectively, where the superscript C denotes central optimisation.

It is clear that $\pi_{TSC}^{NC} < \pi_{TSC}^C$, which means that the conflict of objectives diminishes the profit of the entire TSC. Similarly, $D^C = (s + v + c)/2s > (s + v - c)/4s = D^{NC}$ implies that a lack of coordination in the TSC dissuades tourists from purchasing the package holiday. Hence, from this simple example we can see that it is important for the suppliers in a TSC to coordinate amongst themselves to mitigate the negative impacts of conflicts of objectives on the performance of the entire supply chain.

3.3 Costs of poor information sharing

Poor information sharing amongst TSC members encompasses the scenarios of no information sharing at all, information delay and information distortion. No information sharing mainly arises through distrust amongst TSC members. Information delay is often due to a time lag in processing information by these members, as collecting, analysing, transmitting and reproducing information all take time. The decision-making processes of individual TSC members also cause delays in information sharing.

The distortion of information arises when information passes through different members of a TSC and through interpretation that gradually deviates from its original meaning. Human error, such as the use of imprecise measurements, careless data entry and incomplete records, can also lead to information distortion. The effects of a lack of information sharing on tourism TSCs are highlighted in the following section.

Increased operating costs

If there is no information sharing amongst TSC members, then members will have to collect and analyse information themselves. This requires additional manpower and IT facilities, which in turn increases the operating costs of the individual TSC members. Additional costs may also be incurred by service providers, such as hotels and restaurants, if demand information is not made available on time or is distorted due to improper information processing.

Decision errors

Misunderstandings often occur when there is limited information sharing amongst TSC members. As already highlighted, the misinterpretation of temporary promotion policies by tour operators can cause suppliers to adopt inappropriate capacity expansion strategies. Although these expansion strategies may improve the capacity of the TSC, which benefits the long-term development of the tourism industry, the short-term expansion of the TSC can also lead to the under-utilisation of the capital of TSC members.

Service failure

Lack of information sharing can also cause service failure and loss of customers. For instance, during Chinese New Year 2006, many mainland Chinese visitors joined package holidays that included a visit to HKDL. The admission tickets included in the package were valid for six months from the time of issue. However, many of the visitors who purchased the package tour were refused entry to HKDL when they arrived in Hong Kong during the Chinese New Year period as visitor numbers grossly exceeded the theme park's capacity. The tour operators who sold the package tours did not make this information known to all of the package holiday buyers, and as a result there was extensive negative media coverage of the incident both in mainland China and Hong Kong. The tour operators were accused of not informing their customers about the excessive numbers of visitors to HKDL, and although most of the tourists who were refused entry to HKDL later received compensation, the reputations of the park and the tour operators were badly damaged. Following this incident, it was observed that HKDL was unable to attract enough visitors from mainland China during the Labour Day holiday period in May 2007.

Weakened relationships amongst TSC members

Lack of information sharing can also damage the collaborative relationships amongst TSC members. In a situation in which there is no information sharing amongst these members, individual tourism businesses often assume that they have done their best in contributing to the operation of the TSC and that others should be responsible for any losses incurred. Such lack of trust amongst TSC members threatens existing cooperative relationships and makes further coordination or collaboration more difficult.

3.4 Coordination mechanisms

Increasing numbers of tourism businesses have realised that their overall performance can be enhanced by employing novel methods or technologies to coordinate their relationships with other business partners in their supply chain (Chen *et al.*,

2001). The following two sections focus on strategies that can be adopted to achieve coordination amongst TSC members.

As TSC members are most likely to be independent business entities, coordination in a TSC involves maintaining a decentralised decision-making system so as to improve the overall performance of the TSC through more efficient communication amongst its members. For example, many business hotels in China try to attract weekend leisure visitors to fill empty rooms by offering price discounts. Such action then releases the pressure on the demand for accommodation by holiday makers. Other coordination mechanisms include quantity discounts, capacity exchanges, buybacks, revenue sharing, quantity flexibility and sales rebates. This section introduces two coordination mechanisms – quantity discounts and capacity exchanges – that are frequently used by tourism businesses.

Coordination through quantity discounts

The key to coordinating the decisions of tourism businesses in a TSC is to ensure that the objectives of individual TSC members are aligned with the overall TSC objective, which is to maximise the value or profit of the TSC to be shared by all members. All decisions made by TSC members should thus be evaluated based on their impact on the value or profit of the whole chain, rather than the costs or profits of the individual businesses within it.

When the coordination amongst TSC members leads to an overall TSC profit that is equal to what would be achieved under a centralised system, the mechanism is called perfect coordination. Recall the HKDL-tour operator TSC example in the previous section: the total TSC profit under coordination was higher than that under non-coordination, which drove HKDL to collaborate with the partner tour operator. The following example illustrates a quantity discount coordination mechanism between HKDL and the tour operator.

Shin and Benton (2007) state that quantity discounts are a traditional marketing strategy that is successful because product or service discounts influence the purchasing behaviour of buyers. Suppose that HKDL considers offering a quantity discount to the tour operator at a price w:

$$w = \beta v + (1 - \beta)c + \beta s(1 - q) , \tag{3.4}$$

where the definitions of the variables in equation (3.4) are the same as those given in section 3.2.

Equation (3.4) is the wholesale price (w) function for HKDL with respect to the order quantity q of the tour operator, and suggests that the number of orders is negatively related to the wholesale price of the tour operator. For the tour operator, the total number of admission tickets sold is equal to the market demand for its product $q = D$, and thus $w = \beta p + (1 - \beta)c$. Substituting w into the objective functions of HKDL in equations (3.1) and (3.2) gives the following equivalent equations:

$$\text{Max } \pi_{TO} = (1 - \beta)D(p - c) = (1 - \beta)\pi_{TSC} . \tag{3.5}$$

$$\text{Max } \pi_{TP} = \beta D(p - c) = \beta \pi_{TSC} . \tag{3.6}$$

Equations (3.5) and (3.6) indicate that the objectives of HKDL and the tour operator are consistent with the objective of the TSC as a whole. Hence, the quantity discount strategy constitutes perfect coordination between HKDL and the tour operator, and the resulting profits of HKDL and the tour operator are $\beta \pi_{TSC}^C$ and $(1 - \beta)\pi_{TSC}^C$, respectively.

In this quantity discount strategy, the parameter β represents the profit share of HKDL. In a situation of non-coordination, the profits of HKDL and the tour operator are π_{TP}^{NC} and π_{TO}^{NC}, respectively. For the quantity discount to be accepted by both players, it must first satisfy $\beta \pi_{TSC}^C \geqslant \pi_{TP}^{NC}$ and $(1 - \beta)\pi_{TSC}^C \geqslant \pi_{TO}^{NC}$. Thus,

$$\frac{1}{2} = \frac{\pi_{TP}^{NC}}{\pi_{TSC}^C} \leq \beta \leq 1 - \frac{\pi_{TO}^{NC}}{\pi_{TSC}^C} = \frac{3}{4},$$

which means that HKDL will take about three-quarters of the profit and the tour operator will take the rest. The profit share β thus provides an incentive for each member to cooperate.

The standard Nash bargaining model (Nash, 1950) can be employed to determine β in a quantity discount strategy. HKDL and the tour operator's preferences for their respective share of the TSC profit increase are defined as $\Delta\pi_{TP}$ and $\Delta\pi_{TO}$, where $\Delta\pi_{TP} + \Delta\pi_{TO} = \Delta\pi$. In the bargaining model, HKDL and the tour operator are assumed to jointly maximise the objective function

$$\text{Max } (\Delta\pi_{TP})^a (\Delta\pi_{TP})^b \tag{3.7}$$
$$\text{st. } \Delta\pi_{TP} + \Delta\pi_{TO} = \pi_{TSC}^C - (\pi_{TP}^{NC} + \pi_{TO}^{NC}),$$

where a and b denote the bargaining power of HKDL and the tour operator, respectively. Solving this model for $\Delta\pi_{TP}$ and $\Delta\pi_{TO}$ yields the bargaining result. The profit share of HKDL β in the quantity discount strategy obtained by Nash bargaining is

$$\beta = \frac{3}{4} - \frac{a}{4(a + b)} .$$

HKDL and the tour operator then split the increased TSC profit based on the formulas

$$\frac{a}{a + b}\Delta\pi \text{ and } \frac{b}{a + b}\Delta\pi .$$

If HKDL and the tour operator have the same degree of bargaining power, then they will share the TSC profit equally (i.e., $\Delta\pi/2$), and the parameter β in the quantity discount strategy is $\beta = 5/8$. However, as a core attraction to tourists, HKDL is more likely to have greater bargaining power than the tour operator, and will receive a greater share of the system profit when $a > b$.

Question: HKDL offers a quantity discount on admission tickets to Wing On Travel with a bargaining power ratio of 5:4. What are the profit shares of HKDL and Wing On Travel, respectively?

Answer: In this case, HKDL and Wing On Travel gain the increased system profit at $(5/9)\Delta\pi$ and $(4/9)\Delta\pi$, and the profit share parameter is

$$\beta = \frac{3}{4} - \frac{a}{4(a+b)} = \frac{11}{18}.$$

Thus, the profit share of HKDL is 11/18 and that of Wing On Travel is 7/18.

Coordination under demand uncertainty

Because tourism relies heavily on the economic conditions of source markets and is also very sensitive to natural disasters, terrorist attacks, and one-off social and economic events, the tourism industry often faces demand uncertainty. Moreover, the demand for tourism is also seasonal. Seasonal variations in tourism demand are often perceived as regular changes, but researchers such as Song et al. (2009) find evidence that some of these seasonal variations are stochastic. Another possible uncertainty in tourism demand is changes in consumer taste. These changes tend to be slow and gradual, but their impact can be substantial, and destinations have lost their appeal to tourists from certain countries as a result of consumer taste changes. For example, the attractiveness of Hawaii to tourists from Japan has been declining over the past decade due to changes in the travel preferences of younger Japanese travellers, who tend to be more adventurous than their parents.

Demand uncertainty can result in either excess capacity investment or a lack of such investment. Both situations bring losses to tourism businesses. Capacity exchanges within a TSC, whereby homogeneous firms trade capacity with one another (Hogendorn, 2005), are a method of coordination that can reduce the potential losses caused by demand uncertainty. An example of this method is tour operators with a low capacity but excess bookings purchasing extra capacity from tour operators with excess capacity. The following more detailed example shows how capacity exchanges can be used to mitigate the negative effects of tourism demand uncertainty.

Consider a TSC that consists of two tour operators (TOs) and a hotel in which each tour operator sells the same package holiday product that includes a one-night stay in the hotel. Both operators have the same constant marginal cost − c. Before the holiday season begins, TO_j ($j = 1,2$) reserves a certain number (k_j) of hotel rooms according to its prediction of demand, which is based on the room rate (w) set by the hotel. It then sells the package holiday to tourists at price p_j. The demand forecast of the two TOs also contains a forecasting error, which derives from unforeseen factors that are not included in the forecasting model used by the operator, which is denoted as ϵ_j ($j = 1,2$) and has a constant variance of σ^2 and an expected value of 0.

Under a situation of demand uncertainty, the two tour operators play the following three-stage game.

- **Stage 1** Each tour operator chooses to reserve k_j rooms, which is called *capacity reservation*.
- **Stage 2** Each tour operator realises the size of its forecasting error – ϵ_j and chooses a quantity δ_j to trade with its counterpart at the exchange price (s). If $\delta_j > 0$, then tour operator j is the seller, and if $\delta_j < 0$, then tour operator j is the buyer. This stage is called *capacity exchange*.
- **Stage 3** The quantity that tour operator j will sell to tourists after the exchange is $q_j = k_j + \delta_j$ for a given p_j. This stage is termed the *retail sale* of the package holiday product.

The following sections discuss the non-coordination and capacity exchange coordination cases.

Non-coordination Non-coordination means that there is no exchange between the two tour operators within the TSC, that is, $\delta_j = 0 \; \forall \; j$. In this case, the game is solved backwards to find the Nash equilibrium.

As usual, the linear inverse demand function for TO_j is

$$p_j = \alpha - k_j - \gamma k_i + \epsilon_k \quad (i \neq j) , \tag{3.8}$$

where the parameter γ captures the degree of substitution of the package holiday and $0 < \gamma < 1$.

As each tour operator chooses its reservation k_j, the profit of TO_j is

$$\pi_j = (\alpha - k_j - \gamma k_i + \epsilon_j - c - w)k_j . \tag{3.9}$$

No exchange occurs if there is no coordination and the value of ϵ_j has not yet been realised, and so tour operator j must maximise the expected value of $\pi_j = (\alpha - k_j - \gamma k_i - c - w)k_j$. The reservation capacity pair (k_1^*, k_2^*) suggests that k_1^* is TO_1's best response to TO_2's reservation quantity and k_2^* is TO_2's best response to TO_1's reservation quantity. Solving

$$\text{Max } \pi_j = (\alpha - k_j - \gamma k_i^* - c - w)k_j$$

gives the equilibrium reservation capacity:

$$k_j^{NC} = k_1^* = k_2^* = \frac{\alpha - c - w}{2 + \gamma} , \tag{3.10}$$

where the superscript NC denotes non-coordination.

Substituting equation (3.10) into equations (3.8) and (3.9) gives the expected product price and net profit:

$$E(p_j^{NC}) = E(p_1) = E(p_2) = \frac{\alpha + (1 + \gamma)(c + w)}{2 + \gamma} , \tag{3.11}$$

$$E(\pi_j^{NC}) = E(\pi_1) = E(\pi_2) = \frac{(\alpha - c - w)^2}{(2 + \gamma)^2} \ . \tag{3.12}$$

Capacity exchange coordination If coordination exists, then capacity exchanges will occur. If TO_j needs more rooms than the number that it has reserved, then it will make up the shortage by buying rooms from the other tour operator at a certain exchange price. Conversely, if it has unused rooms, then it will sell them to the other tour operator at the exchange price.

As both k_j and δ_j are given, the quantity that TO_j sells to tourists is $(k_j + \delta_j)$, and the price of the package holiday that TO_j charges is

$$p_j = \alpha - (k_j + \delta_j) - \gamma(k_i + \delta_i) + \epsilon_j \quad (i \neq j) \ . \tag{3.13}$$

The revenue of TO_j is $R_j = p_j(k_j + \delta_j)$.

In stage 2, the reservation capacity k_j is set, but TO_j can choose its exchange capacity δ_j. As no new capacity can be added during stage 2, $(k_1 + k_2)$ remains unchanged despite the trading. TO_j maximises its operation profit in stage 3 from the retail sales minus the operating costs and the trading costs of the capacity exchange. Solving Max $\Pi_j = p_j(k_j + \delta_j) - (c + s)\delta_j$ gives

$$\delta_j = \frac{\alpha - \gamma(k_1 + k_2) - c - s + \epsilon_j}{2(1 - \gamma)} - k_j. \tag{3.14}$$

The total amount of capacity sold through the exchange must equal the total amount purchased $(\delta_1 + \delta_2 = 0)$, and thus the equilibrium exchange price is

$$s^* = \alpha - c - (k_1 + k_2)\bar{\epsilon} \ , \tag{3.15}$$

where $\bar{\epsilon} = (\epsilon_1 + \epsilon_2)/2$.

Substituting equation (3.15) into equation (3.14) gives

$$\delta_j(s^*) = \frac{(k_i + k_j)}{2} + \frac{\epsilon_j - \bar{\epsilon}}{2(1 - \gamma)} \ .$$

As $E(\epsilon_j) = 0$, $E(\epsilon_j, \epsilon_i) = 0 \ \forall \ i \neq j$, and $E(\epsilon_j^2) = \sigma^2$, the expected profit of TO_j is

$$E(\Pi_j) = (1 - \gamma)(\bar{k})^2 + (\alpha - 2\bar{k})k_j + \frac{\sigma^2}{8(1 - \gamma)} \ ,$$

where $\bar{k} = \dfrac{k_1 + k_2}{2}$.

In stage 1, each tour operator maximises its net profit $E(\pi_j) = E(\Pi_j) - (c + w)k_j$ by choosing k_j. Solving $\partial E(\pi_j)/\partial k_j = 0$ gives the equilibrium reservation capacity

$$k_j^{CE} = k_1^* = k_2^* = \frac{\alpha - c - w}{2 + \gamma} \ , \tag{3.16}$$

where the superscript *CE* stands for capacity exchange.

The expected product price and net profit are

$$E(p_j^{CE}) = E(p_1) = E(p_2) = \frac{\alpha + (1+\gamma)(c+w)}{2+\gamma} \quad \text{and} \tag{3.17}$$

$$E(\pi_j^{CE}) = E(\pi_1) = E(\pi_2) = \frac{(\alpha - c - w)^2}{(2+\gamma)^2} + \frac{\sigma^2}{8(1-\gamma)}. \tag{3.18}$$

Capacity exchanges versus non-coordination Under demand uncertainty, tour operators may suffer losses due to unsold rooms or miss the chance to increase their revenue as a result of reservation constraints. The capacity exchange coordination strategy can minimise these losses.

However, there are several questions that arise from the foregoing capacity exchange strategy example. Will the capacity exchange affect the number of rooms reserved by the tour operators? Will the capacity exchange change the price strategies of the tour operators? How do capacity exchanges mitigate the negative effect of demand uncertainty? The following illustration provides answers.

First, from equations (3.10) and (3.16), we can obtain

$$k_j^{CE} = \frac{\alpha - c - w}{2 + \gamma(N-1)} = k_j^{NC},$$

This indicates that the capacity exchange does not affect the level of capacity reservation of the tour operators. Tour operators do not need to change their reservation decisions when they exchange capacity with others, and thus capacity exchanges do not incur additional reservation costs.

Second, from equations (3.11) and (3.17), we can see that the expected product price in the capacity exchange case is the same as that in the non-coordination case:

$$E(p_j^{CE}) = \frac{\alpha + (1+\gamma)(c+w)}{2+\gamma} = E(p_j^{NC}).$$

As the capacity exchange does not alter the price of the package holiday, the tour operators do not need to change their price strategies when opting to exchange capacity.

Third, from equations (3.12) and (3.18), we can arrive at

$$E(\pi_j^{HC}) - E(\pi_j^{NC}) = \frac{\sigma^2}{8(1-\gamma)}.$$

As $0 < \gamma < 1$, the expected net profit for each tour operator is larger if the tour operators adopt a capacity exchange strategy. In fact, the capacity exchange helps the tour operators to deal with the demand shocks better, and when the variance of a random shock is larger, the capacity exchange strategy will be more beneficial still. In addition, when the degree of substitution (γ) of the package holidays increases (the differentiation of the product decreases), the capacity exchange has a greater advantage over the non-coordination scenario.

3.5 Information sharing

Information sharing is an integral part of coordination efforts, as the decisions of TSC members are more efficient and effective when they are based on global rather than individual information. Information sharing also enhances the relationships amongst TSC members.

However, to avoid information overload, TSC members must correctly determine which types of information need to be shared and the most appropriate technologies to use for information processing and sharing.

Types of information

Sales data

Demand information in a TSC is transmitted from customers to upstream suppliers in the form of orders. Sharing order information may reduce the costs arising from surplus capacity investment and unnecessary inventory. However, the transmission of order information may be delayed or distorted for various reasons. If this happens, then the information may confound the planning and forecasting accuracy of the upstream suppliers and result in inappropriate decisions. If tour operators share their sales data opportunely with service providers, such as hotels and airlines, then the providers can adjust their strategies in response to demand changes in a more timely manner.

Business forecasts and plans

Forecasting and planning information from individual firms within a TSC, if shared amongst the members, can help these firms to produce more accurate demand forecasts jointly and can facilitate cooperation amongst members. For example, a one-month promotion by a tour operator would increase demand for that period. Other TSC members need to know when the promotion begins and ends so that they can make their own plans to match the tour operator's promotion, thus rendering the forecasts and plans of the entire TSC consistent.

Capacity information

Capacity information from upstream businesses must be shared with downstream enterprises to avoid overbooking by the upstream businesses. If a hotel discloses the capacity that it has available for allocation to the tour operators in a TSC, then the tour operators can look for additional rooms in other hotels in the peak season to avoid overbooking.

Package holidays schedules

The schedule of a package holiday provides information about a series of pre-arranged tourism activities, such as transportation, sightseeing, dining, accommodation and so on. Information about the package holiday schedules of downstream tourism businesses is a useful and effective input for upstream businesses to ensure reliable and sufficient supply.

Customer information

Customer information comprises demographic and socio–economic data about the tourists who purchase (or may potentially purchase) tourism products or services, and can also indicate tourists' preferences for such products and services. The sharing of customer information amongst TSC members allows tourism businesses to better understand the possible needs and behaviour of their customers so that they can provide appropriate services to satisfy those needs. For example, tour operators in the source markets have a better knowledge of their customers as they share the same culture and language. If information on their customers can be communicated to the other members of their TSC, such as hotels and restaurants at the destinations, these businesses can then design and provide tailor-made services to meet the specific requirements of these customers.

Other information

TSC members can also share their knowledge of markets, technology, logistics, organisation and costs. For instance, on the Greek island of Corfu, tour operators shared their expert knowledge of the tourism market and directed or 'pushed' SMTEs to make productive investments and engage in beneficial synergies[1]. The organisational efficiency of the tour operators also helped the SMTEs to be more organised in keeping records and to focus their attention on satisfying customers.

Value of information sharing

The value of information sharing can be defined as the benefit (excess profit or reduction in operating costs) obtained from such sharing minus the associated costs. For example, sharing information about customers across an entire TSC improves service quality and tourist satisfaction, which leads to repeat custom and ultimately results in an increase in the profit of the entire TSC. Sharing sales and forecast data can help TSC members to mitigate the negative impacts of demand uncertainty and reduce the costs of excess capacity investment and excess inventory.

The costs associated with information sharing include the costs of information acquisition and management. For example, it is very common for tourism firms to initially collect customer data through questionnaires or telephone surveys. However, once the data are collected, they need to be coded, analysed, transformed, stored, maintained and updated, which generates substantial information management costs.

Information sharing amongst competitors

In addition to sharing information with upstream and downstream partners in a TSC, information also can be shared amongst horizontal competitors. The following example illustrates a scenario of demand information sharing between two competing tour operators.

Two competing European tour operators – tour operator 1 and tour operator 2 – sell the same package holiday in the British market. Both operators face a linear demand $p = a - Q$, where p is the market price, a is the market size and Q is the total number of tourists who purchase the package holiday. The market size a is a random variable that can be a^H (high) or a^L (low) with equal probability. For simplicity, the unit cost for both tour operators is assumed to be zero. Suppose that tour operator 1 has obtained information about the market demand – a, whereas tour operator 2 does not have this information.

Further assume that the two tour operators are involved in a two-stage quantity competition. In the first stage, tour operator 1 observes the market size a and decides whether to share its information about a with tour operator 2. The information that is shared is assumed to be truthful. In the second stage, both tour operators compete on quantity based on their information about a.

If in the first stage tour operator 1 conceals the information about market size a, then tour operator 1's output is q_1^H if it observes $a = a^H$ and q_1^L if it observes $a = a^L$ ($a^H > a^L$). Tour operator 2 is not aware of the possible market size, but knows that it has an equal probability of being high or low. Tour operator 2's objective is to maximise its profit:

$$\text{Max } \pi_2 = \frac{1}{2}\left(a^H - q_1^H - q_2\right)q_2 + \frac{1}{2}\left(a^L - q_1^L - q_2\right)q_2 , \qquad (3.19)$$

where q_2 is the number of tourists who buy the package holiday from tour operator 2. Solving equation (3.19) gives the best response of tour operator 2 to tour operator 1's output

$$q_2 = \frac{(a^H + a^L) - (q_1^H + q_1^L)}{4} .$$

In the same way, tour operator 1's best response is $q_1^H = (a^H - q_2)/2$ if the market size is high and $q_1^L = (a^L - q_2)/2$ if the market size is low. Combining the three response functions gives the equilibrium quantities for the two tour operators:

$$\left(q_1^H, q_1^L, q_2\right) = \left(\frac{5a^H - a^L}{12}, \frac{5a^L - a^H}{12}, \frac{a^H + a^L}{6}\right) .$$

If tour operator 1 perceives that the market size is high, then it is likely to sell $(5a^H - a^L)/12$ package holidays, whereas if it observes that the market size is low, then the quantity will be $(5a^L - a^H)/12$ package holidays. Because tour operator 2 has no information about the market size, it always sells $(a^H + a^L)/6$ package holidays.

TABLE 3.1 Profits of the two tour operators without information sharing

	Profit of tour operator 1	Profit of tour operator 2
High market demand	$\left(\dfrac{5a^H - a^L}{12}\right)^2$	$\left(\dfrac{(5a^H - a^L)(a^H + a^L)}{72}\right)$
Low market demand	$\left(\dfrac{5a^L - a^H}{12}\right)^2$	$\left(\dfrac{(5a^L - a^H)(a^H + a^L)}{72}\right)$

TABLE 3.2 Profits of the two tour operators with information sharing

	Profit of tour operator 1	Profit of tour operator 2
High market demand	$\left(\dfrac{a^H}{3}\right)^2$	$\left(\dfrac{a^H}{3}\right)^2$
Low market demand	$\left(\dfrac{a^L}{3}\right)^2$	$\left(\dfrac{a^L}{3}\right)^2$

The profits of the two players in each market demand case are calculated and summarised in Table 3.1.

What happens if tour operator 1 shares its information about the market demand with tour operator 2? In this case, both players know the true market size. If $a = a^H$, then each tour operator sells $a^H/3$ package holidays, and if $a = a^L$, then they each sell $a^L/3$ holidays. Their profits in each instance are presented in Table 3.2.

Comparing the two scenarios, we can see that if tour operator 1 knows the market demand to be high, then it is likely to conceal this information, and the profit of tour operator 1 will be higher without information sharing. However, if tour operator 1 knows the market demand to be low, then it would be better for it to share the information with tour operator 2 to obtain a relatively higher profit. The reason for this is that if the information on low market demand is shared with tour operator 2, then this operator will reduce its supply, which will result in less competition, and both firms will end up with an equal share of the market demand and profit.

We can provide a more detailed example to illustrate this situation. There are 120 or 480 potential tourists who may visit Hong Kong Ocean Park (HKOP) over a weekend depending on the weather conditions. The numbers are known by both Wing On Travel and Hong Thai Travel from historical data: HKOP will receive 480 tourists if it is sunny and 120 tourists if it is rainy. However, assume that only Wing On Travel has knowledge of the weather forecast. If the weather forecast is accurate in predicting rain at the weekend, then will Wing On Travel share this forecast with Hong Thai Travel?

Analysis: In this case, if Wing On Travel conceals the weather condition, then it can sell

$$q_{WO} = \frac{5a^H - a^L}{12} = \frac{5 \times 120 - 480}{12} = 10$$

package holidays and achieve a profit of

$$\pi_{WO} = \left(\frac{5a^L - a^H}{12}\right)^2 = \left(\frac{5 \times 120 - 480}{12}\right)^2 = 100 \ .$$

Hong Thai Travel will provide

$$q_{HT} = \frac{a^H + a^L}{6} = \frac{480 + 120}{6} = 100$$

package holidays and obtain a profit of

$$\pi_{HT} = \left(\frac{(5a^L - a^H)(a^H + a^L)}{72}\right)^2 = \left(\frac{(5 \times 120 - 480)(480 + 120)}{72}\right)^2 = 1000 \ .$$

However, if Wing On Travel discloses the weather conditions to Hong Thai Travel, then although both travel agents provide

$$q_{WO} = q_{HT} = \frac{a^L}{3} = 40$$

package holidays, both will achieve a profit of

$$\pi_{WO} = \pi_{HT} = \left(\frac{a^L}{3}\right)^2 = \left(\frac{120}{3}\right)^2 = 1600 \ .$$

Although tour operators can benefit from horizontal information sharing when the market demand is low, determining whether to share information with competitors depends on many other factors, such as competition strategies (quantity or price competition), types of information (demand or cost information) and the degree of substitution of the product involved (Chen, 2003).

Information sharing technologies

The development of information communication technologies (ICTs) facilitates efficient and effective information sharing amongst TSC members. The main ICTs in the hospitality industry include the computer reservation systems (CRSs) developed in the 1970s, the global distribution systems (GDSs) introduced in the 1980s and the internet, which first became popular in the 1990s.

CRSs are computerised systems used to store and retrieve information and conduct mass transactions related to tourism services. CRSs were first designed and operated by airlines and later adopted by travel agents. Booking holidays and selling transportation tickets are the two main functions of these systems.

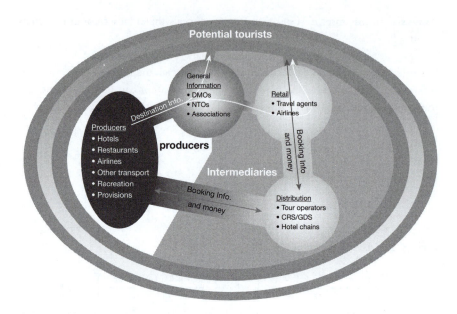

FIGURE 3.1 Tourism supply chains before the internet

Source: adapted from UNCTAD 2001

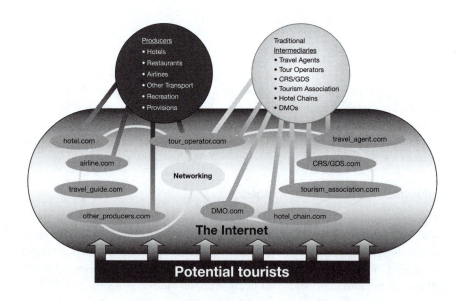

FIGURE 3.2 Internet-enabled tourism supply chains

Source: adapted from UNCTAD 2001

GDSs connect and integrate automated reservation systems to allow reservations to be made through travel agencies worldwide.

The internet has brought revolutionary change to the ways in which tourism businesses are operated, and has become a crucial medium for information acquisition and delivery. The ways in which information can be shared amongst tourism businesses and between businesses and tourists via the internet include email, the world wide web, online chats, blogs, file transfers and streaming media. The low cost and nearly instantaneous acquisition of information on the internet have made TSC coordination much easier. Before the emergence of the internet, tourism suppliers shared travel information amongst themselves and with customers via telephone, fax, post, and radio and television broadcasting (see Figure 3.1). However, in the era of the internet, both service suppliers and traditional intermediaries can communicate directly with their partners and customers (see Figure 3.2). In Chapter 9, we discuss the development of these ICTs and their application to the tourism industry in greater detail.

It should be noted that information sharing is not always beneficial to TSC members due to the high costs of investment in ICT infrastructure. Moreover, sharing key company information is a sensitive and risky issue in the commercial world, as all of the members of a TSC are likely to be financially independent and autonomous.

3.6 Summary

TSC coordination is a pattern of decision making and communication amongst tourism businesses applied to perform tasks to achieve the overall goals of the supply chain. However, conflicts of objective and a lack of information sharing can prevent TSC members from effective coordination, which results in the poor performance of the entire TSC.

Conflicts of business objective generally have a negative impact on the performance of a TSC. In the HKDL example, the conflict between HKDL and the tour operator reduced the overall profit of the TSC, and the lack of coordination dissuaded tourists from purchasing package holidays from the tour operator. Lack of information sharing – including a complete absence of information sharing, information delay and information distortion – can lead to an increase in operating costs, inappropriate business decisions, reduced tourist satisfaction and the deterioration of consumer relations.

Quantity discounts are a traditional market strategy in the tourism industry that has proved effective because the number of orders placed by buyers is negatively related to the price of a tourism product. In the example of HKDL and the tour operator, the two parties achieved perfect coordination through the application of a quantity discount strategy. The quantity discount aligned the objectives of HKDL and the tour operator with that of the overall objective of the TSC and thus maximised the profit of the overall chain.

Capacity exchange refers to the trading of products amongst homogeneous firms. In the tourism industry, it is mainly used to mitigate the negative effects of demand uncertainty. Capacity exchange minimises the losses arising from demand uncertainty without changing the supply capacity or pricing strategies of TSC members.

TSC members can make more effective decisions by sharing global information, including sales data, forecasting and planning data, capacity information, package holiday schedules and customer information. Information sharing can be effectively implemented through established ICTs, such as CRS, GDS and the internet.

Discussion questions

1. Use examples to illustrate why coordination is difficult within a TSC.
2. Consider the example of capacity exchange under coordination. If a new tour operator or more tour operators enter the market, then will the conclusions drawn in the text still hold?
3. Give other examples of beneficial coordination mechanisms amongst TSC members apart from the quantity discount and capacity exchange strategies.
4. Identify further examples of the use of ICTs by tourism businesses to facilitate information sharing and coordination.

Note

1   Source: Bastakis *et al.* (2004).

4

TOURISM SUPPLY CHAIN COMPETITION

Learning objectives

After reading this chapter you will be able to:

1. Identify different forms of competition and market structures in the tourism industry.
2. Understand how tourism businesses adopt competitive strategies to gain competition advantages.
3. Describe four levels of competition in a TSC.
4. Understand the concepts of Nash equilibrium and the Cournot and Stackelberg games.
5. Develop a game-theoretical analysis of a TSC, and understand how market size, costs and product substitution influence the performance of TSC members.

This chapter discusses some of the basic concepts of TSC competition, such as competition types, market structure, level of competition and competitive strategies. It also introduces game theory, a powerful tool used to formulate and analyse the interactions amongst the tourism businesses in a TSC. Three examples – the Nash equilibrium, the Cournot game and the Stackelberg game – are illustrated. A TSC game theory framework is then developed, and the impacts of several market parameters are discussed.

4.1 Tourism supply chain competition

Competition is the rivalry of two or more businesses striving for the same resources, such as customers, markets and profits. Tourism businesses compete with one another other primarily to increase their market share (and consequently their sales volume) and profit margins.

Competition can be interpreted in different dimensions. For example, the implementation of the individual visit scheme (IVS) in Hong Kong in 2003 allowed tourists from major cities in mainland China to obtain visas and travel to Hong Kong more easily. Hong Kong tour operators responded to this opportunity quickly by increasing their product offerings to mainland Chinese travellers. In this instance, the tour operators were mainly competing for quantity. On other occasions, such as in the off-peak seasons, tourism businesses engage in price competition. Competing for market share by reducing product prices constitutes a price war. In addition to quantity and price competition, tourism businesses also compete by providing high-quality services, developing new products and advertising in international markets.

In today's global market, tourism competition is no longer restricted to a specific geographical area or a single product or service. For example, the European package tour market is dominated by large British and German tour operators that offer various types of tourism products comprising multiple services, such as access to tourist attractions, accommodation, transport, dining, shopping, experiences, etc. These tour operators not only compete with one another in terms of products and services, but they also compete with other service providers, such as accommodation providers.

Types of competition

Competition in the tourism industry has traditionally been classified into three types according to the character of the products and services offered: direct competition, substitute competition and budget competition.

Direct competition is the narrowest form of competition, whereby businesses that provide homogeneous tourism products and services compete with one another. For example, two food companies supplying fresh fish to restaurants engage in direct competition.

The second form of competition is known as substitute competition, whereby the products or services that tourism businesses provide are close substitutes. For example, the ground transport services provided by car hire companies compete with the air transport services supplied by airlines. Sometimes, the products or services provided by tourism businesses serve the same purpose but are differentiated from those of competitors by the inclusion of additional services. For example, hotels located in the same area of a destination provide the same accommodation service, but some may also offer shopping and entertainment facilities that provide different experiences to tourists. These hotels are involved in substitute competition.

Budget competition is the broadest form of competition. Tourists' choice of tourism products and services is normally constrained by their income or budget. Once a tourist has allocated a certain amount of money to spend on a holiday, then he or she must decide which tourism products or services to purchase.

The more he or she spends on one such product/service, the less that is available for other products. For example, an American family has allocated $10,000 for a holiday abroad. The family now has to decide how much money will be spent on transport, accommodation, food, shopping, sightseeing and entertainment. In an aggregate sense, all tourism service providers compete for the fixed budgets of tourists.

In the context of a TSC, direct competition often occurs in the upstream of the supply chain amongst the businesses that provide the raw materials and basic services to the midstream tourism businesses. For example, direct competition can be found amongst water and energy suppliers, waste recycling and disposal suppliers and tourism craft producers. The tourism businesses in the midstream can be involved in both substitutive competition with their rivals in the same sector and budget competition with businesses in other sectors. For example, hotels compete with one another for tourists, and they also compete with suppliers in other sectors, such as restaurants, theme parks and entertainment establishments, for a share of tourists' budget, as all of the businesses in a TSC share the same pool of tourists.

Market structure

Market structure describes the state of a market and determines the intensity and characteristics of the competition. In the traditional framework, four major market structures are relevant to the tourism industry, as follows.

Perfect competition

Perfect competition occurs when a very large number of tourism businesses provide a homogeneous product or service. Each tourism business has a relatively small market share, and none has the market power to influence the price of the product. Moreover, there are no barriers to entry, and tourism businesses can enter or exit the market freely. Perfect competition is a theoretical market structure that is rarely found in real life. The closest examples of this type of structure include the high street travel agencies in some European cities and the small local eateries around large resort areas in destinations such as Bangkok and Phuket in Thailand and Hainan Island in China.

Monopolistic competition

Monopolistic competition occurs when a large number of tourism businesses provides a substitutive product or service. Monopolistic competition usually involves non–price competition based on heterogeneous products or services. Each tourism business has a degree of control over the price of its products and services, and there are few barriers to market entry and exit.[1] Examples of monopolistic competition include hotels and restaurants in large resort areas such as Bali in Indonesia.

Oligopoly

Oligopoly occurs when a small number of tourism businesses make up a sector of the tourism industry. These businesses are interdependent in that the decisions of one influence the decisions of the others. Oligopolies also have high barriers to entry. For example, there were twelve super deluxe hotels in Seoul until 1998, but because the high fixed costs of running such hotels form a strong barrier to market entry, only one new hotel has entered this market in the past ten years. Thus, the super deluxe hotel market in Seoul is a typical oligopoly (Chung, 2000). In an extreme case, a market may be composed of only two tourism businesses, a situation normally defined as a duopoly. However, most small tourism markets can be defined as oligopolies (Candela and Cellini, 2006).

Monopoly

Monopoly occurs when a single tourism business dominates the market and has absolute control over a particular product or service; that is, there are no alternative suppliers of this product or service. A monopolist is able to control price by changing the total supply in the market. A good example of the monopoly market structure is the theme park industry in Hong Kong before the opening of Hong Kong Disneyland which consisted only of Hong Kong Ocean Park.

The main criteria that distinguish the different market structures are the number of competitors in the market, the level of differentiation of the products and services on offer and the height of the barriers to entry and exit. The structure of a tourism market may change over time and across geographic boundaries. For example, according to Braun et al. (1992) and Braun and Soskin (1999), from its opening in 1971, Walt Disney World (WDW) dominated the theme park industry in central Florida until the early 1990s, accounting for sixty-eight per cent of the total regional theme park attendance and eighty-six per cent of the theme park revenue in 1988. However, it was not alone in the market: there were more than twenty competing parks and attractions, including Sea World, Busch Gardens, Cypress Gardens and Wet n' Wild. To insulate itself from price competition amongst its rivals, WDW offered multi-day, multi-park admission passes to tourists at a single price. Moreover, WDW continuously invested in new attractions at the existing park and built new park areas. Table 4.1 summarises the distribution of quarterly theme park admission prices in Florida from 1982:Q2 to 1989:Q1. These price data show that WDW could not control the market price, as if it had been able to do so, then there would not have been so many price changes over the sample period. The market structure of the central Florida theme park industry thus changed from an oligopoly to monopolistic competition during the 1970s and 1980s.

In the early 1990s, the market structure of the central Florida theme park industry changed back from monopolistic competition to an oligopoly for the following reasons. First, Anheuser Busch successfully acquired three of Florida's largest parks: Busch Gardens, Sea World and Cypress Gardens. Second, Universal Studios

TABLE 4.1 Quarterly admission price changes from 1982:Q2 to 1989:Q1

Theme park	Average quarterly price change ($)					
	No. of price changes	0.1–0.3	0.4–0.6	0.7–0.9	1.0–1.1	1.2+
Walt Disney World	12	3	1	4	1	6
Busch Gardens	14	3	7	0	2	1
Cypress Gardens	11	6	5	1	4	0
Sea World	6	6	11	0	2	2
Wet n' Wild	17	3	1	2	2	2

Source: Braun *et al.*, 1992

entered the market and introduced its market-proven attractions. At the same time, the growth in park admission prices slowed and eventually converged at a stable level. Over the 1990–95 period, the annual average price increase was less than seven per cent for all of the theme parks, and two thirds of the parks failed to increase their admission prices over this period.

Competition strategies

Members of TSCs adopt certain competition strategies to establish a profitable and sustainable position against the forces that determine industry competition. In his notable book *Competitive Strategy*, Porter (1980) states that three generic alternative strategies can be adopted to expand market share and improve the performance of a business.

The first is the *cost leadership* strategy, which emphasises operational or production efficiency. Maintaining this strategy requires tourism businesses to minimise their costs to achieve overall cost leadership through technological innovation and economies of scale. Economies of scale allow tourism firms to purchase raw materials, labour, capital and other key inputs at preferential prices, which minimises input costs. EasyJet and Ryanair in the UK and Air Asia in Indonesia are good examples of airlines that adopt the cost leadership strategy in their competition with conventional and other low-cost airlines.

The second is the *product differentiation* strategy. The purpose of this strategy is to create something that is perceived to be unique and different to provide insulation against rivalry. This uniqueness can be associated with brand image, product design, service quality, technology and management innovations or with the distribution channel. By adopting the product differentiation strategy, a tourism business can earn above-average returns and secure and maintain strong customer loyalty, thereby also reducing sensitivity to price changes. For example, after the opening of HKDL in 2005, Ocean Park chose to compete with the newcomer by offering different products and services that were equally high in quality. Ocean Park emphasises its strengths, which lie in having real animals, nature-friendly attractions, a cable car with a view and edutainment. As a result of this strategy, Ocean Park has improved its financial performance since 2005.

The third strategy is to *focus* on particular buyer groups or geographical markets. This strategy is most suitable for relatively small tourism businesses that aim to gain competitive advantage through effectiveness, rather than efficiency. The targets selected by a tourism business adopting this strategy are often less vulnerable to substitutes or are subject to weak competition.

Business integration

Integration is a strategic action in response to competition from rivals. It describes the type of management ownership and control adopted by tourism businesses. Two main types of integration occur between tourism businesses: horizontal integration and vertical integration.

Horizontal integration Horizontal integration refers to mergers and acquisitions between businesses that supply similar products or services in the same industry. For example, Whitbread, the largest hotel chain in the UK and owner of the Premier Inn chain, spent £505 million in July 2004 to acquire Premier Lodge and in March 2005 announced that the 141 Premier Lodge hotels had been successfully integrated with the existing Premier Inn chain. This is a typical example of horizontal integration in the hotel sector. Horizontal integration allows a tourism business to reduce the intensity of market competition, enjoy a better economy of scale and enhance operational efficiency. Horizontal integration in the tourism sector can take the forms of ownership transfer, joint reservation arrangements, management contracts and franchising agreements. For example, the major airline alliances – Star Alliance, One World and Sky Team – have frequent flyer and code-sharing arrangements amongst the individual airlines within each alliance. Horizontal integration is also an important strategy for business expansion. The Cendant Hotel Group in the United States saw a business opportunity in China in 2004 after the Chinese government announced its *Provisional Measures for the Supervision of Foreign Invested Enterprises Engaging in Commercial Franchising Businesses*. Cendant teamed up with China's Tian Rui Hotel Corporation and introduced the economy brand Super 8 Hotel chain to China through a franchising arrangement. By the end of 2008, Super 8 China had 124 properties in more than 60 cities across China, of which 65 were up and running. Super 8's fast expansion in China is a good example of transnational horizontal integration.

Vertical integration Vertical integration refers to one tourism business acquiring or merging with another that provides different tourism products and services, for instance, a tour operator taking over an airline. In this case, the tour operator would be looking to benefit from cost reductions through the allocation of tourists to its own air travel services. The same tour operator might also take over a travel agency to find a more profitable way of selling its travel products and services.

A real-life example of vertical integration is Airtours, which is engaged in tour operation, travel agency services, air transport, accommodation and cruises in seventeen countries across Europe and North America. First Choice is similarly involved in tour operation, travel agency services, air transport and car hire in the UK and Ireland. In Hong Kong, HKDL owns and operates two themed hotels (the Hong Kong Disneyland Hotel and Disney's Hollywood Hotel). Vertical integration enables tourism businesses to gain competitive advantage over equally efficient rivals, thereby generating barriers to entry and greater contract certainty (Lafferty and Fossen, 2001). Horizontal integration forms reliable TSCs and allows effective coordination amongst TSC members (see Chapter 3 on TSC coordination)

Competition in tourism supply chains

Competition in TSCs can be grouped into four levels. The first level is *intra-sector* competition between tourism businesses, such as those in the accommodation sector or travel agency sector. The second level is *inter-sector* competition within the same layer of a TSC. For example, the middle layer of a TSC may comprise hotel, bar and restaurant, attraction and theme park sectors. The businesses in these sectors compete for holidaymakers' expenditure knowing that it is constrained by their budgets. The third is *cross-sector* competition, that is, competition amongst sectors located in different layers of a TSC. A good example is the competition between hotels and tour operators. Hotels, which are located in the middle layer of a TSC, rely heavily on the tour operators in the upper layer to sell their rooms. Hotels always try to sell their rooms at high rates to maintain good profit margins, whereas tour operators normally expect hotels to provide high-quality services at a low cost. This conflict of objectives can be interpreted as competition between buyers and sellers for profit margin improvement. The final level is *chain* competition between two or more TSCs, which occurs when substitute package tours are sold by tour operators in the same target market. For example, HKDL and Hong Kong Ocean Park have their own supply chains, both of which compete for package holiday tourists from mainland China.

The complex competitive structure of TSCs requires an effective theoretical tool to identify their distinctive features so as to achieve efficient and effective supply chain management. The following section introduces the game theory approach to analysis of competition amongst TSC members and between TSCs.

4.2 Game theory and its application to TSC competition

Game theory is a powerful tool for formulating, structuring, analysing and understanding strategic scenarios. Since von Neumann and Morgenstern published their seminal work *Theory of Games and Economic Behavior* in 1944, game theory has been broadened and successfully applied in many fields, including economics, sociology and psychology. Game theory is well suited to the study of tourism competition issues, as the structure of TSCs is often very complex, and their members are highly interactive. In this section, the basic concepts of game theory are briefly introduced, and examples of its application to TSCs are given.

Definition of a game

A game is a formal model of interaction between players (individuals or businesses). The formal definition of a game describes the players, their preferences, the information available to them, their strategic actions given that information, and the outcome or payoff (Owen, 1995) of the players' interactive actions. A game with only one player is usually called a decision problem. A game always starts from a given point at which a player (or players) has to make a move. In the business field, this move is often called a strategy. A player must choose a move from several possible strategic actions according to his or her preference and the information available. At the end of a game, there will be a payoff for the player(s), which normally depends on the progress of the game.

A central assumption of game theory is that the players are rational. Rationality means that each player always chooses a strategy that optimises the outcome given the strategies of the other players. The game-theory analyses in this chapter follow a rational framework, although some recent studies have relaxed the rationality assumption.

Classification of games

Games can be classified into groups according to different criteria. A game is *cooperative* if the players are able to form groups or coalitions in which one player can enforce cooperative behaviour. The cooperative game is a competition between groups of players, rather than between individual players. A *non-cooperative* game does not imply that the players do not cooperate, but rather requires that any cooperation amongst players is self-enforcing. Players in a non-cooperative game are unable to make enforceable commitments about which strategy they will choose before they actually make a choice.

According to the sequence of players' moves, games can be also divided into *static* games and *dynamic* games. In static games, players choose their strategies simultaneously, or, if they do not act at the same time, the later players will not know the earlier players' decisions when making their own decisions. If players move sequentially and the later players can observe the actions of the earlier players, then the game is called a dynamic game.

Based on the information available to players, games can also be classified as *complete information* games and *incomplete information* games. A game with complete information means that a player's strategy and payoff are common knowledge to all players. If this is not the case, then we have an incomplete information game.

Nash equilibrium

The Nash equilibrium is a solution to a game in which each player is assumed to know the equilibrium strategies of the other players and no player has anything to gain by changing his or her own strategy. That is, if no player can benefit from unilaterally changing his or her strategy while the other players keep their strategies unchanged, then the current set of strategies constitutes a Nash equilibrium.

Table 4.2 shows a typical 2 × 2 matrix in a two–person game that could represent a duopoly package holiday market with two tour operators: tour operator 1 and tour operator 2. Each tour operator has two pricing strategies: a high price strategy and a low price strategy. If both tour operators supply package holidays at a high price, then tourists have no choice but to accept a high price, and both operators gain a profit of $20. If tour operator 1 sells its package holiday at a high price, but tour operator 2 sells its at a low price, then the former will lose customers and achieve a profit of only $10. Tour operator 2, in contrast, will attract more customers and gain a profit of $30. If both tour operators choose to sell their products at a low price, then they each gain a profit of $15.

In this game, the two tour operators are players with identical sets of strategies (High price, Low price). Obviously, each player prefers to achieve a high profit, and no benefit will be gained if one tries to lower the other's profit.

In Table 4.2, the rows represent the strategies available to tour operator 1, and the columns those available to tour operator 2. Each cell shows the payoff for tour operator 1 on the left and that for tour operator 2 on the right. In this game, the 'Low price' strategy dominates the 'High price' strategy. If tour operator 2 chooses the 'High price' strategy (see the left column of the table), then the 'Low price' strategy for tour operator 1 will generate a payoff of $30 and the 'High price' strategy will bring a payoff of $20. Using a different scenario in which tour operator 2 first chooses the 'Low price' strategy (see the right column of the table), the 'High price' strategy for tour operator 1 will yield a payoff of $10, whereas the 'Low price' strategy will generate a payoff of $15. In both scenarios, the unique Nash equilibrium solution for the game is (Low price, Low price), as regardless of the strategy that one tour operator chooses, the other will always adopt the 'Low price' strategy.

Although (Low price, Low price) is the Nash equilibrium in this game, it is not the best cumulative payoff for the two tour operators. Clearly, if the two tour operators both choose the 'High price' strategy, then each will gain a profit of $20. In reality, however, the 'High price' strategy is difficult to maintain for all players, as there is always an incentive for them to cheat (i.e., to change their strategy) to maximise the payoff. Given that adopting the 'Low price' strategy is beneficial to all players, they will act rationally by offering the holidays at a low price providing there is no collusion.

TABLE 4.2 Pricing strategy game matrix

		Tour operator 2	
		High price	Low price
Tour operator 1	High price	(20, 20)	(10, 30)
	Low price	(30, 10)	(15, 15)

Cournot game

A Cournot game is a typical static non-cooperative game in which complete information is available to all players. Consider a package holiday to Paris sold by only two tour operators (players) in mainland China: tour operator 1 and tour operator 2. The number of tourists buying the package holiday from the two tour operators is q_1 and q_2, respectively. Each tour operator determines the quantity (strategy) of holidays that it will offer without knowing the other's action. The market price for the package holiday is assumed to be the same, and is described by $p = \alpha - q_1 - q_2$, which implies that the market price will decrease if the total quantity of package holidays increases. Parameter α represents the market reservation price, which is the maximum price that the tourists are willing to pay. The operating cost of providing quantity q for tour operator i is $C_i(q_i) = cq_i$ ($i = 1, 2$). This operative's objective is to maximise its own profit π_i (payoff) given the quantity q_i supplied ($i = 1,2$).

$$\text{Max } \pi_i(q_i,q_j) = pq_i - C_i = (\alpha - q_i - q_j)q_i - cq_i \ . \tag{4.1}$$

Thus, tour operator j's best response (function) to the quantity chosen by tour operator i can be explained by

$$q_i(q_j) = \frac{(\alpha - c)}{2} - \frac{q_j}{2} \text{ (see Figure 4.1).}$$

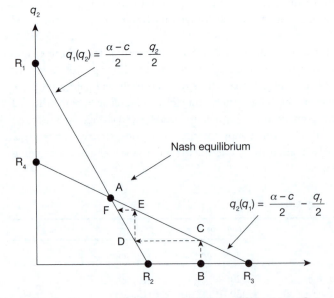

FIGURE 4.1 Response functions and Nash equilibrium in a Cournot game

In Figure 4.1, lines R_1R_2 and R_3R_4 are the response functions of tour operators 1 and 2, respectively. If tour operator 1 chooses the quantity indicated by point B, then the best choice of quantity for tour operator 2 is point C according to line R_3R_4. Believing that tour operator 2 will choose quantity C after it chooses quantity B, tour operator 1 will then choose quantity D based on line R_1R_2. Repeating the decision process, it can be determined that if one tour operator chooses quantity A, then the best choice for the other operator is also point A. Nothing is gained by further changes in strategy. Point A is therefore the Nash equilibrium of this game.

Mathematically, the equilibrium can be solved by combining the two response functions. The quantities and profits of the two tour operators in the equilibrium situation are $q_i^* = (\alpha - c)/3$ and $\pi_i^* = (\alpha - c)^2/9$, $i = 1,2$.

Stackelberg game

In the Cournot game, the two tour operators make their decisions simultaneously. However, if one tour operator moves first and the other moves subsequently after observing the action of the former, then the game is called a Stackelberg game, after the German economist Heinrich Freiherr von Stackelberg, who first described it.

Without loss of generality, it can be assumed that tour operator 2 moves after tour operator 1 in the Stackelberg game, as shown in Figure 4.2. The game is solved by backward induction. Before making any move, tour operator 1 considers how tour operator 2 will respond if the quantity it offers is made available. After making this assessment, tour operator 1 decides on the quantity of package holidays that it needs to offer to maximise its profit.

Based on Figure 4.2, tour operator 1 knows that tour operator 2 will choose quantity

$$q_2(q_1) = \frac{(\alpha - c)}{2} - \frac{q_1}{2}$$

if its quantity is q_1. Thus, the objective of tour operator 1 is to maximise its profit with respect to q_1 given tour operator 2's response.

$$\text{Max } \pi_1(q_1, q_2(q_1)) = \left[\alpha - \beta \left(q_1 + \frac{\alpha - c}{2\beta} - \frac{q_1}{2} \right) \right] q_1 - cq_1 . \qquad (4.2)$$

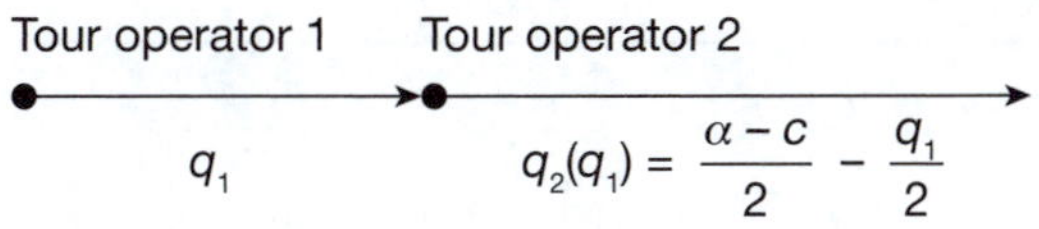

Tour operator 1   Tour operator 2

$$q_1 \qquad\qquad q_2(q_1) = \frac{\alpha - c}{2} - \frac{q_1}{2}$$

FIGURE 4.2 Decision process of a Stackelberg game

Solving equation (4.2) shows that the optimal quantity and profit of tour operator 1 are $q_1^* = (\alpha - c)/2$ and $\pi_1^* = (\alpha - c)^2/8$, respectively. By substituting $q_1^* = (\alpha - c)/2$ into the response function

$$q_2(q_1) = \frac{(\alpha - c)}{2} - \frac{q_1}{2},$$

it can easily be found that the optimal quantity and profit of tour operator 2 are $q_2^* = (\alpha - c)/4$ and $\pi_2^* = (\alpha - c)^2/16$. Clearly, the optimal profit of tour operator 1 is larger than that of tour operator 2. In this situation, tour operator 1 is the market leader with first-mover advantage.

Table 4.3 summarises the equilibrium results of the Cournot and Stackelberg games. The total market output in the latter is higher than that in the former, with a lower market price for the package holidays in the Stackelberg game. Tour operators prefer to be the market leader in a Stackelberg game, as the market leader's profit is much greater than that of the follower in a Stackelberg game and that of all players in a Cournot game.

4.3 Competition in a tourism supply chain

The objective of this section is to establish a game-theory framework for analysing competition in a TSC. Based on the equilibrium results, the impacts of market size, TSC operating costs, and product or service substitution on the performance of TSC members are also discussed.

Competition in a TSC

As noted in Chapter 1, a TSC has a complex structure that consists of multiple layers. Each layer includes various sectors that supply similar or different tourism products or services. To simplify the discussion without loss of generality, the TSC considered here is made up of three sectors: a theme park (TP), multiple hotel accommodation providers (HAs) and multiple tour operators (TOs). Sectors such as transportation, bars and restaurants and retail shops are also included in the TSC. Its products are the package holidays provided by the TOs to tourists. These holidays

TABLE 4.3 Comparison of the payoffs in the Cournot and Stackelberg games

Game		Tour operator 1			Tour operator 2	
	Price	Quantity	Profit		Quantity	Profit
Cournot	$\dfrac{\alpha + 2c}{3}$	$\dfrac{\alpha - c}{3}$	$\dfrac{(\alpha - c)^2}{9}$		$\dfrac{\alpha - c}{3}$	$\dfrac{(\alpha - c)^2}{9}$
Stackelberg	$\dfrac{\alpha + 3c}{4}$	$\dfrac{\alpha - c}{2}$	$\dfrac{(\alpha - c)^2}{8}$		$\dfrac{\alpha - c}{4}$	$\dfrac{(\alpha - c)^2}{16}$

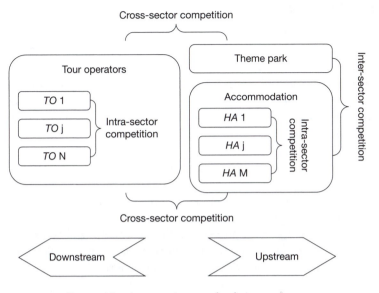

FIGURE 4.3 Competition in a tourism supply chain

include a trip to the TP and a one-night stay in an HA. For example, before 2005 when Hong Kong Ocean Park was the only theme park to serve tourists in Hong Kong, tour operators provided package holidays whose core components were standard admission to Ocean Park, a one-night stay in a Hong Kong hotel and shopping experiences in one of the territory's modern shopping malls, such as Times Square, Harbour City or Pacific Place.

In Figure 4.3, the TOs and HAs are grouped into sectors, and the TSC is represented as a network in which each sector is represented by a node. The three sectors are arranged into two layers or echelons. The TP and HAs in the upstream layer are suppliers of package tour components or options for package holiday products. The TOs in the downstream layer are responsible for the configuration and promotion of the package holidays according to information on tourist demand for the services provided by the upstream sectors. The prices charged by the TOs include payments to the TP and HAs.

Three levels of competition can be identified in the TSC. The first is the intra-sector competition amongst the businesses within a sector, which takes the form of quantity competition in the TO and HA sectors. The second level is the cross-sector competition between the sectors in different layers, such as that between the TP and TO sectors and that between the HA and TO sectors. This cross-sector competition takes the form of coordination in the sense that the sectors must coordinate their product and service provision according to demand. The third level is the inter-sector competition between sectors in the same layer, such as that between the TP and HA sectors at the level below the TO sector.

Game theory framework

All of the entities (TP, TOs and HAs) in the TSC are players in the game. The HAs contract and allocate their capacity to the TOs. This capacity allocation is necessary to satisfy the retail hotel market, in which HAs sell their rooms directly to tourists. For example, tour operators such as Airtours determine quantities one season ahead through long-term contracts. Thus, the HAs and TOs take the tourist quantities as their strategies, and the TP's strategy is the price of the admission ticket. The payoffs for all players in the TSC are the profits determined by the interactive strategies they adopt.

Competition in this case can be described as the following sequential game.

- *First stage* The TP determines the admission ticket price, and the HAs set their room rates through quantity competition.
- *Second stage* Each TO learns the prices set by the TP and HAs and determines the number of tourists (or groups) that they plan to serve, and then allows the market to determine the final price of the package holidays.

Using mathematical notation, there are N TOs and M HAs in the TSC. For simplicity, it is further assumed that there are only two HAs and two TOs, that is, $M = N = 2$. The TOs and HAs have identical variable unit costs c_1 and c_2, and the variable unit cost of the TP is c. A linear inverse price function is assumed for the TO_i:

$$p_1^i = \alpha - q_1^i - \beta q_1^j , \qquad (4.3)$$

where p_1^i is the price of the package holidays offered by TO_i, and q_1^i and q_1^j are the number of tourists served by the two TOs, respectively ($i, j = 1, 2; i \neq j$). Here, α represents the market reservation price or the market size, and has a natural restriction $\alpha > c_1 + c_2 + c$. The parameter β captures the degree of substitution of the package holidays provided by the two TOs. If $\beta = 0$, then the package holidays provided by the two TOs are completely different, whereas $\beta = 1$ indicates that they are perfect substitutes. $0 < \beta \leqslant 1$ thus means that the two package holidays are substitutes of each other and that the degree of substitution depends on the value of β.

Backward induction is employed to solve this sequential game. In the last stage of the game, the TOs simultaneously decide the quantities of tourists that they will serve. Given the prices p and p_2 for the TP and the HAs, the profit function for TO_i is

$$\pi_1^i = q_1^i (p_1^i - p - p_2 - c_1) . \qquad (4.4)$$

Taking the first-order condition of equation (4.4) with respect to quantity and summing the equations for the two TOs in the TSC, the demand for package holidays for each of the TOs and the total demand Q in the TSC can be written as

$$q_1^1 = q_1^2 = \frac{\alpha - p - p_2 - c_1}{2 + \beta}, \quad Q = q_1^1 + q_1^2 = \frac{2(\alpha - p - p_2 - c_1)}{2 + \beta}. \tag{4.5}$$

From the total demand Q, the price p_2 for HA_s can be obtained from

$$p_2^s = \alpha - p - c_1 - \frac{(2 + \beta)Q}{2},$$

where $Q = q_2^s + q_2^t$, and q_2^s and q_2^t are the tourist quantities of HA_s and HA_t, respectively ($s, t = 1, 2; s \neq t$).

HA_s aims to determine the quantity q_2^s that will maximise its profit $\pi_2^s = q_2^s(p_2^s - c_2)$. It is easy to see that the optimal quantity for HA_s would be

$$q_2^s = \frac{2(\alpha - c_1 - c_2 - p)}{3(2 + \beta)}.$$

Thus, the total market demand for package holidays Q in the TSC is

$$Q = \frac{4(\alpha - c_1 - c_2 - p)}{3(2 + \beta)}. \tag{4.6}$$

The objective of the TP is to decide on the price of the admission ticket p that will maximise its profit $\pi_3 = Q(p - c)$. Substituting Q in equation (4.5) with π_3, the corresponding total demand can be obtained as follows.

$$Q = \frac{\alpha - c_1 - c - p_2}{2 + \beta}. \tag{4.7}$$

The equilibrium of the total demand can be solved by combining equations (4.6) and (4.7) as

$$Q^* = \frac{4(\alpha - c_1 - c_2 - c)}{5(2 + \beta)}.$$

Other equilibrium results are summarised in Table 4.4.

TABLE 4.4 Equilibrium results of the game model

	Quantity	Price	Profit
TO	$\frac{1}{2}Q^*$	$\frac{(8 + 3\beta)}{4}Q^* + c_1 + c_2 + c$	$\frac{1}{4}(Q^*)^2$
HA	$\frac{1}{2}Q^*$	$\frac{2 + \beta}{4}Q^* + c_2$	$\frac{2 + \beta}{8}(Q^*)^2$
TP	Q^*	$\frac{2 + \beta}{2}Q^* + c$	$\frac{2 + \beta}{2}(Q^*)^2$

Impact analyses

A TSC is an interactive system, and thus a change in one part of the TSC will pass through the entire chain and influence all members. To capture such interactions amongst TSC members, this section presents some theoretical analyses of the impacts of the three TSC parameters of market size, TSC costs and product substitution on TSC performance.

Impact of market size

Market size describes the volume of potential tourists that can be served by a TSC. In the foregoing game models, it is represented by α. Clearly, the total quantity of tourists Q^* is positively related to market size α, as

$$\frac{\partial Q^*}{\partial \alpha} = \frac{4}{5(2+\beta)} > 0 .$$

Thus, if the market size α increases, then the quantity, price and profit of each TSC member will also increase.

Each TSC member (or sector) has a strong incentive to enlarge the market size of the TSC. There are two ways to achieve market expansion: passive and proactive. For instance, tourism demand, whether for the TSC as a whole or for its members, tends to grow naturally in environments in which the economy is thriving and the political system is stable (passive expansion). An aggressive advertising strategy is a proactive approach to expansion. TPs often advertise their products internationally to strengthen their brand images with a view to attracting more international visitors. Likewise, TOs are more likely to advertise their products and services locally to achieve short-term market expansion. Another advertising strategy for TSC members is to promote package holidays jointly. For example, TPs and TOs may make arrangements to share advertising costs.

Impact of TSC costs

TSC costs include all of the costs that TSC members incur in the provision of the TSC's products. In the foregoing game model, the total demand quantity Q^* is negatively related to the unit costs of the TSC members, c_1, c_2 and c. Hence, an increase in the unit cost of one TSC member may reduce the demand quantity and lead to the poor performance of all TSC members, because their profits are all proportional to the total quantity demanded. The implication is that the profit of a tourism business depends heavily on the costs of all of the members in its supply chain.

Because

$$\frac{\partial p_1^*}{\partial c_1} = \frac{\partial p_1^*}{\partial c_2} = \frac{\partial p_1^*}{\partial c} = \frac{2(1+\beta)}{5(2+\beta)} > 0 ,$$

the equilibrium price of the package holidays in the target market will rise with increases in the unit costs of the TSC members, because the cost increase of each TSC member is passed on to customers.

Taking the first derivative of the equilibrium prices of the HAs and TP gives

$$\frac{\partial p_2^*}{\partial c_1} = \frac{\partial p_2^*}{\partial c} = -\frac{1}{5} < 0, \quad \frac{\partial p_2^*}{\partial c_2} = \frac{4}{5} > 0, \quad \frac{\partial p^*}{\partial c_1} = \frac{\partial p^*}{\partial c_2} = -\frac{2}{5} < 0, \quad \frac{\partial p^*}{\partial c} = \frac{3}{5} > 0 .$$

We can see that the equilibrium price of an HA (TP) changes in the opposite direction to that of the TP (HA) when the costs of either change. This mechanism in fact stabilises the price of the package holidays within the TSC.

Impact of product substitution

The degree of product substitution β defines the level of differentiation of the package holidays offered by the TOs. The lower the degree of substitution, the greater the differentiation. Product differentiation will enhance the competitiveness of the package holidays offered by the different TOs. It is easy to understand that the quantity supplied by each TO will increase if the package holidays are highly differentiated. Upstream businesses such as the TP and HAs will also benefit from product differentiation. Rewriting the equilibrium price of the TOs to reflect greater product differentiation gives

$$p^* = \left[\frac{2}{5(2+\beta)} + \frac{3}{5} \right] \left(\alpha - c_1 - c_2 - c \right) + c_1 + c_2 + c ,$$

which suggests that a TO can charge a higher price if its products are more strongly differentiated from the other package holidays in the market. At the same time, it can also sell more of its products and improve its profitability. The prices of the TP and HAs are independent of β and are thus relatively stable.

These analyses help us to understand some of the impacts on the performance of TSC members generated by changes in market size, TSC costs and product differentiation; however, many questions remain unanswered, for example, what would happen if new TOs or HAs entered the market? Would the incumbent businesses in a sector be forced to reduce their prices? Would other businesses in the same layer benefit from the intensified competition resulting from the market entry? More complicated game models that include more than two TOs or HAs would be needed to analyse the competition dynamics of the TSC in this case.

4.4 Summary

Competition in the tourism industry can be classified into three categories according to the characteristics of the products or services offered: direct competition, substitute competition and budget competition. Direct competition is the narrowest form of competition, and budget competition the broadest.

Market structure describes the state of a market, which determines the intensity and characteristics of competition. The tourism industry can be divided into four market structures based on the intensity of competition: perfect competition, monopolistic competition, oligopoly and monopoly.

Three generic alternative competition strategies can be adopted by tourism businesses. The cost leadership strategy minimises costs to achieve overall cost leadership through technological innovation and economies of scale. The product differentiation strategy involves the creation of something that is perceived to be unique, thereby insulating a business from rivalry. The focus strategy concentrates on a particular buyer group or specific geographical market with a view to better serving customers.

Competition within TSCs can be grouped into four levels: intra-sector competition amongst the tourism businesses within a sector, inter-sector competition amongst the sectors (and their members) in the same layer of a TSC, cross-sector competition amongst sectors (and their members) located in different layers of a TSC and chain competition between two or more TSCs.

Competition in TSCs can be analysed using game theory. The Nash equilibrium is a solution to a game in which each player is assumed to know the equilibrium strategies of the other players, and no player has anything to gain by further changing his or her own strategy.

Players in a Cournot game optimise their payoffs by making their strategic moves simultaneously. In a Stackelberg game, the players make their strategic moves sequentially, with the later players deciding what to do after observing the strategic actions of the earlier players. This type of game is normally solved by backward induction from the strategies adopted by the early players to those adopted by the later players.

A TSC consists of multiple layers. The tourism businesses downstream make decisions to maximise their payoffs after learning the decisions of the upstream businesses. This scenario can be formulated as a sequence game and solved by backward induction.

Various market parameters affect the performance of TSC members. Market size and product substitution have positive impacts on the performance of TSC members, whereas TSC costs are negatively related to their profits.

Note

1 Barriers to entry refer to the hindrances that a business may face when trying to enter a market. These hindrances include investment, government regulations, technology and customer loyalty.

Discussion questions

1. What are the different forms of competition? Give some examples of each form.
2. Describe the major market structures using examples from the tourism and hospitality industry.
3. If you were the manager of a small travel agency in an extremely competitive market, what competitive strategy would you choose and why?
4. Describe the four levels of competition in a TSC and distinguish *inter-sector* competition from *cross-sector* competition.
5. According to a survey conducted by students from a local university on the customers of two restaurants (restaurant 1 and restaurant 2) in a tourist area, 6,000 tourists patronise the two restaurants each year, and 4,000 local customers choose restaurant 2 over restaurant 1 because it is relatively cheaper. Suppose that each restaurant has a choice of three price strategies per customer: $20, $40, $50. If both restaurants charge $20 per customer, then each will obtain 5,000 customers and $100,000 in revenue. If restaurant 1 charges $40 and restaurant 2 charges $20, then restaurant 1 will attract 3,000 customers and obtain $120,000 in revenue, and restaurant 2 will receive 7,000 customers and gain $140,000 in revenue. The full set of payoffs for the two restaurants is shown in the following table (the payoffs are expressed in thousands of dollars).

TABLE 4.5

		Restaurant 2		
		$20	$40	$50
Restaurant 1	$20	(100, 100)	(140, 120)	(140, 150)
	$40	(120, 140)	(200, 200)	(280, 150)
	$50	(150, 140)	(150, 280)	(250, 250)

   Does this game have a Nash equilibrium? If so, what is the solution?
6. What are the differences between a simultaneous game and a sequential game?
7. In the game model in section 4.3, assume that a new accommodation provider enters the market, which means that there will be two tour operators, three accommodation providers and one theme park in the TSC. What will be the impact of the new entrant on the equilibrium price, quantity and profit of each TSC member? If the entry requires a fixed investment F, then will this prevent the new accommodation provider from entering the market? If so, then what is the level of F that deters entry?

5

CHAIN VERSUS CHAIN COMPETITION

Learning objectives

After reading this chapter you will be able to:

1. Extend analyses using the game theoretic approach to analyse the competition between TSCs.
2. Understand how TSC membership, preference and integration affect TSC performance.
3. Understand the managerial implications of chain versus chain competition.

The previous chapter introduced several basic competition concepts and employed game theory to analyse the competition issues amongst the members of a TSC. This chapter extends the discussion of a single TSC to the chain versus chain scenario, and identifies the optimal decisions of tourism businesses in such a scenario. This chapter also examines the impact of such factors as TSC membership, preference and strategic integration on TSC performance and discusses how tourism businesses respond to changes in these factors.

5.1 Chain versus chain competition

As discussed in the previous chapter, the tourism businesses in a TSC benefit from providing package tour components to ensure a consistent supply of these products/services to meet tourist demand. At the same time, however, the performance of one service provider depends on the performance of the others in the TSC, as each tourism business influences tourists' experiences and the payoffs of all enterprises within the TSC. To achieve optimal TSC objectives and satisfy customer needs, the members of a TSC require synthesis as a single entity to compete with similar product/service providers in other TSCs (James and Dale, 2004).

Take the Hong Kong theme park sector as an example. Before 2005, it was dominated by Hong Kong Ocean Park. The opening of Hong Kong Disneyland (HKDL) in 2005 changed the market structure from a monopoly to a duopoly. Each of the two theme parks has developed its own suppliers, including tour operators, accommodation providers and transport services. Hence, there are two competing TSCs in Hong Kong's theme park market. In each of these chains, package tours are compiled from the tourism services/products offered by TSC members and sold by tour operators in target markets. When a customer chooses to purchase a package tour, he or she will consume the products/services provided by the suppliers in one of the TSCs. Thus, the competition between package tours is in fact competition between two TSCs.

In the chain versus chain scenario, three factors have a significant effect on TSC performance. The first is TSC membership, which determines the intensity of competition within each TSC. An increase in the number of TSC members results in TSC capacity expansion, and an increase in the number of suppliers in one TSC sector also leads to an increase in competition within that sector. The second factor is TSC preference, which measures consumer willingness to substitute one TSC's products for those of the other and is associated with product differentiation. A strong TSC preference implies that customers are locked into one TSC. It is difficult for them to change to the other due to high switching costs. The third factor is TSC integration, which refers to the degree of consolidation in the relationships amongst TSC members, activities, functions and processes, and the locations of tourism businesses and their customers and suppliers (Wong et al., 2007). The integration of TSC members significantly alters the structure and mode of competition in the TSCs.

In the next section, we apply the game theoretic model discussed in the previous chapter to analyse chain versus chain competition. The remaining sections focus on the influences of TSC membership, preference and integration on the competition between two TSCs.

5.2 Game-theoretic framework

This section considers a destination dominated by two theme parks (TPs). Each TP works closely and exclusively with its business partners: multiple tour operators (TOs) and accommodation providers (HAs). As a result, two competitive TSCs are formed at this destination. The two TSCs provide package holidays that include a visit to one of the two TPs. One focuses exclusively on package holiday products with a 'fantasy' theme, and the other on those with a 'variety' theme. Tourists can choose only one of the two types of package holidays.

The TOs and HAs in the same TSC are grouped into sectors, and all entities within a sector are assumed to be identical. The TSC is a network in which each sector is represented as a node (see Figure 5.1). The three sectors are arranged into two layers or echelons. The TP and HAs in the upstream layer are suppliers of the package tour components or package holiday product options. The TOs in the downstream layer are responsible for the configuration and promotion of the package holidays based on tourists' demand for the services provided by the upstream sectors. The prices charged by the TOs include the payments made to the TP and HAs.

Several levels of competition can be defined in this game. The first is the intra-sector competition amongst the businesses within a sector. It is illustrated by the quantity competition in the TO and HA sectors. The second is the cross-sector competition between the sectors in different layers, e.g., that between the TP and TO sectors and that between the HA and TO sectors. Cross-sector competition takes the form of coordination in the sense that the sectors coordinate demand. The third is the inter-sector competition between the sectors in the same layer, e.g., that between the TP and HA sectors at the level below the TO sector. The fourth is the chain competition between the two TSCs that supply substitute package tours, and thus compete with each other directly in the target market.

In this model, all tourism businesses (the TPs, TOs and HAs) in the two TSCs are game players and profits are their payoffs. The TOs and HAs aim to increase the number of tourists who use their services, i.e., they adopt the quantity strategy, whilst the TPs take price as their strategy. Competition in the market is described as a two-stage game:

First stage: In each TSC, the TP determines the admission price, and the HA sector achieves its market clearing price through Cournot competition amongst the HAs.

Second stage: Each TO receives the prices of the TP and the HAs and determines the number of package holidays it plans to sell and then allows the market to determine the final price of the package holiday.

In this formulation, TSC_A and TSC_B represent the two TSCs. Subscripts A and B are omitted when a single chain is discussed, and subscript -1 represents the rival (competing) TSC. There are N TOs and M HAs in each TSC, indexed by $i = 1 \ldots N$ and $j = 1 \ldots M$. The variable unit costs of the TP, HA and TO are c, c_2 and c_1, respectively. A linear inverse price function for TO_i is

$$p_1^i = \alpha - Q - \mu Q_{-1}, \tag{5.1}$$

where p_1^i is the price of a package holiday product, and Q and Q_{-1} are the total number of tourists in the two TSCs. The decision variable is tourist quantity q_i for TO_i. Here, α represents the market reservation price or market size. Parameter μ captures tourists' cross-quantity sensitivity or supply chain preference. It is plausible to assume that μ increases and the supply chain preference decreases. As the two TSCs are substitutes for each other, $0 < \mu \leq 1$. If $\mu = 1$, then the two package holidays are also perfect substitutes.

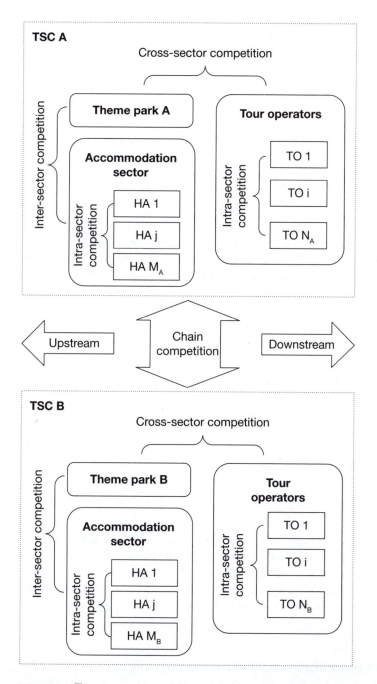

FIGURE 5.1 Two competing tourism supply chains in a destination

Backward induction is employed to solve this sequential game. In the last stage of the game, all of the TOs are allowed to decide the quantities of tourists in the package tour market simultaneously. Given prices p and p_2 for the TP and HA, respectively, the profit of TO_i is

$$\pi_1^i = q_1^i(p_1^i - p - p_2 - c_1) . \tag{5.2}$$

Taking the first-order condition with respect to quantity, and then summing up the equations for all TOs in the TSC, the total demand for package holidays is measured by the total number of tourists as

$$Q = \frac{N(\alpha - c_1 - p - p_2 - \mu Q_{-1})}{N+1} . \tag{5.3}$$

The profits of HA_j and TP are $\pi_2^j = (p_2 - c_2^j)q_2^j$ and $\pi_3 = Q(p - c)$, respectively. Solving p_2 and p from equation (5.3) and then substituting the results into the profit functions of HA_j and TP, we find the optimal quantities for HA_j and TP, respectively. Combine these optimal quantities, and the total number of tourists in the TSC can be obtained as follows.

$$Q = \frac{N M(\alpha - c_1 - c_2 - c - \mu Q_{-1})}{(N+1)(2M+1)} . \tag{5.4}$$

Equation (5.4) is a TSC's best response function with regard to its rival TSC. Solve this equation for both TSCs, and the equilibrium of the total tourist numbers for the two competing TSCs is

$$Q_s = \frac{m_s n_s f_s - \mu m_s n_s m_t n_t f_t}{1 - \mu^2 m_s n_s m_t n_t} , \tag{5.5}$$

where $n_s = \dfrac{N_s}{N_s + 1} \in \left[\dfrac{1}{2}, 1\right]$, $m_s = \dfrac{M_s}{2M_s + 1} \in \left[\dfrac{1}{3}, \dfrac{1}{2}\right]$, $C_s = c_{s1} + c_{s2} + c_s$ and

$$f_s = \alpha_s - C_s , s,t = A,B .$$

If $Q_A < 0$ or $\delta < \mu m_B n_B$, where $\delta = (\alpha_A - C_A)/(\alpha_B - C_B)$, then TSC_A has to withdraw from the market if its product loses market attraction due to cost disadvantage(s), and TSC_B will then dominate the package holiday market as a monopoly. To ensure that the demand for each TSC at its equilibrium quantity is positive, we must additionally assume that $(1/(\mu m_A n_A)) > \delta > \mu m_B n_B$. Additional equilibrium results are summarised in Table 5.1.

5.3 Impact of tourism supply chain membership

This section focuses on the influences of TSC membership on the performance of the supply chain members and sectors and the chain as a whole. In the game model, an increase in TSC memberships is represented by an increase in the number of tour operators and accommodation providers.

TABLE 5.1 Equilibriums of TSC_S

	Quantity	*Price*	*Profit*
TO	$\dfrac{Q_S}{N_S}$	$(\dfrac{1}{N_S} + \dfrac{N_S + 1}{N_S M_S} + \dfrac{N_S + 1}{N_S}) Q_S + C_S$	$(\dfrac{Q_S}{N_S})^2$
HA	$\dfrac{Q_S}{M_S}$	$\dfrac{N_S + 1}{N_S M_S} Q_S + c_{S2}$	$\dfrac{N_S + 1}{N_S}(\dfrac{Q_S}{M_S})^2$
TP	Q_S	$\dfrac{N_S + 1}{N_S} Q_S + c_S$	$\dfrac{N_S + 1}{N_S} Q_S^2$

Let us first consider the impacts of TSC membership on each supply chain member. Table 5.2 presents the theoretical results, with the variables transformed. For example, the equilibrium price of a tour operator can be rewritten as

$$\left(1 - \frac{1 - \mu^2 m_B n_B}{\dfrac{1}{m_A n_A} - \mu^2 m_B n_B}\right)\left(f_A - \mu m_B n_B f_B\right) + C_A .$$

Assuming the other variables remain unchanged, an increase in N_A/M_A leads to a rise in n_A/m_A or a decrease in $1/(n_A m_A)$. Hence, the price of the tour operator decreases. Additionally, because Q_t is negatively associated with N_s and M_s ($s \neq t$), the quantities, prices and profits of the TSC_B members decrease with an increase in N_A/M_A.

The results in Table 5.2 show that an increase in membership in one sector of the TSC boosts the profits of enterprises in other sectors of the same TSC, but adversely affects those of their counterparts in the corresponding sector of the rival TSC. Such an increase also leads to a decrease in the prices of both TSCs' package holidays. From the TP's perspective, encouraging more TOs and HAs to join a TSC can result in greater market share and greater profits. From that of the TO and HAs, profits will be maximised if the sector is dominated by a single firm (monopoly).

We next analyse the impacts of TSC membership on each sector of the TSC and the entire TSC. The total profit of the TO sector in TSC_A can be rewritten as

$$\Pi_{A1} = N_A \pi_{A1} = \frac{f_B^2 (\delta - \mu m_B n_B)^2}{\left[\sqrt{N_A}\left(\dfrac{1}{m} - \mu^2 m_B n_B\right) + \dfrac{1}{m_A \sqrt{N_A}}\right]^2} . \tag{5.6}$$

Intuitively,

$$K(N_A) = \sqrt{N_A}\left(\frac{1}{m_A} - \mu^2 m_B n_B\right) + \frac{1}{m_A \sqrt{N_A}}$$

TABLE 5.2 Impact of tourism supply chain membership on each TSC member

		Quantity	Price	Profit
	TO	$\uparrow(M_A\uparrow),\downarrow(N_A\uparrow),$	$\downarrow$	$\uparrow(M_A\uparrow),\downarrow(N_A\uparrow),$
TSC_A	HA		$\downarrow(M_A\uparrow),\uparrow(N_A\uparrow),$	
	TP		$\uparrow$	

has minimal value when $N_A = (1/(1 - \mu^2 m_A m_B n_B))$ if the other parameters remain unchanged. Hence, if $N_A \leqslant (1/(1 - \mu^2 m_A m_B n_B))$, then Π_{A1} increases when N_A increases; if $N_A > (1/(1 - \mu^2 m_A m_B n_B))$, then Π_{A1} increases when N_A decreases. Because $(1/(1 - \mu^2 m_A m_B n_B)) < 4/3$ and $K_{A1}(1) < K_{A1}(2)$, Π_{A1} decreases in $N_A \in [2, +\infty]$.

The total profit of the HA sector in TSC_A can be written as

$$\Pi_{A2} = M_A \pi_{A2} = \frac{n_A f_B^2 (\delta - \mu m_B n_B)^2}{\left[\sqrt{M_A}\left(2 - \mu^2 n_A m_B n_B\right) + \dfrac{1}{\sqrt{M_A}}\right]^2}. \tag{5.7}$$

Using the same logic as in the TO sector, we know that Π_{A2} decreases if M_A increases.

The total profit of TSC_A can be rewritten as

$$\Pi_A = \frac{(f_A - \mu m_B n_B f_B)^2}{\left(\dfrac{1}{m_A n_A} - 1\right) + \left(\dfrac{(1 - \mu^2 m_B n_B)^2}{\dfrac{1}{m_A n_A} - 1}\right) + 2\left(1 - \mu^2 m_B n_B\right)}. \tag{5.8}$$

Note that $(1/m_A n_A - 1) \in [1, 5]$ and $1 - \mu^2 m_B n_B < 1$; thus,

$$\left(\frac{1}{m_A n_A} - 1\right) + \left(1 - \mu^2 m_B n_B\right)^2 \Big/ \left(\frac{1}{m_A n_A} - 1\right)$$

decreases when n_A or m_A increases. Hence, Π_A increases with an increase in N_A or M_A.

To sum up, an increase in TSC membership leads to an increase in the total profit of the TSC, but a decrease in the profits of the respective sectors.

We can divide the competitors into two groups: direct and indirect competitors. The former are TSC members in the same sector of the same TSC, whilst the latter are those in the corresponding sector of the competing TSC. According to the foregoing analysis, new entrants in a specific TSC reduce the profits of the incumbent businesses in the corresponding sector of the competing TSC and vice versa. The example in Table 5.3 illustrates the impact of a new entrant. The figures in this table are percentage changes relative to the benchmarks provided at the

TABLE 5.3 Influence of a new entrant

Profit	$\mu = 1$				$\mu = 0.75$			
(TSC$_A$)	$N_A + 1$	$N_B + 1$	$M_A + 1$	$M_B + 1$	$N_A + 1$	$N_B + 1$	$M_A + 1$	$M_B + 1$
TO	−15.68	−0.87	2.71	−1.32	−15.82	−0.61	2.48	−0.94
TO sector	−7.25	−0.87	2.71	−1.32	−7.40	−0.61	2.48	−0.94
HA	1.18	−0.87	−24.54	−1.32	1.01	−0.61	−24.71	−0.94
HA sector	1.18	−0.87	−11.97	−1.32	1.01	−0.61	−12.16	−0.94
TP	1.18	−0.87	2.71	−1.32	1.01	−0.61	2.48	−0.94
TSC	0.57	−0.87	0.76	−1.32	0.40	−0.61	0.54	−0.94

Profit	$\mu = 0.5$				$\mu = 0.25$			
(TSC$_A$)	$N_A + 1$	$N_B + 1$	$M_A + 1$	$M_B + 1$	$N_A + 1$	$N_B + 1$	$M_A + 1$	$M_B + 1$
TO	−15.91	−0.40	2.34	−0.60	−15.96	−0.20	2.26	−0.30
TO sector	−7.50	−0.40	2.34	−0.60	−7.55	−0.20	2.26	−0.30
HA	0.91	−0.40	−24.81	−0.60	0.85	−0.20	−24.87	−0.30
HA sector	0.91	−0.40	−12.28	−0.60	0.85	−0.20	−12.35	−0.30
TP	0.91	−0.40	2.34	−0.60	0.85	−0.20	2.26	−0.30
TSC	0.30	−0.40	0.40	−0.60	0.24	−0.20	0.32	−0.30

(Benchmarks: $N_A = 10$, $M_A = 6$, $f_A = 1000$, $N_B = 9$, $M_B = 5$, $f_B = 950$)

bottom. As can be seen from the table's numerical illustrations, the influence of a new direct competitor on the sector's profits is greater than that of a new indirect competitor in another sector. Furthermore, the negative influence of the entry of direct competitors on the profits of the TSC's members also increases with a decrease in μ; that is, the TSC preference can serve as a buffer to reduce competition intensity.

5.4 Impact of tourism supply chain preference

This section discusses the impact of TSC preference on supply chain performance. TSC preference is determined primarily by the product differentiation between the two TPs concerned, as they provide the main motivation for tourists to choose a package holiday. In the game model, parameter μ characterises the supply chain preference. A stronger preference implies a lower value of μ.

Taking the first-order condition of Q_A with respect to μ gives

$$\frac{\partial Q_A}{\partial \mu} = \frac{\mu Q_A - f_B/2}{18(1 - \mu^2/36)}. \tag{5.9}$$

Thus, if $\partial Q_A/\partial \mu < 0$ or $\delta < 1/2(\mu m_B n_B + (1/(\mu m_A n_A)))$, then the quantity of tourists in TSC_A increases with a TSC preference increase (a decrease in μ). Otherwise, if $\partial Q_A/\partial \mu > 0$ or $\delta > 1/2(\mu m_B n_B + (1/(\mu m_A n_A)))$, then the quantity of tourists in TSC_A increases with a decrease in the TSC preference (an increase in μ).

Because the profits are all proportional to the square of the quantity (see Table 5.1), they have the same properties as the demand quantity. In other words, an increase in the TSC preference does not necessarily improve TSC performance.

Under the condition $\delta < 1/2(\mu m_B n_B + (1/(\mu m_A n_A)))$, the overall performance of TSC_A increases along with an increase in the TSC preference (a decrease in μ). In this situation, the small value of δ indicates that TSC_A has no cost or market size advantage. A possible strategy for this TSC is to differentiate its products/services, i.e., to increase the TSC preference. Not only does tourism product differentiation increase profits, but it also avoids the possibility of a price war.

The curve of $g(\mu) = 1/2(\mu m_B n_B + (1/(\mu m_A n_A)))$ is presented in Figure 5.2, from which it can be seen that $g(\mu)$ is minimised when $\mu = 1/(m_A n_A m_B n_B)^{1/2}$ ($\mu m_B n_B = 1/(\mu m_A n_A)$), denoted by μ'. We can see that $\mu' > 1$ within $m_i - n_i$. As $1 \geqslant \mu > 0$ and $1/(\mu m_A n_A) > \delta > \mu m_B n_B$, we can also conclude that

$$\mu \leq \mu^{max} = \min \left\{ \frac{1}{\delta m_A n_A} , \frac{\delta}{m_B n_B} , 1 \right\}.$$

Curve $g(\mu)$ shows that it is monotonically decreasing with parameter μ in the domain $(0, \mu^{Max})$. Accordingly, if the current value of μ satisfies $\delta < g(\mu)$, then a decrease in μ will lead to an increase in $g(\mu)$, which would not change the in-equal relationship because of the monotonic nature of $g(\mu)$. The differentiation strategy will thus be effective in the long run.

Under the condition $\delta > 1/2(\mu m_B n_B + (1/(\mu m_A n_A)))$, TSC_A cannot improve its performance through product differentiation (decreasing μ), although a larger value of δ implies that TSC_A has lower supply chain costs when the two TSCs have the same market size, and vice versa. This cost or market size advantage may motivate TSC_A to practise a cost leadership strategy in the long run. A low-cost position

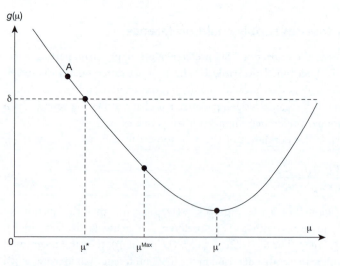

FIGURE 5.2 Graph of $g(\mu)$

would place TSC_A in a favourable position vis-à-vis substitutes relative to its rival (Porter, 1998).

5.5 Impact of cross-sector integration

The operations of TSC members can be strategically integrated and managed as a single entity or system. There are two types of integration in TSCs (see Figure 5.3): cross-sector integration, in which a TO integrates with a HA, and inter-sector integration, in which a TP integrates with a HA. In this section, we consider the impact of cross-sector integration on a TSC, with analysis of inter-sector integration relegated to the next section. For simplicity, the following analysis assumes that there is only one TO and one HA in each TSC, although the conclusion is the same when multiple TOs and HAs are involved.

There are three cross-sector integration possibilities in the chain versus chain scenario: none of the TSCs has cross-sector integration; only one TSC, for example, TSC_B, has cross-sector integration; and both TSCs have cross-sector integration. The response functions for each of these possibilities are given in Table 5.4.

If the TO integrates with an HA, then the profit of the integrated TO is $\pi_{12} = Q(p_1 - p - c_2 - c_1)$. Combining the demand function (5.1), the optimal quantity of package holidays is $Q = (\alpha - \mu Q_{-1} - p - c_2 - c_1)/2$, which is also the demand curve for the TP. Substitute Q into the profit function of the TP, and it is easy to see that the optimal quantity of tourists is $Q = (f - \mu Q_{-1})/4$. If the rival TSC is not integrated, then its response function is (5.4). If this rival is cross-sector integrated, then it has the same response function: $Q_{-1} = (f_{-1} - \mu Q)/4$.

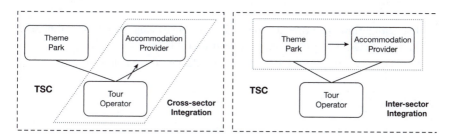

FIGURE 5.3 Cross- and inter-sector integration in a TSC

TABLE 5.4 Response functions of cross-sector integration

TSC_A	TSC_B	
	Integrated	*Not integrated*
Integrated	$\left(Q_A = \dfrac{f_A - \mu Q_B}{4},\ Q_B = \dfrac{f_B - \mu Q_A}{4}\right)$	$\left(Q_A = \dfrac{f_A - \mu Q_B}{4},\ Q_B = \dfrac{f_B - \mu Q_A}{6}\right)$
Not integrated	$\left(Q_A = \dfrac{f_A - \mu Q_B}{6},\ Q_B = \dfrac{f_B - \mu Q_A}{4}\right)$	$\left(Q_A = \dfrac{f_A - \mu Q_B}{6},\ Q_B = \dfrac{f_B - \mu Q_A}{6}\right)$

TABLE 5.5 Equilibrium of cross-sector integration

TSC	Quantity	Profit of TO	Profit of HA	Profit of TP
No integration				
TSC_A	$\dfrac{f_A-(\mu/6)f_B}{6-(\mu^2/6)}$	$\left(\dfrac{f_A-(\mu/6)f_B}{6-(\mu^2/6)}\right)^2$	$2\left(\dfrac{f_A-(\mu/6)f_B}{6-(\mu^2/6)}\right)^2$	$2\left(\dfrac{f_A-(\mu/6)f_B}{6-(\mu^2/6)}\right)^2$
TSC_B	$\dfrac{f_B-(\mu/6)f_A}{6-(\mu^2/6)}$	$\left(\dfrac{f_B-(\mu/6)f_A}{6-(\mu^2/6)}\right)^2$	$2\left(\dfrac{f_B-(\mu/6)f_A}{6-(\mu^2/6)}\right)^2$	$2\left(\dfrac{f_B-(\mu/6)f_A}{6-(\mu^2/6)}\right)^2$
Cross-sector integration of TSC_B				
TSC_A	$\dfrac{f_A-(\mu/4)f_B}{6-(\mu^2/4)}$	$\left(\dfrac{f_A-(\mu/4)f_B}{6-(\mu^2/4)}\right)^2$	$2\left(\dfrac{f_A-(\mu/4)f_B}{6-(\mu^2/4)}\right)^2$	$2\left(\dfrac{f_A-(\mu/4)f_B}{6-(\mu^2/4)}\right)^2$
TSC_B	$\dfrac{f_B-(\mu/6)f_A}{4-(\mu^2/6)}$	$\left(\dfrac{f_B-(\mu/6)f_A}{4-(\mu^2/6)}\right)^2$		$2\left(\dfrac{f_B-(\mu/6)f_A}{4-(\mu^2/6)}\right)^2$
Cross-sector integration of both TSCs				
TSC_A	$\dfrac{f_A-(\mu/4)f_B}{4-(\mu^2/4)}$	$\left(\dfrac{f_A-(\mu/4)f_B}{4-(\mu^2/4)}\right)^2$		$2\left(\dfrac{f_A-(\mu/4)f_B}{4-(\mu^2/4)}\right)^2$
TSC_B	$\dfrac{f_B-(\mu/4)f_A}{4-(\mu^2/4)}$	$\left(\dfrac{f_B-(\mu/4)f_A}{4-(\mu^2/4)}\right)^2$		$2\left(\dfrac{f_B-(\mu/4)f_A}{4-(\mu^2/4)}\right)^2$

The equilibrium quantities are derived by jointly solving the response functions of the two TSCs. The results are presented in Table 5.5.

We can now compare the equilibrium results before and after integration.

TSC quantity

Let

$$g(x)=\frac{f_A-(\mu/x)f_B}{6-(\mu^2/x)} \quad \text{and} \quad g'(x)=\frac{(6\mu/x^2)(f_B-(\mu/6)f_A)}{6-(\mu^2/x)^2}>0.$$

Thus,

$$\frac{f_A-(\mu/6)f_B}{6-(\mu^2/6)}>\frac{f_A-(\mu/4)f_B}{6-(\mu^2/4)}.$$

Using the same logic, we can prove that

$$\frac{f_B-(\mu/6)f_A}{4-(\mu^2/6)}>\frac{f_B-(\mu/4)f_A}{4-(\mu^2/4)}.$$

That is, the integration of TSC_B reduces the product quantity of TSC_A. The cross-sector integration of TSC_A also reduces the quantity of TSC_B even if TSC_B is integrated. Cross-sector integration therefore reduces the competing TSC's quantity and profits. Moreover, because

$$\frac{f_B-(\mu/6)f_A}{4-(\mu^2/6)} > \frac{f_B-(\mu/6)f_A}{6-(\mu^2/6)} \quad \text{and} \quad \frac{f_A-(\mu/4)f_B}{4-(\mu^2/4)} > \frac{f_A-(\mu/4)f_B}{4-(\mu^2/4)} ,$$

the total tourist quantity of the TSC increases after integration.

Profit of the TO

Given that TSC_A is not integrated, the profits of the TO and the HA in TSC_B before and after TSC_B integration are

$$3\left(\frac{f_B-(\mu f_A/6)}{6-(\mu^2/6)}\right)^2 \quad \text{and} \quad \left(\frac{f_B-(\mu/6)f_A}{4-(\mu^2/6)}\right)^2 ,$$

respectively. Proving that

$$3\left(\frac{f_B-(\mu f_A/6)}{6-(\mu^2/6)}\right)^2 > \left(\frac{f_B-(\mu/6)f_A}{4-(\mu^2/6)}\right)^2$$

is the same as proving that

$$\sqrt{3}\frac{f_B-(\mu f_A/6)}{6-(\mu^2/6)} > \frac{f_B-(\mu/6)f_A}{4-(\mu^2/6)} ,$$

and the latter requires that

$$\left[\left(\sqrt{3}-1\right)\frac{\mu^2}{6}-\left(4\sqrt{3}-6\right)\right]\left(f_B-\frac{\mu}{6}f_A\right)<0 .$$

Because

$$f_B-(\mu/6)f_A > 0 \quad \text{and} \quad \mu^2 \le 1 < \frac{6(4\sqrt{3}-6)}{(\sqrt{3}-1)} ,$$

the in-equal relationship holds, that is,

$$3\left(\frac{f_B-(\mu f_A/6)}{6-(\mu^2/6)}\right)^2 > \left(\frac{f_B-(\mu/6)f_A}{4-(\mu^2/6)}\right)^2 .$$

If TSC_B is cross-sector integrated, then the profits of the TO and HA in TSC_A before and after this integration are

$$3\left(\frac{f_A-(\mu/4)f_B}{6-(\mu^2/4)}\right)^2 \quad \text{and} \quad \left(\frac{f_A-(\mu/4)f_B}{4-(\mu^2/4)}\right)^2 , \text{respectively.}$$

Using the same logic, we can prove

$$3\left(\frac{f_A - (\mu/4)f_B}{6 - (\mu^2/4)}\right)^2 < \left(\frac{f_A - (\mu/4)f_B}{4 - (\mu^2/4)}\right)^2.$$

Thus, the cross-integration of TSC_B reduces the TO's profit.

Profit of the TP

Because the TP's profit is quadratic of the quantity, it increases after cross-sector integration.

To sum up, cross-sector integration can improve a TSC's market share irrespective of whether its rival TSC is integrated. Following integration, the TSC can supply more lower-priced package holidays, thus increasing consumer surpluses. The TO's profit in fact drops after it integrates with the HA. The only sector to benefit from this integration is the TP, whose profit increases after integration. In this case, the TO would not normally have an incentive to integrate with the HA, but such integration may still occur, as it gives the TO priority access to hotel services, increases its market share and, in turn, enhances its long-run competitive advantages over the TOs within other TSCs.

5.6 Impact of inter-sector integration

This section identifies how the inter-sector integration of the TP and HA influences the performance of the two TSCs. It also discusses the joint impacts of inter-sector integration and product differentiation on TSC performance.

Similar to cross-sector integration, as we saw in the previous section, there are also three possibilities for inter-sector integration: neither of the TSCs is inter-sector integrated, only one of them is inter-sector integrated, and both are inter-sector integrated.

If the TP is integrated with the HA, then the TO will have to buy accommodation and park access from the TP at price p_{23}. The TO's decision will not change, and the optimal quantity remains $Q = (\alpha - p_{23} - c_1 - \mu Q_{-1})/2$. The demand curve for the integrated TP becomes $p_{23} = \alpha - \mu Q_{-1} - c_1 - 2Q$, and the profit function is $\pi_{23} = Q(p_{23} - c - c_2)$. Thus, the optimal package quantity is $Q = (f - \mu Q_{-1})/4$. The best response functions of the rival TSC are those in equation (5.4) if it is not integrated and $Q_{-1} = (f_{-1} - \mu Q)/4$ if it is. The equilibrium of the game is thus derived by jointly solving the response functions of the two TSCs, which are listed in Table 5.6.

Conclusions can be derived by comparing the equilibrium before and after inter-sector integration. The proof is similar to that for cross-integration, and is thus omitted here. The results show that all of the tourism businesses (i.e., the TP, HA and TO) benefit from inter-sector integration between the TP and HA. The volume of the integrated TSC increases, but the profit of the rival TSC decreases.

TABLE 5.6 Equilibrium of inter-sector integration

TSC	Quantity	Profit of TO	Profit of HA	Profit of TP
Inter-sector integration of TSC$_B$				
TSC$_A$	$\dfrac{f_A - \mu f_B/4}{6 - \mu^2/4}$	$\left(\dfrac{f_A - \mu f_B/4}{6 - \mu^2/4}\right)^2$	$2\left(\dfrac{f_A - \mu f_B/4}{6 - \mu^2/4}\right)^2$	$2\left(\dfrac{f_A - \mu f_B/4}{6 - \mu^2/4}\right)^2$
TSC$_B$	$\dfrac{f_B - \mu f_A/6}{4 - \mu^2/6}$	$\left(\dfrac{f_B - \mu f_A/6}{4 - \mu^2/6}\right)^2$		$2\left(\dfrac{f_B - \mu f_A/6}{4 - \mu^2/6}\right)^2$
Inter-sector integration of both TSCs				
TSC$_A$	$\dfrac{f_A - (\mu/4)f_B}{4 - (\mu^2/4)}$	$\left(\dfrac{f_A - (\mu/4)f_B}{4 - (\mu^2/4)}\right)^2$		$2\left(\dfrac{f_A - (\mu/4)f_B}{4 - (\mu^2/4)}\right)^2$
TSC$_B$	$\dfrac{f_B - (\mu/4)f_A}{4 - (\mu^2/4)}$	$\left(\dfrac{f_B - (\mu/4)f_A}{4 - (\mu^2/4)}\right)^2$		$2\left(\dfrac{f_B - (\mu/4)f_A}{4 - (\mu^2/4)}\right)^2$

The theoretical results presented in Table 5.6 suggest that inter-sector integration is the optimal strategy for the TP if the rival TSC is not integrated. If its rival also pursues inter-sector integration, then this type of integration is still the best response strategy for the TSC under consideration. The TO benefits from the lower TP price and large tourist volume after integration, and the TP consolidates its dominant position by offering a more attractive price.

Returning to the case of the Hong Kong theme park industry, the entry of HKDL in 2005 changed the market structure from a monopoly to a duopoly. Different from Ocean Park, HKDL operates two hotels: the Disneyland Hotel and the Hollywood Hotel. To compete with HKDL effectively, Ocean Park recently announced a master plan to redevelop the park and build three themed hotels costing HK$5.5 billion. The park hopes to attract more overseas tourists through integration with its own hotels.

Both of the TPs in our two TSCs would like to integrate with HAs, but inter-sector integration does not guarantee an increase in total profits for the TP and TO compared with the scenario in which neither TSC is integrated. Table 5.7 illustrates three possible outcomes: the total profits of the TP and HA increase in

TABLE 5.7 Total profits of the *TP* and the *TO* before and after integration

Case	μ	f_A	f_B	Total profit of the TP and the HA before integration		Profit of integrated TP	
				TSC$_A$	TSC$_B$	TSC$_A$	TSC$_B$
1	0.5	10	12	0.91	1.41	0.93	1.50
2	1	10	18	0.58	3.14	0.43	3.42
3	1	10	10	0.82	0.82	0.80	0.80

both TSCs (case 1), the profits of the integrated TP increase in one TSC and decrease in the other (case 2), and the profits of the integrated TP decrease in both TSCs (case 3). Case 3 is particularly interesting because the optimisation of each TSC results in worsened performance for both TSCs.

The foregoing analysis assumes that inter-sector integration has no effect on TSC preference. A hotel operated by a theme park is often elaborately designed, with the same theme as the park or a similar one. It offers a differentiated experience to tourists visiting the park, thereby enhancing their recreational experience. As a result, inter-sector integration not only changes the TSC structure, but also differentiates the package holidays supplied by the two TSCs. This change is particularly significant when one of the TSCs opts not to pursue inter-sector integration.

Consider a scenario in which neither of the TSCs is initially integrated. To identify the inter-sector integration of one TSC, we assume that the original TSC preference is μ, changing to μ' after the inter-sector integration of TSC_B. Note that $\mu' < \mu$ or $\theta = \mu'/\mu < 1$. The product quantities of TSC_B before and after inter-sector integration are $(f_B - \mu f_A/6)/(6 - \mu^2/6)$ and $(f_B - \mu'f_A/6)/(4 - \mu'^2/6)$, respectively. It is clear that

$$\frac{f_B - (\mu'f_A/6)}{4 - (\mu'^2/6)} - \frac{f_B - (\mu f_A/6)}{6 - (\mu^2/6)} > \frac{f_B - (\mu f_A/6)}{4 - (\mu'^2/6)} - \frac{f_B - (\mu f_A/6)}{6 - (\mu^2/6)} > 0 ,$$

which means the product quantity of TSC_B increases following inter-sector integration.

The total profits of HA and TP in TSC_B before and after inter-sector integration are

$$4\left(\frac{f_B - (\mu f_A/6)}{4 - (\mu^2/6)}\right)^2 \text{ and } 2\left(\frac{f_B - (\mu'f_A/6)}{4 - (\mu'^2/6)}\right)^2 ,$$

respectively. Proving that

$$2\left(\frac{f_B - (\mu'f_A/6)}{4 - (\mu'^2/6)}\right)^2 > 4\left(\frac{f_B - (\mu f_A/6)}{4 - (\mu^2/6)}\right)^2$$

requires that

$$\frac{1 - (\mu'/6)\,\delta}{4 - (\mu'^2/6)} > \sqrt{2}\,\frac{1 - (\mu/6)\delta}{6 - (\mu^2/6)} .$$

Because

$$\frac{1 - (\mu'/6)\,\delta}{4 - (\mu'^2/6)} \geq \frac{1 - (\mu/6)\delta}{4 - (\mu'^2/6)} ,$$

this should suggest that

$$\frac{1-(\mu/6)\,\delta}{4-(\mu'^2/6)} > \sqrt{2}\,\frac{1-(\mu/6)\delta}{6-(\mu^2/6)} \quad \text{or} \quad \frac{1}{4-(\mu'^2/6)} > \frac{\sqrt{2}}{6-(\mu^2/6)}.$$

The latter in-equal relationship means $\theta^2 > 0 > (1.456/\mu^2) + 0.707$, which always holds for $\mu \in [0,1]$.

Hence, inter-sector integration improves both the demand quantity and profits of TSC members.

It should be noted that if package holiday products are adequately differentiated through integration, then the performance of the rival TSC is not necessarily adversely affected by inter-sector integration, which differs somewhat from the finding obtained in the previous analysis. For example, if $\mu = 0.6$, $f_A = 10$ and $f_B = 12$, then the quantity of TSC_A is 1.48 when neither TSC is inter-sector integrated. If TSC_B is integrated in this manner, and μ changes to 0.5, then the quantity of TSC_A decreases to 1.43. If inter-sector integration changes μ to 0.3 (thus implying a higher degree of product differentiation), then the quantity of TSC_A increases to 1.52. It is clear that the inter-sector integration and greater product differentiation of TSC_B improve the performance of both TSCs. In summary, if both TSCs adequately differentiate their products through inter-sector integration, then they will both achieve a win–win outcome.

5.7 Summary

In the tourism industry, competition between TSCs is common. In such competition, the businesses in one TSC compete not only with their competitors in the same TSC, but also with their counterparts in other similar TSCs. The performance of a business in one TSC thus depends on the performance of other TSCs.

This chapter formulates chain versus chain competition as a two–stage game that extends the analysis of TSC competition in Chapter 4. Four types of relationships are analysed theoretically: intra-sector competition amongst the suppliers within a sector, inter-sector competition amongst the sectors in a TSC, cross-sector coordination amongst the sectors in different layers and competition between two TSCs.

The impacts of TSC membership, preference and strategic integration are analysed based on the equilibrium results. These results have several managerial implications, which can be summarised as follows. First, a greater number of members in a TSC strengthens its overall capacity. However, the increased competition resulting from greater TSC membership in a sector reduces the profits of each service provider and that of the sector as a whole, whilst the service providers in other sectors benefit from the greater competition. Second, a stronger supply chain preference does not necessarily improve the performance of a TSC. When a TSC has no cost or market size advantage over its rival, it should consider differentiating its products as a long-run strategy. However, from the supply chain's perspective, a cost leadership strategy would be the optimal choice. Third, integration with accommodation providers does not necessarily result in greater profitability for tour operators, although theme parks do have an incentive to engage in such integration. If theme parks can effectively differentiate themselves from their competitors through strategic integration with accommodation providers, then all of the TSCs involved will benefit.

Discussion questions

1. Based on the game model presented in this chapter, analyse the impact of the market size α and unit costs ($c/c_1/c_2$) on the quantity, price and profit of each TSC member.
2. What is the impact of TSC membership on a TSC? Why has HKDL increased its number of contractual tour operators from 50 to 130 since it opened in 2005?
3. Does product differentiation necessarily improve TSC performance? If not, then why not?
4. Consider a game played by two TSCs: TSC A and TSC B (see Figure 5.4). Each has two possible strategies: cross-sector integration or no integration. What is the equilibrium of this game? If the two strategies available were inter-sector integration and no integration, then what would the equilibrium be?
5. Explain case 3 in Table 5.7 as a prisoner's dilemma game.
6. Formulate a game model to explain the impact of two tour operators' integration (merger) in the following supply chain structure.

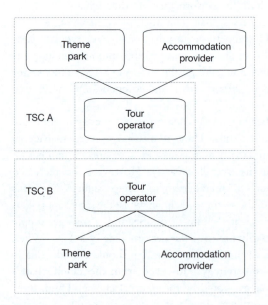

FIGURE 5.4 TSC integration

6

TOURISM DISTRIBUTION CHANNELS

Learning objectives

After reading this chapter you will be able to understand:

1. The basic concepts of distribution channels and why they are necessary.
2. The main functions of tourism intermediaries.
3. The structure of tourism distribution channels.
4. How to create new channels and rebuild existing ones.
5. The factors that influence the development of tourism distribution channels.
6. The roles played by tour operators and travel agents in distribution channels.

6.1 Tourism supply chain and distribution channels

One of the objectives of TSCM is to coordinate and integrate all of the functions and activities performed by the supply chain members in the provision of tourism products and services to tourists. From the entire TSC's perspective, it is important that all of the tourism product/service suppliers reduce production costs, maximise operational efficiency and enhance tourist satisfaction at each level of the supply chain to increase the competitiveness of the overall chain. The tourism businesses within a TSC thus need to build close relationships with both upstream and downstream partners. The upstream suppliers provide individual tourism products and services to their midstream partners to ensure that individual products/services are packaged and assembled. In the downstream of the chain, these packaged and assembled products/services are sold to tourists through a variety of distribution or marketing channels. A tourism distribution channel is an organised service system that consists of tourism product/service suppliers, intermediaries and customers. The terms *supply chain* and *distribution channel* are interchangeable in some of the literature, as both are recognised as links between tourism suppliers and final customers. However, the directions of the two networks differ: when looking at the upstream suppliers from the lower stream we see a supply chain; when looking at the downstream buyers and customers from the upstream we see a distribution channel (Smith and Xiao, 2008). In this book, a TSC is defined as the connected chain of tourism businesses that perform and/or support the channel functions (McDaniel *et al.*, 2006), whereas a tourism distribution channel is considered to be part of a downstream TSC, focusing primarily on the distribution of tourism products/services to tourists.

The channel intermediaries can be individuals or organisations, such as tour operators or travel agents, operating between the tourism suppliers and their final customers, i.e., tourists. Every tourism distribution channel contains tourism suppliers and final tourists, and no intermediaries are involved if suppliers sell their products/services directly to tourists. In this case, the distribution functions are performed by the suppliers, although they remain part of the supply chain. For example, even if a hotel sells all of its guest rooms directly to walk-in guests instead of through travel agents, it still needs to retain sales personnel to perform a variety of marketing activities. Hence, the key question is not whether the distribution functions are performed by suppliers, but rather whether these functions are performed efficiently and effectively and by whom.

Organisations that assist the channel members in handling tourist, information and financial flows are also recognised as parts of the tourism distribution channel. Examples of such organisations include banks, credit card companies, insurance companies, financial institutions, marketing research firms, advertising agencies, visitor information centres and IT providers.

Different from manufacturing product distribution channels in which raw materials form part of the production flows, tourism distribution channels deal primarily with final products/services. For example, the distribution channel of a hotel sells only an integrated accommodation product – hotel rooms to guests and food and beverage (FB) products that support the accommodation provision. It does not distribute any raw materials, such as furniture, water and energy supplies.

Another difference between tourism and manufacturing distribution channels is the direction of the goods/service flows (Ujma, 2001). In the manufacturing industry, the physical flow of products moves within the distribution channel from suppliers to customers. Tourism products and services, in contrast, are consumed by mobile customers who visit the destination in which the product/service or experience is consumed (Page, 2006). The flows within a tourism distribution channel thus refer to the movements of tourists rather than to physical products. Furthermore, tourism distribution channels are usually shorter than those in the manufacturing industry, as the former involve close face-to-face interactions between suppliers and tourists, thus rendering a stock or inventory of tourism products/services unnecessary.

6.2 Channel intermediaries

Channel intermediaries work as a bridge between tourism suppliers and their customers. As discussed previously, a tourism supplier can sell its products/services directly to its customers without channel intermediaries. In practice, though, the majority of tourism suppliers utilise channel intermediaries to sell their products/ services. For example, around seventy per cent of international travellers in Europe employ intermediaries to arrange long-haul travel (Williams and Richter, 2002). Why do both tourism suppliers and tourists use channel intermediaries? To answer this question, we need to understand the main functions of these intermediaries and the benefits that tourism suppliers derive from employing them.

Matching supply and demand

Demand for tourism products/services rarely matches supply in terms of either quantity or type, and channel intermediaries can eliminate the gap between the two. Quantity discrepancy occurs in two cases. First, tourism suppliers typically offer a relatively large number of tourism products/services to achieve economies of scale. Under monopolistic or perfect competition conditions in which alternative suppliers exist, demand for the products/services offered by a supplier may be restricted. If this is the case, then a channel intermediary can play an important role in closing the gap between the demand for, and supply of, tourism products/ services by purchasing them from the supplier and selling them to its customer base. For example, HKDL's Hollywood Hotel has a capacity of six hundred hotel rooms, but actual demand for these rooms by park visitors is limited, as more than sixty per cent of these visitors are local residents. To increase the hotel's occupancy rate, HKDL offers a significant percentage of the rooms to contracted tour operators and travel agents, which then sell them to a much wider customer base.

Second, there are situations in which demand for certain tourism goods/services is high, but the supply of these goods/services is limited due to capacity constraints. Intermediaries can buy the same tourism goods/services from different suppliers and sell them in the market to meet the strong demand.

The product/service-type discrepancy exists when consumers demand a wide range of tourism products/services, but tourism suppliers provide only a limited range. In this situation, tourism intermediaries can combine various tourism products/services to meet tourist demand for a more diverse range.

Improving efficiency

Channel intermediaries can improve distribution efficiency by reducing the number of transactions and the relative costs. For example, assume that five Japanese tourists want to take their holidays in Las Vegas. Without an intermediary, they will have to purchase directly from at least four suppliers (a transport operator, hotel accommodation provider, tourist attraction supplier(s) and FB suppliers), thus resulting in 20 (5 × 4) direct business transactions. The number of transactions is reduced to nine (5 + 4) if all five tourists and the tourism suppliers and customers go through a channel intermediary (see Figure 6.1). The transaction costs related to the holiday purchases of these five Japanese tourists are also greatly reduced, saving not only resources but also search time.

Distribution channel intermediaries also improve distribution efficiency by reducing the distribution costs resulting from geographic distances. Tourism suppliers are often located in destinations that are far away from their source markets. Intermediaries can buy tourism products/services from suppliers in the destinations and sell them in the source markets through their agents.

Facilitating information exchange

Given the geographical distances between a destination and its source markets, an important task for tourism suppliers is to provide sufficient information about their products/services to potential tourists in the source markets with a view to influencing their purchase decisions. Transferring valuable information to customers can be very costly or even impossible for small suppliers due to budget constraints. Although IT may reduce the costs of information flows to a large extent, ensuring that information penetrates the right markets and reaches the right customers still requires a huge investment. For example, although small hotels and businesses on a Mediterranean island cannot afford to advertise their products/services in an emerging market such as China, a channel intermediary can gather the information that they provide and disseminate it in this source market at a much lower cost.

Channel intermediaries also often collect satisfaction data from tourists who purchase holidays from them and then share this information with their suppliers, thereby helping the latter to improve service quality. Furthermore, these intermediaries can effectively collect, organise and process information from a variety of tourism suppliers and share it with potential tourists, which simplifies, and reduces the cost of, the information search process for the latter.

Providing extra services

Channel intermediaries can perform a variety of extra services to ensure the efficient operation of the supply chain. For example, tour operators often offer credit to travel agents, thus allowing them to delay paying for the products they sell. Channel intermediaries are usually experienced in managing tourist satisfaction, and they can help small and medium suppliers to improve operational efficiency and service quality. Additionally, the affiliated channel members also supply complementary services, such as finance, credit, insurance and consultancy services, to both tourism suppliers and customers.

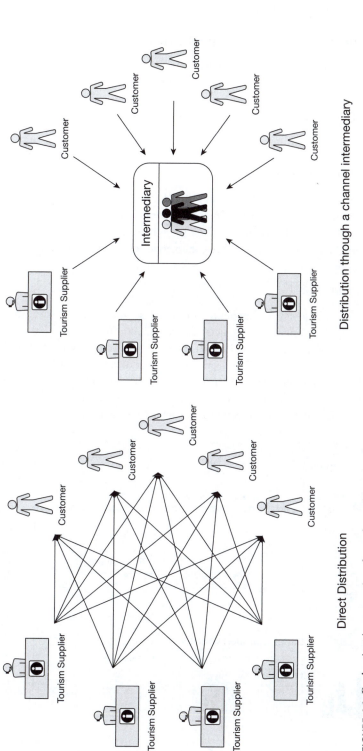

Direct Distribution

Distribution through a channel intermediary

FIGURE 6.1 Reduction in transactions by a channel intermediary

6.3 Tourism distribution channel structure

The distribution channel structure defines the way in which the suppliers of tourism products/services are organised to perform various distribution functions, and can be examined from two dimensions: the vertical dimension, which describes the length of the distribution channel, and the horizontal dimension, which depicts its width.

The vertical dimension

The vertical dimension, or length, of a distribution channel is determined by the number of member categories within it. Traditionally, the length of a channel is measured by the number of intermediary levels between tourism suppliers and final customers. Figure 6.2 illustrates three alternative tourism distribution channels.

Direct channel

The direct, or zero-level, channel has the simplest and shortest vertical structure: tourism suppliers sell their products/services directly to customers without the involvement of intermediaries. Low-cost airlines and economy hotels usually sell their products in this manner, for example. The fast development of internet-based technologies has created new opportunities for tourism suppliers to distribute their products/services directly to consumers. For instance, the UK-based low-cost carrier easyJet sells its airline seats directly to customers only online.

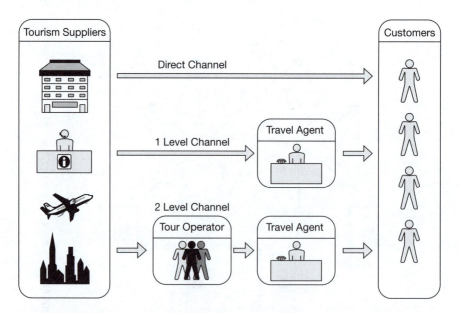

FIGURE 6.2 The vertical dimension of tourism distribution channels

A tourism supplier chooses this selling method for a variety of reasons. For example, it may believe that it can perform the distribution functions itself more efficiently and effectively than intermediaries (e.g., it may offer lower distribution costs, a more prompt response and greater customer satisfaction, etc.). If a supplier depends too heavily on intermediaries to sell its goods/services, then these intermediaries are likely to enter into a bargaining process that may diminish the supplier's profit margin. Hence, such tourism suppliers as hotels, theme parks and airlines usually employ their own sales force that engages in direct sales.

Indirect channel

In the indirect channel, a tourism supplier works closely with intermediaries in selling its products/services. These intermediaries perform some of the distribution functions in addition to those performed by the supplier itself. Figure 6.2 shows two indirect channels: a 1-level channel and a 2-level channel. An N-level channel means there are N levels of intermediaries between the supplier and its final customers. For example, the 2-level channel in Figure 6.2 has two levels of intermediaries: tour operators and travel agents. Some channels have more than two levels. For example, a package tour to Hong Kong for mainland Chinese visitors may involve local inbound travel agents, international tour operators, outbound travel agents in mainland China and, finally, the tourists themselves.

In practice, tourism suppliers usually sell their products/services through both direct and indirect channels, making for a complex distribution system. An example of the distribution channels for heritage and cultural tourism attractions in New Zealand is presented in Figure 6.3.

The horizontal dimension

The horizontal dimension, or width, of a tourism distribution channel is determined by the number of players that offer the same types of products/services and are located at the same channel level. Referring again to Figure 6.2, a tourism supplier such as an airline may sell its tickets through five travel agents in a 1-level channel. The channel width is thus five at the travel agent level. If a tourism distribution channel has more than one level, for example, a theme park sells its admission tickets through three tour operators and ten travel agents in a 2-level distribution channel, then the channel width is three at the tour operator level and ten at the travel agent level.

6.4 Tourism distribution channel development

In practice, tourism suppliers at both the destination and sectoral level within a destination are very active in developing efficient tourism distribution channels with a view to increasing their sales volumes and revenues. Some of these channels have been in place for many years and have proved to be efficient, which is not to say

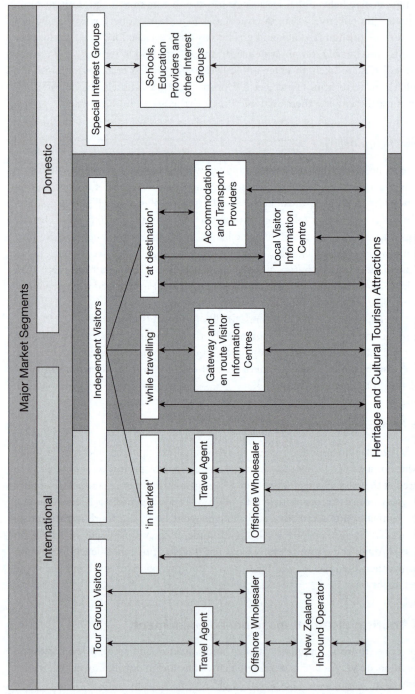

FIGURE 6.3 Distribution channels for heritage and cultural attractions in Rotorua and Wellington

Source: adapted from Pearce and Tan (2004, p.230)

that there is no room for further improvement. Channel development is a continuous and iterative process. The evolution of tourism distribution channels generally requires tourism suppliers to respond to the complex and dynamic environment in a timely and effective manner.

Factors influencing channel development

In general, there are five main factors that affect the development of distribution channels: the market, suppliers, intermediaries, the competition and the environment. It is important that tourism businesses understand these factors if they are to develop effective distribution channels.

Market

Effective distribution channel development must be based on the characteristics of the market, such as tourists' purchasing behaviour, the scale and scope of the market, and its geographical density or dispersion.

Tourists are generally segmented according to their cultural, economic, and social backgrounds and demographic characteristics. Different segments tend to exhibit different types of purchasing behaviour. Younger and better-educated tourists usually purchase their holiday products online and pay for them with credit cards, whereas senior or retired tourists are more likely to purchase their travel products from traditional channel members such as travel agents or retail travel shops using cash. Package holidays are very popular with Asian tourists, particularly those from emerging markets such as China. Tourist attractions, hotel accommodation providers and airlines targeting these tourists thus need to work closely with tour operators and travel agents to reach a much wider customer base. To capture different market segments, for example, HKDL has contracts with the main tour operators and travel agents in China to sell the park to package holiday makers and offers an online purchase channel through its own website.

The size of the potential customer base for a particular product/service determines the scale of the market, whereas the number of customer segments affects its scope. A supplier with a large customer base may need to engage intermediaries to help it with product/service distribution. If, in contrast, a supplier provides only customised tourism products/services to certain market segments, then direct sales may be more effective, as the supplier tends to have more specific knowledge than intermediaries about the type of tourists it serves.

Market density measures the number of potential customers per unit area, such as a square mile or square kilometre. Generally speaking, a tourism supplier needs to cover a much broader area when market density is low. In this type of market, the supplier tends to employ channel intermediaries to boost product/service penetration. The geographical dispersion of customers also influences channel development. Direct sales are more effective when the potential customer base is closer to the supplier, whereas selling through channel intermediaries is more effective when the customer base is far away from the supplier, which is the case with long-haul tourists. Long-haul package tours are often sold via international tour operators.

Suppliers

The features of tourism suppliers, such as their business objectives, availability of resources and business capacities, also affect the development of distribution channels. For example, one of HKDL's main objectives is to attract visitors from within Asia, particularly China, as the region is where their future customers are based. Given the huge size of the Chinese market, HKDL develops, supports and manages a large number of intermediaries that are contracted to distribute its products in Asia, including China. Smaller tourist attractions in Hong Kong, such as museums, art galleries and shops selling local handicrafts, in contrast, have to rely on traditional direct sales channels.

Intermediaries

Intermediaries' level of resources, capacities and network coverage influence the way in which distribution channels are developed. Specialised intermediaries, such as the tour operators that deal with special interest groups (for example, senior travellers and travellers interested in health tourism products), tend to be small in scale and to have limited capacity and coverage. The suppliers of such tourism products may have to work with a greater number of intermediaries or engage in direct sales if the costs of contracting intermediaries are too high.

Competition

Market structure defines the competitive intensity of the tourism industry. Tourism suppliers operating in a perfect or monopolistic market, for example, such as the handicraft vendors or cafés and shops in a resort area, have to sell their products directly to tourists, as their profit margins are so small that there is no incentive for them to employ intermediaries. Tourism suppliers competing with rivals in an oligopolistic market, in contrast, such as the luxury (high-tariff) hotels in Hong Kong, may have to work with several intermediaries to increase market share.

Business environment

The business environment includes the economic, technological, social, cultural, ethnic, political and legal environment in which the tourism businesses operate. Economic recessions may reduce market demand and result in the closure of these businesses, and thus higher level distribution channels may be reduced to lower level channels (that is, these channels may be reduced in both length and width). The more widespread coverage of the internet today encourages direct B2C sales.

Social, cultural and ethnic factors have a great impact on customers' preferences and purchasing behaviour, which requires that businesses design and operate distribution channels that are able to meet the demands of consumers with different cultural, social and ethnic backgrounds. Political and legal factors also encourage or restrict the behaviour of channel members, and can in turn affect the channel structure. For example, the Competition Commission and Office of Fair Trading in the UK is a public body that regulates and investigates business mergers and acquisitions with a view to ensuring fair competition and restricting monopoly power. Anti-monopoly regulations and laws also affect the design and structure of the distribution channels within the tourism industry.

Tourism distribution channel development

The development of tourism distribution channels involves either designing a new channel or improving the performance of existing channels. A tourism supplier decides to develop distribution channels for the following reasons: a new business wants to enter its target market; an existing tourism business is interested in expanding to a new market; the business environment has changed; or the existing channels are unable to respond to changes in the business environment. Channel development is an iterative process that includes the five general steps shown in Figure 6.4.

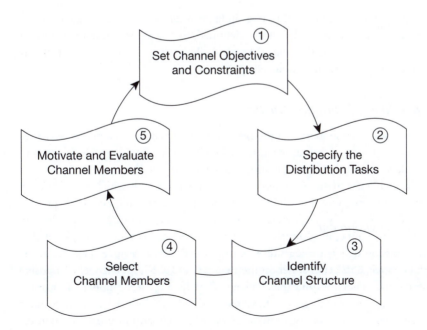

FIGURE 6.4 Five stages of channel development

Step 1: Set channel objectives and constraints

The first task in developing new distribution channels is environmental scanning (ES), which helps the supplier to evaluate both the external and internal factors that may affect its operations and management of its business. Analysis is normally carried out on the basis of either historical data (if they exist) or information collected through market surveys. The analysis should be able to assess the overall demand conditions sufficiently and accurately, including the strengths and weaknesses of the business and the opportunities and challenges it faces. At the same time, it should also point out the availability of and constraints on the resources needed to develop the distribution channels.

After ES, the supplier needs to set its distribution objectives. Although distribution channel objectives differ from one business to another, the following are the most common factors that need to be considered in their establishment. First, the channel should be able to transfer information and feedback between the supplier and customers quickly and accurately; second, it should allow the supplier to achieve the planned market share and growth within the development period; and, third, it should minimise distribution costs and maximise profits.

The distribution channel's objectives should be consistent with the supplier's overall strategies, and should match its strengths given the constraints identified in the ES exercise. The objectives should also be easy to implement and evaluate.

Step 2: Specify the distribution tasks

To achieve the distribution objectives in light of the resource constraints, a series of distribution tasks need to be clearly identified. In other words, the supplier needs to ensure that the distribution tasks are sufficiently specific to be effectively executed and their results evaluated.

Step 3: Identify channel structure

In this stage, the supplier determines the most effective channel structure to perform the various distribution tasks specified in the previous stage. Decisions must be made concerning the most appropriate channel length and width.

Channel length defines the number of channels through which a supplier can reach its end–user customers. Multi–channel distribution is the most common practice in the tourism industry. Tourism suppliers tend to sell their products/services through two or more competing channels to reach their target markets. For example, HKDL sells admission tickets through three alternative channels: a direct channel at the park entrance, a direct channel on the internet, and a 2-level channel comprising multiple tour operators and travel agents. Clearly, a greater number of channels provides customers with greater flexibility and reduces the risk of failing to meet the channel distribution objectives. However, competition amongst multiple channels aimed at the same target markets may result in reduced profit margins for

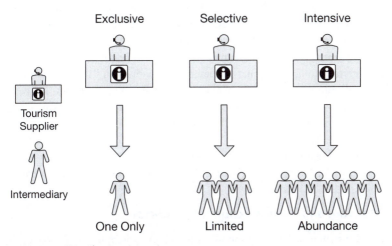

FIGURE 6.5 Distribution intensity

the travel intermediaries. Hence, the suppliers within TSCs need to coordinate with other TSC members to eliminate unnecessary competition amongst them.

Suppliers also need to determine the channel width or distribution intensity, i.e., the number of channel members at each level. Three alternatives are available: exclusive, selective and intensive distribution (see Figure 6.5). Exclusive distribution refers to the tourism supplier granting only one intermediary the exclusive right to distribute its goods in the target market. The intermediary therefore has no competitors and receives strong support from the supplier. In an exclusive distribution channel, the intermediary tends to have much stronger negotiating power with the supplier, and this type of channel works well only when the equilibrium pay-offs are reached for both the supplier and the intermediary. The intensive distribution channel, in contrast, puts the supplier in the dominant position, and multiple intermediaries have to compete amongst themselves to meet the sales targets specified by the supplier. Between exclusive and intensive distribution lies selective distribution, which allows only a limited number of intermediaries to distribute the supplier's products/services. Of the three distribution channels, intermediaries prefer the exclusive arrangement, whilst suppliers generally prefer the intensive channel arrangement. The final structure of the distribution channel is therefore determined by negotiations between the supplier and the channel members in a cooperative game setting.

Step 4: Select channel members

The common selection criteria for channel members include service coverage in terms of geographic area and market mix; distribution experience in terms of the length of business operations (normally measured in years); reputation factors, such as the business's brand image; financial performance; operational and managerial capabilities; service quality; and willingness to cooperate. It is difficult to select channel members based on all of these criteria, and hence suppliers usually prioritise them in the selection process. For example, consider a newly completed independent luxury hotel in Hong Kong that specialises in meetings and conventions and wants to set up distribution channels in mainland China. The hotel operator discovers that there are only a limited number of intermediaries that specialise in meeting and convention tourism, some of which work closely with its competitors. This hotel operator will thus have to lower its standards and employ less reputable or experienced intermediaries or attempt to build a more effective and efficient direct distribution channel to its target market via the internet or its customer database.

Step 5: Motivate and evaluate channel members

To encourage distribution channel members to achieve distribution objectives, it is important to provide them with incentives. The key to motivating channel intermediaries effectively is understanding their needs and wants and linking them closely to incentives (Jobber, 2001). Table 6.1 illustrates the needs and wants of tour operators and travel agents in order of priority.

Possible incentives, based on Table 6.1, can be categorised into two groups: direct and indirect incentives. Direct incentives refer primarily to financial rewards, including price, quantity, cash, seasonal discounts, commission payments, sales rebates, financial assistance and allowances. The aim of indirect incentives is to help intermediaries to improve operational and managerial efficiencies. The major indirect incentives include sales and management education and training, marketing

TABLE 6.1 Needs and wants of tour operators and travel agents

Tour operators	Outbound travel agents	Inbound travel agents
Sales volume	Sales volume	Sales volume
High profit margins	High profit margins/commissions	High profit margins
Producer reliability	Image	Active customers
Low risk	Regular innovation in products	Reliable partners
Mixture of large and small operators	Good service	Low risk
Loyal clientele	Prompt commission payments	Mixture of large and small operators
Prompt payments	Maximum range of products	Loyal clientele
Mixture of markets	Up-to-date information	Prompt payments
	Loyal clientele	Mixture of markets

Source: Buhalis and Laws, 2001

information research support, product and service assistance and promotion and advertising support.

Most of these incentives focus on short-term objectives. The most important and effective long-term incentive is the development of a close partnership between the supplier and its distribution channel members, thus enabling in-depth cooperation and coordination, as well as benefit/risk sharing.

An evaluation of channel members can help the supplier to decide which intermediaries' contracts to renew to achieve distribution objectives and improve channel efficiency. In practice, tourism suppliers usually evaluate the performance of their members periodically. The frequency of such evaluation depends on the number of channel members and their degree of power. Evaluating a distribution channel with a large number of channel members may take a long time and incur substantial costs. Small- and medium-sized suppliers depend largely on channel members that may be reluctant to provide performance information. Thus, evaluation may take place less frequently and be narrower in scope.

Possible evaluation criteria include the sales volume or revenue, number of new customers generated, profit margins achieved, service quality measured by customer satisfaction, number of customer complaints, and expenditure on promotion and marketing. Different weights are normally assigned to each of these criteria during the evaluation process, and the final score of each member is the weighted sum of all criteria values.

6.5 Tourism distribution channel members

Tour operators and travel agents are the main tourism distribution channel members. They are also often referred to as travel intermediaries, and they generally act as wholesalers and retailers in the tourism industry. This section briefly introduces their characteristics, classifications and major functions in tourism distribution channels.

Tour operators

Tour operators play the principal role of intermediaries in distribution channels to bring together tourism suppliers and customers by packaging a variety of tourism products/services into a single product and then selling it to the target tourist (Tepelus, 2005). The European Union's Package Travel Regulations (EUPTR, 1992) define tour operators as 'organizers who, otherwise than occasionally, organize package holidays and sell them directly or through a retailer to potential tourists'.

Package holidays constitute tour operators' most important product in the distribution channel (Buhalis, 2001). A package holiday or inclusive tour is a:

> pre-arranged combination of at least two of the following components when sold or offered for sale at an inclusive price and when the service covers a

period of more than 24 hours or includes overnight accommodation: (a) transport; (b) accommodation; and (c) other tourist services not ancillary to transport or accommodation.

(EUPTR, 1992)

For example, a package holiday to Hong Kong, as marketed and operated by tour operators, usually consists of overnight accommodation in Hong Kong, visits to one of its two theme parks and other tourist attractions, shopping and the use of transport services.

Thus, tour operators not only perform various distribution functions, but they also lead the development of package holidays, which distinguishes them from other tourism intermediaries and intermediaries in other industries, which tend to only execute distribution functions. Package holiday development consists of a series of activities that include idea generation, feasibility evaluation, product design and implementation, and the final launch of the products in target markets. The four general stages of package holiday development by tour operators are summarised in Table 6.2. Note that not all stages and activities are involved in such development. At each stage, the tour operator needs to decide whether to redo the stage, proceed to the next one or even stop the process. In some cases, tour operators skip some steps to generate new products quickly and occupy the market.

TABLE 6.2 Four general stages in the development of package holidays

---

Idea generation and concept development
Analyse customers' needs and preferences
Identify marketing opportunities and trends
Generate the ideas and concepts of package holidays
Define package features
Target customer groups
Measure market size and growth
Identify the technical and resource feasibilities
Analyse the costs and profit margins
Analyse the accumulative benefits for both tour operators and customers

Business analysis
Analyse the critical success factors
Estimate likely selling price and sales volume
Estimate profitability and break-even point

Implementation
Select qualified tourism suppliers and travel agents
Contact and negotiate with these suppliers and travel agents
Plan resources and coordinate suppliers
Package and schedule the activities of package holidays

Commercialisation
Launch the package holidays
Place advertisements and promotions
Administer tours

Tour operators can be classified into two categories according to their size: large tour operators, which usually operate in multiple countries and provide a wide range of tourism products/services to the mass tourism market, and small-to medium-sized tour operators that normally specialise in certain market segments and often provide high-quality tourism goods. Because of their scale advantage, large tour operators tend to emphasise costs, market share and attractive prices rather than quality, whereas small- to medium-sized operators normally pursue success through product differentiation, quality and brand image.

Today, the main international holiday markets, especially those in Europe, are dominated by a few large tour operators that have become highly integrated with other travel product suppliers, including travel agents, airlines, hotels, resorts, restaurants and local transport providers. For example, TUI, the European market leader and the world's largest tour operator, owns 81 brands, operates 3,700 outbound travel agents, 285 hotels and 88 aircrafts, manages inbound agents in 32 countries, provides car hire services in the Mediterranean, and even produces its own television travel programmes (Theuvsen, 2004). Market concentration and vertical integration have led to oligopolistic competition amongst European tour operators. As a result of the greater economies of scale enjoyed by the giant tour operators such as TUI, small- and medium-sized tour operators find it difficult to compete. The large operators also exercise their bargaining power in negotiations with tourism suppliers (airlines, hotels, restaurants, cruises, etc.) and 'force' them to accept inferior contracts.

The main tour operator association in Europe is the European Tour Operators Association (ETOA), which was founded in 1989 and now has more than four hundred members. The main associations in the US are the National Tour Association (NTA) and the United States Tour Operators' Association (USTOA).

Travel agents

A travel agent sells tourism products, particularly package tours, to target customers on behalf of tour operators and tourism suppliers, such as airlines, hotels and cruise lines. Unlike retailers in other industries, travel agents do not carry any stock, and thus they bear little financial risk. Based on the number of sales, travel agents receive a price discount known as a commission from tourism suppliers.

UK-based Thomas Cook is recognised as the first modern travel agent in the world. In 1841, it arranged for a group of 570 temperance campaigners to travel from Leicester's London Road railway station to a rally in Loughborough. Early travel agents operated independently, and their main business was selling travel dockets from hotels and transport providers to middle-class customers. The emergence of air travel and the post-war boom in mass-market package holidays resulted in the greatest changes in travel agents' operations. Following a series of mergers and acquisitions, many travel agents successfully expanded in scale, implemented IT and became involved in tour operation targeted at the mass market. The typical travel agent today deals with a diverse range of activities, including airline seat reservations, hotel room bookings, car hire, the development of travel itineraries for both national and international travellers, the sale of package tours, travel insurance, travellers' cheques and foreign currency, the advertising and promotion of destinations and a variety of tourism product/service providers, and communicating with customers and coordinating with tourism suppliers.

Travel agents are usually outbound-oriented, making reservations and providing related services to outbound tourists. Some agents, however, known as inbound or incoming agents, also conduct business with incoming passengers at a particular destination. Therefore, the terms 'outbound' and 'inbound' are sometimes used to distinguish agents' business type and interrelationships with other operations (Gee et al., 1990), although agents are not obligated to engage exclusively in inbound or outbound business. For example, some agents in Southern Europe offer both types of services.

Travel agents can also be categorised into three types depending on their size: independent, mintiple and multiple agents. Independent agents are privately owned and often have a single location. They own fewer than six outlets and usually serve a special or niche market or concentrate on a particular area or group. Multiple travel agents, in contrast, generally have more than a hundred outlets, which are located on the high streets of most cities in a given country, operate on a nationwide basis and are often owned by large travel corporations. They focus on tourism product distribution to the mass market, and most are integrated by large tour operators that can easily control the distribution process. Mintiple agents often target particular regions or districts, provide high-quality travel services and enjoy high profiles. Travel agents may be additionally characterised as leisure travel agents, which cater primarily to the package holiday market, or business travel agents, which specialise in commercial and business travellers.

A travel agent's profits come primarily from the sale of holidays and the booking commissions it receives from tourism suppliers. Some tourism suppliers, such as airlines in the US, pay no commission to travel agents, as they tend to sell their tickets directly to customers over the internet. Agents thus have to add an additional fee to protect their profit margins when they sell the services provided by these suppliers

6.6 Summary

The tourism distribution channel is the downstream component of a TSC, and is focused on distributing tourism products/services to final customers. It comprises tourism suppliers, consumers, interdependent intermediaries and related organisations. The distribution functions may be performed by the tourism suppliers themselves or by intermediaries.

The main role played by distribution channel members is matching the demand for and supply of tourism products/services in terms of quantity and assortment. The employment of channel intermediaries can effectively improve distribution efficiency by reducing the number of transactions and related costs. The use of intermediaries also facilitates the effective exchange of information between tourism suppliers and final customers. Intermediaries can also provide extra services in addition to performing the standard distribution functions.

The vertical dimension, or length, of a distribution channel is measured by the number of intermediary levels between tourism suppliers and final customers. The horizontal dimension, or width, of a tourism distribution channel is determined by the number of channel members engaged in the same type of business operations and located at the same level of the distribution channel.

A variety of factors influence the development of tourism distribution channels, including market factors (customers' purchasing patterns and the scale, density, and geographic dispersion of the market), tourism suppliers (their objectives, resources and capabilities), intermediaries (their resources, capacities and distribution costs), competitive intensity and the business environment.

The five general stages in the creation of new channels, or the rebuilding of existing ones, are: identifying the channel objectives and constraints; specifying the distribution tasks; designing the channel structure; selecting the channel members; and motivating and evaluating these members.

Tour operators package a variety of tourism service components into a single product, and then sell that package directly to the target market or indirectly through travel agents. A travel agent sells travel-related products/services, particularly package tours, to final customers on behalf of tour operators and/or tourism product/ service suppliers.

Discussion questions

1. Describe the differences between a TSC and a tourism distribution channel.
2. Do you have any experience with package holidays? If so, then when did you purchase them, and how many types of services were included?
3. Please give practical examples of a tourism distribution system that includes more than two channel members (the supplier and customers) and identify the length and width of each channel.
4. Suppose that you are the manager of a new theme park that recently opened in Shanghai. How would you design the distribution channels? What factors should you consider when you design the structure of these channels?
5. Suppose that you are planning your summer holiday in Phuket, Thailand. How could tour operators or travel agents help you in making your holiday a reality?

7

CAPACITY AND INVENTORY ISSUES IN TSCM[1]

Learning objectives

After reading this chapter you will be able to:

1. Understand that tourism is a capacity-constrained service.
2. Describe the strategies for matching supply and demand.
3. Describe the overbooking strategy.
4. Understand the definitions and key elements of revenue management strategies.
5. Describe a typical hotel revenue management process.

7.1 Introduction

A TSC can be categorised as a push supply chain because the production of tourism products is normally based on demand forecasting, and demand for these products is forecast on the basis of historical sales data (Zhang *et al.*, 2009). We will see in this chapter that the tourism products in a TSC are perishable and that tourism services are capacity-constrained. The nature of these products/services renders it difficult for tourism managers to balance supply and demand in the short run by varying production capacity. This chapter begins with a consideration of the perishable inventory of tourism products, followed by a discussion of the distinct characteristics of tourism service capability. Classifying the primary constraints that restrict tourism capacity helps us to understand the strategies adopted to deal with the related supply and demand issues.

The airlines, hotels and other tourism enterprises in a TSC often employ overbooking and revenue management as the main strategies to deal with limited service capacity and meet fluctuating demand. This chapter introduces the basic ideas of the overbooking strategy and illustrates the history, definition and key elements of revenue management. As the best revenue management examples are found in the airline and hotel industries (Kimes, 2000; Cross, 1997), a typical hotel revenue management process is provided as a step-by-step example of the way in which a revenue management system operates in practice.

7.2 Tourism capacity management

Perishable inventory

Due to their unique nature, services cannot be saved, stored, resold or returned. A primary issue that the tourism industry faces in relation to perishable services is the inability to inventory these services. Unlike manufacturing firms, tourism firms cannot build up inventories during periods of slow demand to use later when demand increases. A guest room that remains unsold on one night cannot be resold the following night. The room's productive capacity has perished. Demand forecasting and creative planning for capacity utilisation thus constitute important and challenging decision issues in the tourism sector.

Not all service organisations face equal challenges in managing supply and demand (Lovelock, 1983), although tourism firms face greater challenges than those in other service industry arenas, as they experience wide fluctuations in demand, and peak demand for hospitals, attractions and restaurants, for example, frequently exceeds capacity. To identify effective strategies for managing supply and demand fluctuations, the tourism industry requires a clear understanding of underlying demand patterns and the constraints on its capacity.

Capacity constraints

Tourism is a capacity-constrained service industry whose critical fixed-capacity factors include time, labour, equipment, facilities and a combination of the four. The primary constraint on production for tourism businesses is time. For example, airlines and hotels primarily sell flight time and the time spent overnight in a room, respectively. If this time is not used productively, then profits are lost.

Tourism is typically also a labour-intensive industry. The primary capacity constraint in this arena is staffing levels. A restaurant, attraction or hotel may face the reality that at certain times demand for its services cannot be met because staff are already operating at peak capacity, although it does not always make sense to hire additional service providers when demand is low at other times.

Equipment can also constitute a critical constraint for the tourism industry. For air-freight delivery services, for example, the aircraft needed to service demand may not have additional capacity. During peak periods, such as holidays, hotels and attractions face the same issue, whereas restaurants may be affected on a daily basis, such as during the lunch and dinner hours.

Finally, tourism businesses faces restrictions brought about by their limited facilities. For example, hotels have only a certain number of rooms to sell, airlines are limited by the number of seats on aircraft, attractions are constrained by their number of rides, and restaurant capacity is restricted by the number of tables and seats available.

Tourism businesses' service capacity is generally fixed over the short run, although some firms are able to change their capacity by adjusting the amount of space or time available. Understanding their primary capacity constraints, or the combination of factors that restricts capacity, helps TSC members to identify the strategies needed to deal with supply and demand issues.

Demand patterns

Understanding tourism capacity issues fully requires identification of tourism demand patterns, and a number of questions concerning the predictability and underlying causes of that demand require answers.

Predictable demand

Demand for capacity-constrained tourism organisations comes from both walk-in customers and those who make reservations. Although both forms of demand can be managed, they require different strategies. The two types of customers constitute an inventory from which managers can select the most profitable customer mix. To forecast demand, managers need to compile information on the percentage of reservations and walk-ins, customers' desired length of service use and the likely service duration.

Time-varying demand

Tourism demand varies over time. For some tourism businesses, demand may be greater on the weekends, during the summer months or at particular times of the day. Managers must be able to forecast time-related demand to ensure that they are able to make effective pricing and allocation decisions that manage the shoulder periods of high demand. It is also essential that tourism businesses can accurately predict the length of time a customer will use the service. For example, in a restaurant, it is usually true that lunches are shorter than dinners. If the restaurant's manager can accurately predict customers' meal durations, then he or she can make better reservation decisions and better estimates of service capability.

Demand fluctuations

Demand patterns sometimes appear to be random, that is, there is no apparent predictable cycle. Yet, even when this is true, causes can often be identified. For example, day-to-day changes in the weather may affect the use of recreational or entertainment facilities. Although the weather cannot be predicted very far in advance, it may still be possible to anticipate demand a day or two before the weather changes. Natural disasters such as floods, hurricanes or epidemics have a dramatic impact on tourism demand, and, once they occur, tourism businesses can expect a drastic decline in demand.

Demand patterns by market segment

A tourism organisation that has detailed records of tourist behaviour may be able to disaggregate demand by market segment, thereby revealing patterns within patterns or demand that differs from one segment to another. For example, hotels usually host business travellers on weekdays, whereas leisure travellers are more likely to visit on weekends or holidays. By identifying such patterns, hotels can provide discounts or special celebration events to attract flexible leisure travellers during weekends.

Strategies for matching capacity and demand

Once a TSC member has a clear understanding of its capacity constraints and demand patterns, it is in a good position to develop strategies to match supply and demand. There are two general approaches to accomplishing this goal. The first is to smooth demand fluctuations by shifting demand to match the existing supply, an approach which implies that the peaks and valleys of demand will flatten to match as closely as possible the horizontal optimum capacity line. The second approach is to adjust capacity to match fluctuations in demand (Zeithaml *et al.*, 2006).

Shifting demand to match capacity

TSC members who adopt the first strategy seek to shift tourists/travellers away from periods in which demand exceeds capacity, perhaps by convincing them through some incentive to instead purchase the service during periods of lower demand. Such a change will be possible for some, but not for all. For example, many business travellers are unable to shift their travel demand for flights, hire cars and hotel services. Leisure travellers, in contrast, are often able to change their travel arrangements if a TSC member's offers, for example, of a lower price or more comprehensive service coverage, are sufficiently attractive.

During periods of slow demand, TSC members seek to attract a greater number of and more diverse customers to utilise their productive capacity. A variety of approaches, detailed in the following paragraphs, can be employed to shift or increase demand to match capacity. Tourism firms frequently adopt a combination of these approaches.

Vary the service offering

One approach is to change the nature of the service offering, depending on the season of the year, day of the week or time of the day. For example, Whistler Mountain, a ski resort in Vancouver, Canada, offers its facilities for executive development and training programmes during the summer months when skiing is not possible. Airlines can change the configuration of seating to match the demand arising from different market segments. Some aircraft may have no first-class section at all for certain routes, but a significant portion of seats in first class on routes with strong demand for such seating. In all of these examples, the service offering and associated benefits are altered to smooth customer demand with a view to matching the organisation's resources.

Communicate with customers

Another approach to shifting demand is to communicate with customers, informing them of periods of peak demand to allow them to choose alternative periods to avoid crowding or delays. For example, informing customers of how long the queues are at different rides in an amusement park permits them to decide whether they would prefer to opt instead for another ride or entertainment programme within the park. Forewarning customers about busy times and possible waits can also have the added benefits of decreasing their expectations and reducing dissatisfaction levels. Research has found that customers who are forewarned about the busiest hours at tourist attractions are more satisfied than customers who are not, even when the former have to wait (Clemmer and Schneider, 1989). In addition to signage communicating peak demand times to customers, advertising and other forms of messages and promotion can emphasise different service benefits during peak and off-peak periods and remind customers of the peak demand times.

Modify timing and location of service delivery

Some attractions and restaurants adjust their hours and days of service delivery to reflect customer demand more directly. Many public attractions, such as public parks and museums, currently open during normal business hours on weekdays, thus presenting an obvious mismatch with tourist demand for such attractions, which tends to be greater on weekends and holidays. It is thus recommended that these attractions adjust their opening hours to better reflect tourist demand patterns.

Differentiate by price

A common strategy during seasons of slow demand, and one that is rooted in the basic laws of supply and demand, is to discount the price of the service. The effectiveness of the price differentiation strategy, however, depends on an accurate assessment of tourists' sensitivity to price changes, which is measured by the price elasticity of demand. Such elasticity is usually negative. Consumers are relatively sensitive to a change in price for tourism products/services with greater price elasticity, meaning they are likely to consume more of those products/services when their price decreases. For example, luxury hotels such as the Island Shangri-la, Mandarin Oriental Hong Kong and Four Seasons Hong Kong attract more mainland Chinese leisure tourists when they reduce their room rates on the weekends.

Any hotel, airline, restaurant or other tourism service establishment can reach maximum capacity if the price is low enough, but the goal is always to ensure the highest level of capacity utilisation without sacrificing profits. The complex relationship amongst price, market segment, capacity utilisation and profitability is discussed in greater detail in the revenue management section of this chapter (see section 7.4).

Adjusting capacity to meet demand

The second strategic approach to matching supply and demand focuses on capacity adjustment. The fundamental idea is to adjust, stretch and align capacity to match tourism demand (rather than trying to shift demand to match capacity, as in the first approach). During periods of peak demand, TSC members attempt to stretch or expand capacity as much as possible. During periods of slow demand, in contrast, they try to shrink that capacity to avoid wasting resources. The general strategies for adjusting the four primary service resources (time, labour, equipment and facilities) are discussed in the remainder of this section.

Stretch existing capacity

The existing capacity of service resources can often be expanded temporarily to match demand. In this case, no new resources are added; rather, existing staff, facilities and equipment are required to work harder and longer to meet demand.

Stretch time. It is possible to extend service hours temporarily to accommodate demand. For example, restaurants and retail shops often stay open longer on weekends and/or holidays.

Stretch labour. In the tourism industry, employees are quite often required to work longer and harder during peak seasons. Frontline service personnel in hotels, tourist attractions and restaurants, for instance, are asked to serve more customers per hour during busy times than during slow periods.

Stretch facilities and equipment. Theatres, restaurants and meeting facilities can sometimes be expanded temporarily by adding more tables, chairs or other equipment to cater for increased demand. Computers, power lines and maintenance equipment can also be stretched beyond what would be considered their maximum capacity for short periods of time to meet occasional surges in demand.

Caution should be exercised when employing any of these stretching strategies to solve the issue of excess demand, as wear and tear may occur, thus leading to the provision of inferior services. They should be employed infrequently if possible, and employees, facilities and equipment should be given time to re-charge or rejuvenate themselves when the peak period is over.

Align capacity with demand fluctuations

By adjusting service resources creatively, TSC members can also adjust the basic mix of time, labour, facilities and equipment to match their capacity with tourist demand patterns. The specific methods of adjustment are explained in the following.

Use part-time employees. The employment of part-time staff allows an organisation to align its labour resource with demand. Hotels usually hire part-time employees during the holiday rush, tourist resorts bring in extra workers during the peak season and restaurants often ask employees to work split shifts during peak mealtime hours.

Hire facilities or equipment. Some tourism organisations hire additional equipment or facilities during peak seasons. For example, travel agencies hire or lease buses during the peak holiday season, as buying them would make little sense when they would sit idle during the rest of the year.

Cross-train employees. If employees are cross-trained, then they can be shifted amongst tasks, filling in wherever they are most needed. Cross-training increases the efficiency of the entire TSC and avoids underutilising employees in some areas and overtaxing others. Many airlines cross-train their employees to ensure that they can move from ticketing to the gate counters and assist with baggage if needed. In fast-food restaurants, employees usually specialise in one task during busy hours, operating specialist teams as large as ten staff members during peak hours. The number of team members may then shrink to as few as three during off-peak hours, with each person performing a variety of functions.

Modify or move facilities and equipment. It is sometimes possible to adjust or creatively modify existing capacity to handle demand fluctuations. Hotels utilise this strategy by reconfiguring their guest rooms. For example, two guest rooms with a connecting door can be sold to two different parties with the door locked during the peak season and turned into a suite during the slow season. The airline industry provides another good example. Adopting an approach known as demand-driven dispatch, airlines determine flight schedules on the basis of market needs. This approach depends on accurate forecasts of the demand for airline seats and the ability to shift flight assignments quickly for airplanes with different seating capacities to match demand.

Combining demand and capacity strategies

Many TSC members adopt multiple strategies, combining marketing- and operations-driven demand management approaches. Figuring out which is the best set of strategies to maximise capacity utilisation and ensure customer satisfaction and profitability can be a challenging task, particularly when there is a constellation of service offerings within one service setting, for example, theme parks with rides.

A complexity of service offerings requires that TSC managers have a good understanding of the benefits and limitations of the available demand and capacity strategies to ensure that an appropriate combination of strategies is adopted. The ultimate goal of combining strategies or adopting different ones is to sustain the long-term development of the entire TSC.

7.3 Overbooking strategy

Tourism service suppliers usually accept reservations for their services. When reservations are taken, additional demand is deflected to other time slots at the same facility or to other facilities within the same organisation. Reservations also benefit customers by reducing waiting times and guaranteeing service availability. Problems arise, however, when customers fail to honour their reservations, a fairly common occurrence. Unfulfilled reservations result in empty seats, rooms or tables, which means wasted service capacity for tourism service providers.

To compensate for late cancellations, early departures and no-shows, many service organisations employ an overbooking strategy. Overbooking involves selling more capacity than actually exists to counterbalance the effects of cancellations and no-shows. It reduces the risk of unsold capacity and thus helps to maximise revenues. It also enables a larger number of customers to book their first-choice service, as the offering of additional capacity reduces the likelihood of a service being declared fully booked (Humphreys, 1994).

Service providers usually set a level (for example, a given number of rooms in a hotel) at which they are prepared to overbook. This level depends upon the market mix forecast for the given dates and the associated drop-out rate and demand for those dates.

There are two ways to approach the problems of overbooking in relation to the allocation of capacity to different price categories:

1. The real physical capacity can first be divided amongst the price categories by means of an allocation process. Overbooking limits are then set separately for each category.
2. Alternatively, an overbooking limit can be determined for the total actual capacity. The resulting capacity is then split amongst the various price categories.

Although the first method is theoretically the most effective in approaching the optimum limits, the second is the most often used because it is simple to implement and involves less cost. Just as the technique for allocating capacity involves a trade-off between the risks of spoilage and spill, the overbooking process seeks a balance between the risks of spoilage and denied access. The cost of spoilage is the revenue lost by not selling units of the service. Denied access may entail both a direct financial cost and an indirect cost that is much more difficult to quantify, that is, the harm done to the company's image by giving customers an impression of poor service.

The direct financial cost is the compensation that the service supplier agrees to pay to customers who have been denied the service. Depending on the organisation's commercial policy, this compensation may be very small, very large or even non-existent. In the United States and Europe, governments impose rules to ensure that, as far as scheduled airlines are concerned, at least some compensation is paid to overbooked passengers. The non-quantifiable cost is the poor image of suppliers that will remain in the minds of customers who have booked and then been denied the service.

A good overbooking strategy minimises the expected opportunity cost of idle service capacity and the expected cost of turning away customers. To develop a good overbooking strategy, a tourism service supplier must collect information on no-shows and cancellation rates over time. Companies can also develop other methods, such as guarantees, customer reminders or deposits, to reduce the likelihood of no-shows. In addition, tourism service suppliers must also develop internal methods for dealing with displaced customers. If employees are not trained in how to handle this potential unpleasant situation, then both customer and employee satisfaction may suffer.

7.4 Revenue management

The revenue management strategy was first initiated by the airline industry in the early 1980s. It was pioneered by American Airlines as a technique to draw additional revenue from inventory that would otherwise remain unsold. Recognising that the initial investment to purchase aircraft and the cost of maintaining that aircraft were both substantial, airlines attempted to sell every seat possible to compensate for these fixed costs. Airline companies realised that selling empty seats at any price was always preferable to leaving them unsold. The revenue management system was thus introduced to calculate the best pricing strategy to optimise the profits generated by the sale of airplane seats based on real-time modelling (Kimes, 1989; Cross, 1997). Employing differentiated pricing categories and the systematic control of the airline seats for sale in each category allowed airlines to increase turnover and profits and customers to enjoy lower prices for the same service quality.

The hotel industry started to adopt revenue management in the early 1990s. As airlines and hotels share similar characteristics (i.e., relatively fixed capacity and variable pricing structures), it was a decade before the latter caught on and began to implement their own revenue management practices. Computerised revenue management programs were slower to develop in the hotel sector than the airline sector, due in part to software limitations in handling complicated booking situations (Koss-Feder, 1994). The hotel industry also faces a different competitive situation because its supply runs so far ahead of demand. Over the past decade, however, this industry has begun to evolve its own revenue management system that is applicable to different hotel properties.

Revenue management has gained widespread acceptance in the airline and hotel industries, and research has addressed the theoretical and practical problems facing these industries although in actuality the entire tourism industry, including tour operators and retail agencies, also apply revenue management principles and employ revenue management-type practices to manage revenue flows and market share (Kimes, 2001). Laws (2000) argued that a revenue management policy should be coordinated through the entire tourism industry, as low-price holiday offers constrain the industry's ability to function systematically as a network of long-term business relationships and create tourism products and experiences that are enjoyable for clients, rewarding for entrepreneurs and staff and welcomed by destination area residents, local businesses and politicians.

Definitions

The fundamental component of revenue management is recognising any opportunity to maximise revenue potential on a real-time basis. Revenue management has been described as the application of information systems and pricing strategies to allocate the right capacity to the right customer at the right place and the right time (Kimes, 1989). An effective revenue management strategy separates price-insensitive customers from price-sensitive customers according to the time the service is rendered or the reservation made (Donaghy et al., 1995). Lieberman (1993) defines revenue management as 'the practice of maximizing profits from the sale of perishable assets, such as hotel rooms, by controlling price and inventory and improving service to selected customer segments' (p. 36). Although the strategy's purpose remains constant, its applications can be very different. Today's service industry has generally embraced revenue management, but varies its practices by the nature of each individual business.

Figure 7.1 shows a typology of revenue management that categorises several service industries with different characteristics. Successful revenue management applications are generally found in Quadrant 2 industries, in which both capacity and price can be managed (Kimes, 2000).

Revenue management has been most effective when applied to operations with the following characteristics: fixed capacity, predictable demand, perishable inventory, appropriate cost and pricing structures and variable and uncertain demand (Jagels and Coltman, 2004). As a result, the best revenue management examples are found in the airline and hotel industries and in other tourism industries that share these characteristics with them.

Key elements of revenue management

To manage and increase revenue, a revenue manager must possess the ability to segment customers based on their willingness to pay in addition to forecasting, pricing and overbooking abilities.

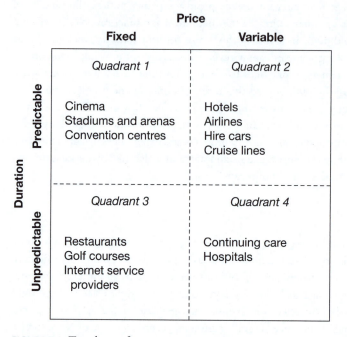

FIGURE 7.1 Typology of revenue management

Source: adapted from Kimes (2000, p. 6)

Customer segmentation

To employ revenue management effectively, a company must be able to segment customers by price sensitivity. By segmenting customers in this way, the restrictions associated with low prices encourage price-conscious travellers to book ahead. Business travellers, in contrast, are typically more time-sensitive and thus unable to qualify for the lower rates.

Forecasting

Accurate forecasts are essential to any revenue management system, and they require extensive information on demand and booking patterns by rate level and length of usage. Most companies have information on historical sales patterns, but they may fail to track the dates/times that customers make reservations. Without such information, it is almost impossible to make accurate forecasts.

Pricing

Revenue management is a form of price discrimination (Kimes, 2000). Tourism service suppliers need to classify customers and charge them different rates on the basis of their different needs and types of behaviour. This type of pricing strategy adopts a number of rational rules and restrictions to differentiate between guests who are willing and able to pay higher prices and those who are willing to change their behaviour in exchange for a lower price (Hanks et al., 1992). For example, price-sensitive customers can enjoy a lower price, but be subject to such restrictions as having to book ahead and agreeing to a non-refundable deposit. Customers who are willing to pay full price, in contrast, can book at any time and select any kind of room. The advantage of this kind of segmentation is that the tourism company can sell discounted products to one customer segment without losing any income from other segments. At the same time, such a pricing system is relatively easy to explain to customers, as each price category is established according to reasonable rules.

Price discrimination is a growing trend. Charging customers different prices based on their needs not only yields greater revenue, but also results in more satisfied customers. The key is to build a rational price structure in case customers from the high-price segment need to purchase a low-price room.

Overbooking

As previously discussed, an overbooking policy is also essential to a good revenue management system. Companies overbook to protect themselves against the possibility of no-shows. Although customers have made reservations in advance, they may cancel those reservations or fail to show up for a variety of reasons. The resulting unsold hotel rooms or vacant airline seats mean lost profits. Overbooking does carry a risk, however: if all customers who have made reservations show up, then the company will have insufficient capacity and facilities. It is thus essential that tourism companies identify the optimal overbooking rate.

Typical hotel revenue management process

As previously noted, the best revenue management examples are found in the airline and hotel industries (Kimes, 2000; Cross, 1997). Hence, for illustration, we consider a typical hotel revenue management process. The objectives of revenue management in this sector are first introduced, followed by a step-by-step illustration of how it is performed and a description of the development of a computerised revenue management system.

Objectives

To manage and increase revenue, a manager must follow a series of processes depending on the targeted objectives. Common objectives are to maximise revenue, optimise the average daily rate (ADR) or capture the number of room nights sold. These objectives determine what revenue strategy a hotel property should implement to attain its revenue target.

Maximising revenue potential

With this goal in mind, a hotel should theoretically take any business opportunity that comes through its door and turn no business away. Most hotel sales personnel are trained to sell as many available rooms as possible to minimise the amount of perishable inventory and achieve greater revenue potential.

Optimising the ADR

Optimising the ADR at a proper level enables hotels to sell rooms at the most profitable prices, thereby adding more value to the bottom line. The ADR can be influenced upward by directing sales efforts towards higher-priced rooms. This strategy is usually achieved by selling a product at a certain specified rate to reach a desired target. Revenue may suffer, however, because the hotel may have to turn away potential business to attain a high ADR.

Capturing room nights (length of stay)

The ideal way for a hotel to achieve strong revenue is to capture a longer length of stay. Hosting more long-term guests allows a hotel to save on labour hours in the front office and housekeeping department. Although the daily rates for transient guests are generally higher than those for weekly or monthly guests, the hotel will attain better profits over the long term by filling more rooms with long-term guests (Blank, 2002).

Objectives give managers a direction and target area to set controls on the available rates for different types of reservations. It is always important to bear them in mind during the revenue management process to ensure that all revenue efforts increase the profitability of the bottom line.

Typical hotel revenue management process

Before beginning the actual process, the manager begins with some type of comparative or historical data that apply to the hotel area or a specific timeframe for the targeted forecast. After analysing these data, a proper forecast can be made and strategies implemented. The following five steps are presented to illustrate the revenue management process and explicate the common practices and functions of hotel revenue management.

Collect data

The first step is the collection of data. There are three important pieces of data that need to be collected and analysed before a manager can make any revenue maximisation decisions: historical data; information about the competition; upcoming events.

Historical data include past occupancy rates, room rates and any hard copies or system-generated reports on the hotel property. These data inform managers of the trends in guest stay patterns and reflect business growth over the past few years. There is no rule for how far back a manager should track historical data; the ideal is to include as many years as possible. It is better to collect and keep all available data until comparative analysis is complete. It is important that the historical information gathered is applicable to the specific timeframe (or time interval) to be forecast, whether fourteen days or thirty, sixty, ninety days. Managers also need to ensure that the data are relevant and contribute to the accuracy of the analysis and forecast.

Information about the competition, or in today's jargon, the competitive set, is developed by each individual hotel and depends on the classification of competition. The competition can be properties in the same area or region or, more specifically, direct competition, such as hotels with the same rating, scale, service and targeted customers. Any type of information that can be gathered about a hotel's competitors will be helpful in the data analysis process. Although information about their past occupancies and rates may be proprietary, it is often possible to obtain through proper networking.

Gathering data about the competitive set's rates for the next year at the year-end is strongly recommended. Comparing these rates with competitors' current rates renders it easier to identify their strategies.

Upcoming events – revenue managers must always be aware of any current/upcoming holidays and events during the forecast period, as well as any events that will occur in the upcoming year but did not occur in the past, and vice versa. These data will definitely have an impact on demand, although demand will also be affected by the nature of the events and when they will take place. Because there is no tracking device for upcoming events, managers need to develop the habit of reviewing the news on a daily basis. Most relevant information is obtainable from the internet, magazines and newspapers that cover the economy. As revenue managers read through these materials and save copies on file, they are developing a valuable resource for future review.

It is also important to learn the goals and objectives of other tourism organisations (i.e., convention and visitors' bureaus and local tourism associations) and their plans for the upcoming financial year. Such information also gives managers an idea of where the major players are in terms of business promotion and marketing focus.

These three types of data should be gathered prior to analysis and forecast, although other information can also prove invaluable. Successful revenue managers also collect any data that relates to people. By learning which events draw people, managers also learn when and from where demand will come.

Analyse data

At the data analysis stage, managers need to compare historical and current trends, distinguish the economic differences between them, and decide which information is valid and which is not. Although historical information reveals consumer buying/ spending patterns, the peaks/valleys of business and marketing/promotional emphases, it is not necessarily an accurate indicator of future trends. Management thus needs to use good judgment when analysing historical data. For example, if a revenue manager were forecasting Christmas 2003 based on only two years of historical data, then he or she would make a fictitious reading because of the significant impact of the 9/11 crisis in 2001. When employing historical data, it is thus wise to recognise economic differences and perform comparative analysis only at a normal business level.

As previously mentioned, it is also always wise to collect as much data as possible to make sure that trending is representational. For instance, if a manager wanted to make a forecast for the Christmas/New Year holidays in 2004, then his or her historical data should be prior data for the same holidays in 2003, 2002, 2001, etc., as far back as possible. Year-to-year comparisons help managers to identify any changes or aberrations (i.e., the 9/11 crisis in 2001). In the case of an aberrant event, comparison of data from before and after the even allows better measurement and forecasting of the current year's business volume.

After reviewing the historical information they have collected, managers should have a rough idea of the likely trends for the forecast timeframe. The next step is to review the competitive set and determine what competitors' rate strategies are likely to be in the forecast period. Comparing competitors' historical rates with a pre-set future rate should produce some kind of percentage change. Based on this information, a revenue manager can determine whether a rate increase or decrease is appropriate. If he or she is able to discover competitors' strategies for different customer segments (i.e., foreign independent travellers [FITs], tour groups and conventioneers), then he or she will have a better basis for adjusting rates to an advantageous level.

Finally, knowing about upcoming events provides managers with another revenue advantage, as events have a direct or indirect impact on occupancy rates. If an event is to be held in the vicinity of a hotel property, then management will know that there will be a time demand. In other words, if individuals want to attend the event, then they will need to attend it during its scheduled time period. No alterations in travel dates are possible, which directly affects hotel occupancy and confers a big revenue advantage. If the event is to take place outside the property's vicinity, then it will have an indirect impact on demand. Unless all of the hotels within the event area are sold out, the property will experience only secondary demand.

Perform forecast

After analysing the collected data, managers enter the core stage of the revenue management process, that is, the forecast stage. All of the aforementioned preliminary work is performed for the purpose of obtaining an accurate forecast of future business volume. An accurate projection will indicate whether the hotel property needs to pursue more business, whether business will be coming directly or whether there will be enough business to meet its budget. Analysis of these data provides a revenue manager with a rough idea of what business level to expect. As far as determining a forecast based on real numbers, however, the most commonly used measure is the booking pattern or booking pace.

A booking pattern refers to how long prior to arrival guests generally make their reservations. If we break this length of time into smaller time intervals, then we should obtain the pace of booking, which indicates any increase in reservations. The booking pace can be a percentage change or real data. For example, if, from a Monday to a Monday (a seven-day period), a hotel property realises a 200 room night increase for a certain demand period (i.e., the 24–31 December Christmas holiday), then the hotel will be 200 room nights ahead of its targeted seven-day period. If the manager employs this statistic as the starting point, then next week he should have 200 more room nights on the books for the 24–31 December period.

If this pace holds true to the current statistic, then the revenue manager will have quite an accurate forecast. Based on the concrete measurement of the booking pace from the current day to next week, and from next week to the next seven-day period and all the way to the demand period, the revenue manager can take the factor (200 room nights) over the course of one week, determine how many weeks remain before the demand period and easily see the number of room nights the hotel will have available.

When tracking the booking pace and employing it as a viable measure for forecasting purposes, revenue managers need to 'take pictures' constantly, that is, they need to gather reservation statistics between the beginning and end of each time interval and compare the percentage change (or change in the number of room nights) between each interval to adjust that pace. The booking pace will also vary by market segment (as explained in the next step). It is therefore important to divide customers into segments based on their willingness to pay, which allows the rate setter to know the expected booking pace for each segment as a preliminary step to allocating rooms amongst the segments. Because of seasonal demand changes, a new forecast should be prepared every month according to the booking and competition pace.

Set revenue controls

The forecast will indicate the hotel property's business level for the forecast period. The next step is to set some controls on rates in a way that achieves revenue maximisation. First, the manager needs to compare the forecast values (ADR, occupancy percentage) of any chosen time interval (i.e., next week, fourteen days, thirty, sixty, ninety days or a full year) with the annual budget. Revenue controls will differ depending on whether the property is meeting or falling behind its annual budget.

If, according to the booking pace, demand will exceed the number of room nights available for the specified period, then the next step is to identify the rate that customers are paying at this booking pace. If they are buying at a rate that is lower than the targeted ADR, then there is an opportunity to drive up the ADR. The revenue manager could close out the lower rates and establish revenue controls to gain business at a higher rate. Making such a rate adjustment should slow down the booking pace, perhaps from 200 room nights per week to 95. Other controls, such as requiring a two-night stay or payment thirty days in advance, are also commonly employed by hotels. Making proper rate adjustments or setting hurdles often achieves the best combination of ADR and occupancy, thus optimising revenue in an effective manner. After all, the purpose of long-range forecasting is to allow sufficient time to set revenue controls to filter out unwanted business and obtain the ideal business mix for revenue maximisation.

If, in contrast, the forecast business level is less than the budget, then revenue managers need to look at three key areas: revenue, ADR and room nights. For example, if the room nights forecast meets or exceeds the budget, then it is possible that the ADR will not; consequently, revenue may not meet the budget either. The logic of setting revenue controls then becomes obvious. Managers must first decide which goal is easier to achieve – increasing ADR or simply driving up revenue. If they opt for the former, then the hotel will need to hold off any rate rise, and, as a result, revenue will suffer, which is the downside of pursuing the ADR. The art of revenue management is achieving a balance between the ADR and occupancy to optimise revenue. Revenue, ADR and room nights are thus critical, not only to an interpretation of the forecast, but also to how the property will meet its budgeted objectives.

In an ideal hotel environment, another effective way to set controls for better revenue management is to allocate rooms into different market segments. Such allocation depends on the occupancy mix and the demand for a different mix. The hotel itself constitutes one huge segment, and there are usually three major segments – FITs, wholesales and groups. A revenue manager will normally sit on the FIT. FITs usually pay the highest rates and thus provide the greatest revenue for the property. The sales department, in contrast, usually sits on the inventory that goes into the group segment.

A revenue manager can move inventory between segments based on each segment's booking pace. For example, if the booking pace for groups (or wholesales) is declining, and the FIT pace is on the rise, then it is necessary to cut a number of rooms from the group (or wholesale) inventory and sell them to FITs. Once all rooms are allocated, no one needs to know the strategy employed because each segment has a certain portion of room nights to sell. The sales staff selling to groups (or wholesales) cannot sell the inventory reserved for FITs.

In short, revenue controls involve deciding what kind of business the hotel can allow on its books and what kind it should turn away. These controls can be established on the basis of various distribution channels, that is, market segments.

Monitor controls

Effective revenue management requires constant attention and monitoring. A revenue manager needs to follow up the outcome of the revenue controls he or she sets to ensure the best revenue for the hotel property. In addition to adjusting rate hurdles, setting duration controls and moving inventory between market segments, managers must make sure that reservations and sales personnel are aware of these controls and know how to implement them.

To ensure better coordination between departments and hotel managers in terms of revenue management, it is common practice for a revenue manager to conduct a Revenue Maximisation (RevMax) meeting on a weekly or bi-weekly basis. In the RevMax meeting, managers identify opportunities for revenue optimisation and coordinate responsibilities to a team that should include the General Manager, Director of Sales and Marketing, Controller, Reservations Manager and Revenue Manager. Every decision taken in the RevMax meeting is a business decision. Revenue managers should always present their data from a statistical standpoint and have numbers to back up their recommendations to ensure that the decisions taken and effort exerted by the team are beneficial. During the RevMax meeting, these managers focus on managing low-demand periods, from the current month to the next thirty-, sixty-, ninety-day periods, and discussing the best sales strategy to implement.

These are the five key steps of a typical hotel revenue management system whose aim is to maximise revenue and optimise revenue potential. This revenue management system does not inform hotel personnel of an actual strategy; it is instead a set of dynamics, mainly to deal with the establishment of controls (rates). The revenue system is a filtering system, and it helps hoteliers to decide what business to keep and what business to turn away.

Development of computerised revenue management systems

Before computerised central reservation systems (CRSs) or property management systems (PMSs) became prevalent in the hotel industry, managers performed all of the revenue steps manually. It was not until the early 1990s that hotels began to benefit from the many automated revenue management systems and software available on the market.

Whilst international hotel chains such as the Marriott Corporation, Holiday Inn and Hilton all have their own company- and brand-specific computerised revenue management systems, a variety of made-to-order automated revenue management systems are available in the market to cater to individual hotels and motels of all sizes and configurations. These automated systems, which feature numerous built-in gadgets and bells and whistles, assist managers in accessing available computer-generated reports and in the preliminary analysis of these reports, thereby enhancing the accuracy and efficiency of the revenue process with real-time results.

Computerised revenue management systems can predict future occupancy patterns and demand based on a complex and detailed analysis of current levels of activity and the historical pace of bookings at a certain property for each market segment (Adams, 2000). Automated systems not only confer real-time benefits, but eliminate human error and produce relatively more accurate forecasts. Many automated revenue management systems have the ability to collect and analyse historical data relative to the booking pace, no-shows, walk-ins, average length of stay, customer stay patterns and daily market segment performance. In addition to analysing capacity, some of these systems have hundreds of built-in revenue controls that accept or reject reservations according to a preset strategy. In terms of performance monitoring, a computer is able to track forecast accuracy and the competitive environment to indicate whether a property is achieving its fair market share.

Automated systems do have several disadvantages, however. No matter how complex or sophisticated an automated system is, revenue management involves a mental process that no computer can substitute for. For example, a hotel may have three rooms that remain unsold for a certain day. If the system has a $200 per room night parameter set, and a reservation request comes in for five nights at $150 per night, then the system will reject it, thus turning away $750 of business (relative to the $600 desired rate limit according to the parameter). Another possible scenario is a long-stay request with a split: guests wish to split a six-night stay, with two nights this week and four nights next week. The computer is unlikely to recognise such a complex situation, and is thus likely to turn away some profitable potential business. Hence, unless all possible scenarios are input/programmed into the system, which would be very difficult to achieve, human involvement is still required in making the correct decisions. Computers can produce trustworthy sophisticated reports and forecasts, but what matters most is how management acts upon these data. Another disadvantage of automated systems is that staff are often trained 'how' to operate them, but not 'why'. The fundamental principles of revenue controls are far more critical than computer functions.

In deciding whether a hotel requires an automated or manual system, hospitality practitioners should first consider the return on investment. It is necessary to evaluate the extent to which revenues will be optimised and what the ADR will be if an automated system is installed. If a manual system can produce ninety per cent optimisation, and an automated one perhaps ninety-seven per cent, then decision makers should consider whether an investment that increases productivity by seven per cent is one worth making. The scale of the hotel may also be a decision factor. For example, a small hotel with fifty to eighty rooms and the ability to maintain its integrity level and produce sufficient results for strategic decisions may have little need to invest in an advanced computerised system.

Manual systems give managers the flexibility to arrange data, spreadsheets or charts freely to obtain the desired results. The limits set in such systems are up to the revenue manager, who decides on the complexity of the report format and the dividing line between market segments. Automated systems, in contrast, incorporate boundaries that limit the report format. Revenue managers must still manipulate the automated report to obtain omitted measurements.

Effective revenue management in a hotel does not require an advanced computerised management system or a seasoned veteran to play the role of revenue manager. Although it is better for the hotelier if the revenue manager understands the intricacies of the hotel business, it is more important that he or she is logical and comfortable with theory, has excellent knowledge of the destination in which the hotel is located, and the ability to identify the peaks and valleys of the business and react accordingly. Revenue management is both an art and a strategy to attract valuable business and maintain good relationships amongst consumers, wholesalers and the hotel property.

Hotel revenue management has become an indispensable tactical tool, regardless of the size, segmentation or rating of a hotel property. All things being equal, the systematic application of revenue management will always have a positive impact on sales turnover. The revenue management process requires the solid implementation of all of the aforementioned revenue steps and frequent attention to the system, regardless of whether it is manual or automatic.

7.5 Summary

Because the suppliers in a TSC lack the ability to inventory their products, the effective use of capacity can be critical to success. This chapter provides an understanding of the issues surrounding the management of supply and demand in the capacity-constrained tourism industry by exploring the lack of inventory capability, the nature of service constraints (time, labour, equipment and facilities) and the causes of fluctuating demand.

Based on these fundamental issues, the chapter has presented a variety of strategies for matching supply and demand. These strategies fall into two main categories: demand strategies (shifting demand to match capacity) and supply strategies (adjusting capacity to meet demand). The former seek to flatten the peaks and valleys of demand to match the flat capacity constraint, whereas the latter seek to align, flex or stretch capacity to match these peaks and valleys. Tourism organisations often employ several strategies simultaneously to solve the complex problem of balancing supply and demand.

Overbooking and revenue management have been presented as sophisticated forms of supply and demand management that balance capacity utilisation, including market segmentation, forecasting and pricing. Revenue management guides decisions on how to allocate undifferentiated units of capacity to available demand in a way that maximises profit or revenue. The problem then becomes one of determining how much to sell at what price and to which market segment.

Revenue management offers the potential of increased revenue to the tourism industry, but it needs to be approached with caution, as it carries the risk that the tourism organisation will lose focus or inadvertently alter its image in pursuit of increased revenue. The potential long-term impact on the organisation's reputation should be considered carefully.

Discussion questions

1. Why do tourism suppliers lack the capability to inventory their products?
2. What are the common constraints on tourism service capability? Please give an example for each.
3. Describe the basic strategies employed to match supply and demand.
4. What is the overbooking strategy? Discuss the risks of adopting such a strategy.
5. What is revenue management? List the key elements of revenue management strategies.
6. Discuss how revenue management is applied in the hotel industry.

Note

1   This chapter is jointly written with Wenli Li.

8

CUSTOMER RELATIONSHIP MANAGEMENT IN TSCs

Learning objectives

After reading this chapter you will be able to:

1. Understand what customer relationship management (CRM) is about and the critical concepts it involves.
2. Describe the key components of Tourism Supply Chain (TSC) customer management.
3. Calculate customer lifetime values and identify the most valuable customers.
4. Understand the concept of service quality and the factors that affect customer satisfaction.
5. Know how e-CRM can affect the performance of TSC members.

8.1 Introduction

Competition within the tourism industry has intensified over the past two decades. In the 1980s, tourism was largely a supply-driven industry that saw a boom in the hotel sector worldwide due to a favourable tax environment featuring accelerated depreciation schedules and easy access to bank loans in North America and Europe (see Vogel, 2006, p. 98). At that time, the focus of tourism enterprises' marketing strategies was on attracting more customers to purchase their products and services through traditional sales tactics such as transactional pre-purchase activities. The economic prosperity of the 1990s saw the further evolution of the industry, with increasing numbers able to travel following deregulation of the airline industry and the rapid expansion of low-cost carriers in Europe and North America, which reduced travel costs significantly. As a result of these factors, tourism marketing strategies have shifted from tactical sales to strategic marketing, including CRM, whose purpose is not only to attract additional customers, but to retain customers after they have purchased a product/service. Globalisation and the development of ICTs in the twenty-first century have forced tourism businesses to pay even greater attention to CRM to achieve their objectives.

Porter (1985) suggests two strategies for achieving competitive advantage: cost leadership and product differentiation. Both have become increasingly difficult to achieve in the tourism industry, however, given that most, if not all, tourism businesses in the same sector/layer of a TSC face the same market conditions and possess similar ICTs. They are thus able to change their cost strategies and adapt to new technologies very quickly if they discover that other businesses have competitive advantages in terms of cost or differentiation. The cost advantage and product differentiation strategies are difficult to sustain in the long run. Cost leadership and product differentiation are known as competitor-centred strategies for achieving competitive advantage (Day and Wensley, 1988). Increasing numbers of businesses in the tourism industry have actually switched from competitor-centred to customer-focused competition strategies in recent years. For example, the philosophy of Shangri-la Hotels and Resorts is 'Shangri-La Hospitality from Caring People', which is in line with the company's commitment to providing guests with distinctive Asian standards of hospitality and service. Five of its eight guiding principles are customer-focused (www.shangri-la.com). The primary market segments of Shangri-la Hotels and Resorts are high-end business and leisure travellers, whose loyalty depends very much on service quality and superior customer management skills.

The CRM concept is particularly important to TSCs, relative to supply chains in the manufacturing industry, as their end users are tourists, whose attention is focused on the quality of their interactions with tourism product/service suppliers. The following section presents some of the basic concepts related to CRM in the TSCM context.

8.2 Definitions of CRM

Greenberg (2001) suggests that CRM is a complete system that: provides a means to enhance the experience of individual customers to ensure the construction of a loyal customer base; supplies both technological and functional solutions to identify, capture, and retain customers; and provides unified information about customers within the enterprise. Day and Van den Bulte (2002) state that CRM is a cross-functional process for achieving on-going dialogue with customers across all contact and access points, with personalised treatment provided to the most valuable customers, to increase customer retention and the effectiveness of marketing initiatives. Another definition of CRM is that provided by Jespersen and Skjøtt-Larsen (2005): 'CRM is a business strategy – an attitude towards employees and customers – that rests on a number of processes and systems. The goal is to construct long-term relationships and thereby add value for the customer and the company through understanding of individual needs and preferences' (p. 86).

All of these definitions suggest that the goal of CRM is to anticipate and react to the needs of customers with effective and efficient actions. Contemporary CRM

TABLE 8.1 Traditional marketing versus CRM approaches

Traditional marketing	CRM
Transaction focus	Customer focus
Short-term focus	Lifetime focus
One transaction	Multiple transactions
Broadcast approach	Sniper approach
One-way, one-time communications	Two-ways continuous dialogue
Segment of many	Segment of one

Source: Özgener and İraz, 2006

differs from traditional marketing activities. It is a cross–functional philosophy that integrates all business functions within an organisation. Table 8.1 presents a comparison of traditional marketing and CRM approaches.

Table 8.1 suggests that CRM is a customer-oriented, multi-faceted, and dynamic process relative to the traditional marketing approach. Its goal is to construct a bond between tourism businesses and their customers. To establish this bond, tourism firms need to identify who their customers are, how to reach preferred customers and what services are required to meet those customers' needs.

In the TSC context, CRM refers to the ways in which the employees, technologies, and processes of individual TSC members or the entire TSC can best be utilised to satisfy TSC customers and sustain a close relationship between customers and partners. Please note that TSC customers are not always tourists. Tourists are the end-customers of these chains, whereas their intermediate customers are the TSC members themselves. For example, hotels are the customers of tour operators and vice versa.

The principles of CRM in TSCs are considered to comprise three critical concepts (see Figure 8.1).

1. *The product concept* relates to the provision of high-quality products/services that possess the features required by customers. A method known as the customer value requirement map (CVRM), which is discussed later in this chapter, can be used to identify customers' wants and needs.
2. *The selling concept* relates to the development of new selling concepts that are conducive to TSCM. Traditional selling focuses primarily on transactional pre-purchase activities, with attention paid to sales presentations, handling customer complaints, closing sales deals and signing contracts. The aim of traditional selling is to increase sales of products/services with a view to generating more profits and gaining new business. However, the traditional selling concept is tactical in nature and lacks a strategic orientation, and it is thus in many ways counterproductive to TSCM. The new selling concept within the TSCM framework, in contrast, advocates the development of a new selling orientation, interfaces more effectively with logistics, and adopts cooperative behaviour in TSC planning, the evaluation of TSC performance, and demand forecasting (Mentzer, 2004, pp. 130–31).

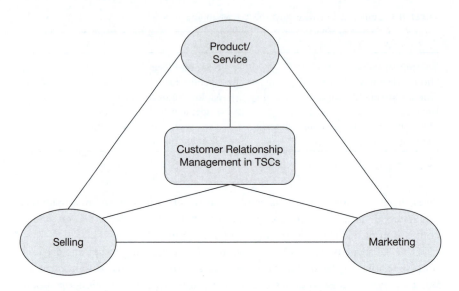

FIGURE 8.1 Principles of CRM in TSCs

3. *The marketing concept* refers to effective promotional campaigns, including customer relationship marketing by TSC members to communicate the benefits, features, and values of their products/services to their customers. The marketing concept within TSCM also requires the free sharing of information between TSC members and customers.

8.3 Key components of CRM

CRM cycle

The CRM cycle concept introduced by Nykamp and McEachern (1999) can be employed to describe the CRM process in TSCs. The CRM cycle begins with the identification and understanding of customers' needs. Once these needs have been identified, TSC members can develop appropriate or tailor-made products/services to satisfy customers on the basis of differentiated needs or customer segmentation. The resulting new products/services then need to be communicated and delivered to existing and potential customers. Those who are satisfied with the products/services provided will then become loyal customers of the TSC, with the possibility of lifelong bonding with TSC members.

Similar to the CRM cycle concept, Mentzer (2004) describes CRM as a supply chain value strategy, as shown in Figure 8.3. According to Mentzer, the goal of CRM is to obtain/sustain competitive advantage in the marketplace.

Identifying customers is the first step in CRM. As Mentzer (2004) notes, not all customers are created equal. Accordingly, their needs and demand for tourism products also differ. International luxury hotel chains often find themselves attracting primarily high-end business and leisure travellers whose income level, tastes, and preferences are clearly different from those of their mass tourism counterparts. Once tourism businesses have identified who their customers are, they can then emphasise the appropriate values in their product design and development. TSC members also need to provide and communicate these values to their customers (both existing and potential). Most importantly, TSC members need to assess customer satisfaction with the values delivered on an ongoing base.

The identification of customers is normally driven by supply considerations. When entrepreneurs start a new tourism business, they tend to design and develop their products based on a certain target market. Before investing in a hotel property, for example, an entrepreneur will carry out an investment feasibility study. One aspect of this study is the identification of the hotel's target customers and how much demand there will be for hotel rooms among those customers. One method adopted by tourism businesses to select customers is discrimination pricing. For example, the customers for such luxury tourism products as high-end resort

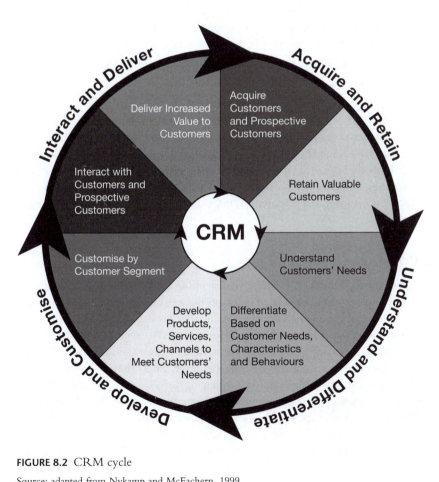

FIGURE 8.2 CRM cycle

Source: adapted from Nykamp and McEachern, 1999

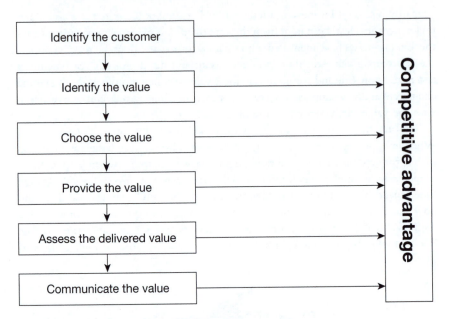

FIGURE 8.3 Tourism supply chain value strategy

Source: adapted from Mentzer (2004, p. 92)

hotels and business class airline seats are selected through the price discrimination strategy. However, the simple identification of target customers is insufficient for the success of TSC operations. The most crucial task for TSC members is to identify the values that customers place on the products provided by TSC businesses and whether those products possess the values that customers prefer. A customer value requirement map is a useful analytical tool that allows TSC businesses to identify customer values.

Customer value requirement map

Most international hotel chains carry out in-house customer surveys to gauge the level of customer satisfaction with their products/services through pre-designed customer satisfaction questionnaires. Such surveys are a good way to understand how customers view these hotels' existing services and to identify ways to improve service quality if customers are dissatisfied with certain service attributes. They are far from sufficient to ensure good CRM, however. Effort should also be devoted to identifying customer value requirement changes over time. The in-depth study of high-end customer values and their implications for future product development can be a highly complex process that requires carefully trained personnel (Mentzer, 2004). A relatively simple and effective device for identifying the value requirements of customers in a TSC setting is the aforementioned CVRM (Woodruff and Gardial, 1996).

The typical CVRM illustrated in Figure 8.4 can be employed as a guide for tourism business executives in carrying out customer interviews. It also provides useful suggestions for the formulation of TSC strategies to deliver these values.

This map looks like a normal questionnaire, but it should not be simply distributed to customers for completion. Rather, it should be filled out by trained executives and managers of the TSC member firms during the interview process. The typical questions the interviewer should ask the customer include: 'We cannot serve your needs unless we understand what you want from us, so please tell me what it is about our products/services that is important for you?'; 'What is it about our products/services that worries you the most?'; 'If you made a wish list for our products/services, what would be the top three items on that list?' Once this wish list or customers' value requirements have been established, the interviewer should ask the customers to rank the importance of these requirements on a scale of 1 to 5. Please note that it is acceptable for a customer to give certain requirements an equal ranking. The next step is to ask the customer to rate the performance of the focal business's products/services on a scale of 1 (excellent) to 5 (terrible) based on the value requirements he or she has identified. Afterwards, the customer should be asked to rate the performance of the products/services provided by a competitor (it is important to specify this competitor). Suppose that we are evaluating the customer value requirements of a restaurant in a TSC that primarily serves international tourists who have identified the following value requirements for the restaurant's service: food taste, food hygiene, dining ambiance, service speed and price. Upon completion of the interview, the interviewer should have a CVRM that looks like that in Figure 8.5.

The results of the foregoing CVRM provide a number of strategic insights for the focal business of the TSC. They show, for example, that the restaurant has

Value requirement	Importance rating*	Performance rating**				
		1	2	3	4	5
Requirement 1						
Requirement 2						
:						
:						
:						
Requirement N						

Note: *Importance rating: ranges from 1 = essential to 5 = not important; **1 = Excellent, 2 = Good, 3 = Fair, 4 = Poor, 5 = Terrible (rate both focal [F] and competing [C] businesses).

FIGURE 8.4 Customer value requirement map

Source: adapted from Mentzer (2004, p. 96)

Value requirement	Importance rating*	Performance rating**				
		1	2	3	4	5
Food taste	1	F	C			
Food hygiene	1		FC			
Dining ambiance	2			C	F	
Speed of service	3	F		C		
Price	4	C	F			

Note: *Importance rating: ranges from 1 = essential to 5 = not important; **1 = Excellent, 2 = Good, 3 = Fair, 4 = Poor, 5 = Terrible (rate both focal [F] and competing [C] businesses).

FIGURE 8.5 Customer value requirement map for a restaurant

competitive advantage, according to the customer's assessment, with respect to the taste and fast delivery of food, but is less competitive in terms of dining ambiance and price compared with a competing restaurant. The restaurant manager can draw on this information to further improve service. It is possible, however, that the customer's perception concerning price relative to the restaurant's competitor may be incorrect. If this is the case, then it is clear that the focal restaurant requires better communication with its customers about the price of its products/services. The CVRM thus provides both operational and communication insights to TSC members.

Logistics leverage

The previous subsection introduced a simple method for obtaining customer value requirements for the individual products/services provided by individual TSC members. If we take a much broader perspective, then the number of tourism businesses that sell homogeneous products/services such as accommodation, package holidays and restaurant meals in a specific market are likely to be numerous. In many situations, the customer value requirements for these products/services are the same, and tourism businesses thus often find it difficult to compete with one another through product differentiation and value enhancement. Instead, they often opt to increase market share through price competition. If all of the tourism businesses selling homogeneous products/services are engaged in a price war, then the consequences may be devastating for both customers and the TSC, as the outcome tends to be reduced service quality and profits for TSC members. As noted, tourists are the end-customers of TSCs, and the quality of the products/ services provided to them depends on more than one service provider, which are themselves engaged in B2B relationships. Under these circumstances, smart TSC managers try to achieve competitive advantage not through product differentiation but through *logistics leverage*. Logistics leverage refers to 'the achievement of excellent and superior, infrastructure-based logistics performance, which – when implemented through a successful marketing strategy – creates recognizable value for customers' (Mentzer and Williams, 2001, p. 103). The key to logistics leverage is to create a cluster of services around a product (such as a package holiday, air transport, or a cruise holiday) through the supply chain and its partners to give the focal business a distinct advantage over its competitors. This type of competition is supply chain-based rather than product-based. Logistics leverage is likely to generate sustained competitive advantage in the market if it is implemented through changes in corporate infrastructure, including employees, ICTs, facilities and strategic corporate relationships. Liang *et al.* (2009) examined the impact of improved logistics service management on the satisfaction and loyalty levels of 654 international tourists visiting Taiwan and using a supply chain connecting the airport, accommodation, attractions and retail shops, and found the efficiency of the logistics service to be one of the most important factors in positively influencing tourist satisfaction and loyalty.

Resource requirements for CRM

Logistics service improvement requires resources, particularly when such improvement involves investment in corporate infrastructure, facilities and human capital. Similar to many other businesses, tourism enterprises are also constrained by resources. To achieve competitive advantage, TSC businesses must thus prioritise their resource allocation to meet customers' value requirements. Logistics leverage in TSCM is also considered to be a type of product differentiation strategy, as it offers customers efficiency and reliability in the consumption of the product/service that other firms cannot emulate. The imitation of a logistics service is more difficult than the imitation of a product, as it requires considerable financial and human resources to achieve logistics leverage. Adoption of an effective logistics leverage strategy derived from a CVRM also requires thorough market research and coordination among TSC members. The logistics leverage strategy is customer-centred, and TSC members need to shift resources from the areas customers do not care about to areas customers do care about as illustrated in Figure 8.6.

Successful CRM within a TSC requires TSC members to move scarce resources from the inefficient services quadrant to the ineffective services quadrant (see Figure 8.6) to improve customers' level of satisfaction. The excellent services quadrant indicates that TSC members are meeting the customer value requirement, although this designation does not mean that TSC members should no longer pay attention to these services. In fact, to maintain excellent services, TSC members need to maintain investment in those services to avoid any decline in service quality.

Segmenting customers

In the CRM cycle model, customer segmentation is employed to develop and customise products/services. Hence, in conjunction with the identification of

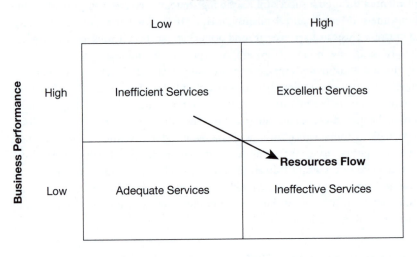

FIGURE 8.6 Managing resources for effective CRM
Source: adapted from Mentzer (2004, p. 109)

customer value requirements, TSC members should also be actively engaged in analysis of such segmentation. Not all customers are equally profitable, and thus TSC members need to identify who the most profitable customers are and how to encourage them to spend more on products and services. Analysis of customer information allows TSC members to segment customers based on their socio-economic and demographic characteristics. Once TSC members understand their customer mix, they can adopt appropriate marketing strategies to target the most profitable customers and reduce marketing costs. Tourism businesses use different criteria to identify their most valuable customers. For example, airlines consider the frequency with which passengers travel with them as an indicator of customer value, whereas tour operators may use revenue generated per customer. In fact, customer segmentation can also help TSC members to design and modify their products/services according to their value requirements. Market segmentation further helps TSC members to take better care of their customers, which is the core of CRM.

Predicting customer behaviour

Analysis of customers' past purchasing behaviour can help TSC members to predict their future purchasing intentions, thereby allowing tourism enterprises to anticipate what products/services customers are likely to purchase next and how much they are willing to pay for them. Such predictions can also help tourism businesses to adjust their pricing and promotion strategies without resulting in a loss in demand for their products/services. For example, Hilton's CRM system frequently analyses the demographic information of guests in its Hilton Honors Program. Behavioural patterns are identified to support direct mail campaigns with a view to helping Hilton to plan seasonal activities for its business travellers (Wisner et al., 2008).

Customer profitability assessment

One purpose of customer segmentation is to evaluate customer profitability. Although it is difficult for most CRM systems to determine such profitability, it is important to obtain this information as it directly affects CRM resource allocation. Certain customers may be profitable now, but become unprofitable in future. For instance, business travellers who book air tickets through a travel agency rarely purchase other package products from that agency. Although this type of customer may be seen as unprofitable, if he or she is satisfied with the services the travel agency provides, then it is likely that he or she will recommend the agency to family and friends, who may subsequently purchase package products. It is thus essential that tourism businesses pay attention to customers' lifetime profitability rather than their profitability for a fixed period of time.

Calculation of a customer's lifetime profitability is based on his or her current purchases, the average profit margin on the items he or she purchases, and the value of his or her lifetime purchasing power (Wisner et al., 2008). The following example illustrates how to calculate customers' lifetime profitability.

Example 8.1

Assume that Wing On Travel has two top customer types in terms of profitability: Type A and Type B. The company wishes to calculate the expected lifetime profitability of these two types to design cost-effective targeted marketing strategies. The following table presents their purchasing data.

	Avg. Sales/yr.	Avg. Profit Margin	Expected Lifetime
Type A	$300,000	20%	5 years
Type B	$240,000	15%	15 years

Assuming an annual discount rate of 8%, the present values of these customers' lifetime profitability are

$$NPV_A = \alpha \left[\frac{(1+i)^n - 1}{i(1+i)^n} \right] = \$300,000 \times 0.2 \times \left[\frac{(1+0.08)^5 - 1}{0.08 \times (1+0.08)^5} \right] = \$238,475$$

and

$$NPV_B = \alpha \left[\frac{(1+i)^n - 1}{i(1+i)^n} \right] = \$240,000 \times 0.15 \times \left[\frac{(1+0.08)^{15} - 1}{0.08 \times (1+0.08)^{15}} \right] = \$307,843 \, ,$$

where

α = average annual profit;
i = annual discount rate;
n = expected lifetime in years.

We can see that Type B customers are more profitable than Type A because they have a much longer expected lifetime use of the business provided by Wing On Travel, although the former's average sales and profit margins are less than those of the latter.

In addition, TSC members also need to focus on the total revenues generated by customers in a given period with a view to mobilising resources to attract those that are most profitable. Consider, for example, two customers who purchase air tickets from Hong Thai Travel. One spends $10,000 per year, and the other $5,000. Although the first customer appears to be more valuable than the second as he or she generates twice as much income, if the second customer also books air tickets from other travel agencies, spending a total of $30,000 per year, but the first books only through Hong Thai Travel, then the second customer actually has greater revenue-generating potential for Hong Thai Travel. This agency thus needs to make every possible effort to attract and better manage the second customer.

Personalising customer communications

As today's tourists, especially younger tourists, prefer the convenience of the internet for communication and transactions, it is essential that tourism firms engage in personalised communication with their customers through the internet and e-mails to maintain a positive relationship. Effective communication also improves customer satisfaction and enhances customer loyalty. For example, Cathay Pacific Airways, an effective user of CRM applications, draws on customer information to create a mutually beneficial relationship with its customers. In case of any flight delays, the airline's Marco Polo Club members receive personalised text messages, thereby allowing them to plan their departure to the airport accordingly.

From TSC members' perspective, knowledge of customers, including their past behaviour and preferences, enables the customisation of communication to specific customer groups. Such customised communication can result in greater sales and profitability for tourism businesses. For instance, the online booking systems of these businesses can remember customers' names, payment details, click sequences within the online booking website, and the products purchased. These data constitute useful information for travel agencies, tour operators, and accommodation providers in designing personalised products and services for customers who use their online booking systems.

8.4 Customer service management

Customer service management

Customer service in the SCM context describes a host of different but critically interrelated activities that provide customer utility or optimum levels of service. La Londe *et al.* (1988) describe customer service as the process of providing significant value-added benefits to the supply chain in a cost-effective way. Customer service management (CSM) is the system that manages these critical activities. Band (1991) defines CSM as a system in which customer needs, wants, and expectations are met or exceeded over the transaction cycle, thereby resulting in repurchase behaviour and loyalty.

CSM has changed dramatically over the past thirty years. In the beginning, customer service in tourism businesses consisted of receiving and answering personal letters from customers who had questions about or problems with travel and tourism products/services. The establishment of help desks enabled customers to communicate directly with service representatives about their requirements. By the 1990s, the purpose and function of CSM had evolved beyond the provision of a toll-free telephone number to encompass a wide range of customer care activities. In the late 1990s, the functions of customer service centres, also known as contact centres or customer interaction centres, developed to include the deployment of a wide range of multimedia tools to manage every component of the business operation that may affect customer satisfaction (Ross, 2004). More recently, the functions of these centres have expanded into areas in which CSM integrates the internet, wireless communications, speech recognition and video into a single system that provides effective and interactive services to customers. Such applications integrate all channels of customer interaction into a central platform, thereby significantly reducing customer service costs. In addition, interaction centres can improve knowledge of customer behaviour to support customised sales and services, in turn boosting customer satisfaction and loyalty (Ross, 2004).

Service quality gaps

The identification of customer value requirements, customer segmentation, CRM investment and effective CSM are all aimed at improving the service quality of TSC members. To improve that service, it is important that TSC members understand the gaps that exist between tourism product/service suppliers and customers within the TSC. Possible such gaps are illustrated in Figure 8.7.

TSC customers (whether final or intermediate customers) form their expectations of the tourism products/services provided by the suppliers in a TSC on the basis of both their past experiences and the quality of the same/similar such products/services provided by competing firms as a benchmark. TSC members do not always understand customer expectations for their products/services, which leads to Gap 1. In package holiday sales, for example, there are two reasons for

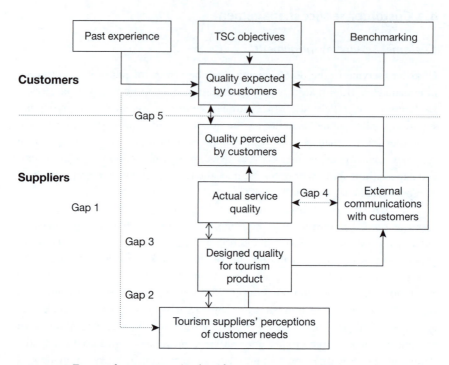

FIGURE 8.7 Expected versus perceived performance in a TSC

Source: adapted from Parasuraman *et al.*, 1988

this gap. First, the travel agent who sells the package holiday fails to communicate tourists' needs to the tour operator clearly, and hence the latter is uncertain of its customers' exact requirements. Second, because the tour operator does not know exactly what tourists' demands are, it is unable to convey those demands to accommodation and transportation providers, and so on. As tourists pass through the supply chain, this process continues, and the gap widens.

Even if TSC suppliers understand exactly what their customers' needs are, the retailers of tourism products/services may be unable to interpret correctly the designed characteristics of those products/services to potential tourists, thereby leading to Gap 2. Furthermore, differences often exist between what is designed and what is produced or provided (Gap 3), which is often caused by a lack of coordination and information sharing among TSC members. Gap 4 results from ineffective communication between TSC members and final customers (tourists). Not surprisingly, the retailer's (travel agent's) resultant perception of what is delivered by the supplier (tour operator) is often very different from tourists' original expectations, which constitutes Gap 5. All of these gaps are interrelated and may be widened if earlier gaps are not closed in a timely fashion. The end result is dissatisfied customers (including tourists, tourism product suppliers and retailers), reduced revenue, and a smaller customer base.

Service quality attributes

To understand the service quality gaps that exist between customers and TSC businesses, it is important to know what service attributes customers are actually looking for when they purchase and consume a tourism product. According to Zeithaml *et al.* (1990), these service attributes include the following (although they were developed on the basis of generic consumer products, they can also be applied to analysis of tourism services):

1. *Tangibles.* Tangibles are what can be seen, such as new facilities and the latest equipment. They give customers a sense of confidence and assure them that the services they are receiving are of good quality.
2. *Reliability.* TSC businesses should continually deliver on their promises to customers. Service reliability enables TSC members to lock in customers who are willing to pay a premium for their products/services.
3. *Responsiveness.* A helpful attitude and timely service will always make customers feel that they are dealing with a winner.
4. *Competence.* TSC businesses that support their products with cost-effective and competent services will always be leaders in the marketplace.
5. *Courtesy.* If TSC members do not respond to their customers with politeness, respect, consideration and professionalism through their frontline staff, then they will lose their customers to competitors.
6. *Credibility.* Service leaders succeed through high standards of honesty, trustworthiness and believability.
7. *Security.* TSC customers, including tourists, often pay a great deal of attention to the security of tourism product/service delivery and monetary transactions between TSC members.
8. *Access.* Access refers to the degree of ease with which customers can purchase tourism products or contact sales and service functions. Customer convenience and access to products/services are important factors in determining competitive advantage.
9. *Communication.* Effective customer communication is a fundamental criterion for service leadership.
10. *Understanding customers.* TSC members that provide tourism products/services that customers really want will always enjoy an advantage over their competitors.

Measuring customer satisfaction

It is reasonable to believe that large service quality gaps lead to a higher degree of customer satisfaction. Understanding these gaps is thus only the starting point of service quality improvement. TSC members must also assess how large the gaps are to mobilise resources to close them and increase customer satisfaction. Customer satisfaction can be expressed by the following ratio (Ross, 2004):

$$\text{Customer satisfaction} = \frac{\text{Perceived quality}}{\text{Needs, wants, and expectations}}.$$

If the customer satisfaction value is greater than 1, then the quality of the service provided exceeds the expectations of the customer. If it is less than 1, then it falls below those expectations. A value of 1 means the service quality just meets customer expectations.

Different from the classification developed by Zeithaml *et al.* (1990), Fuchs and Weiermair (2003) group service attributes into three categories that have different impacts on customer satisfaction: basic factors, performance factors, and excitement factors.

Basic factors are minimum customer requirements. They cause dissatisfaction if unfulfilled, but do not lead to customer satisfaction if fulfilled or exceeded. In other words, they are necessary but insufficient for customer satisfaction. Customers consider them to be prerequisites. The basic components of a package holiday, such as shopping, sightseeing and entertainment, are the basic services that tourists expect the tour operator to provide. If one of these services is missing, then tourists will be dissatisfied, although the inclusion of all of them does not necessarily lead to an increase in tourist satisfaction.

Performance factors will lead to satisfaction if fulfilled or exceeded and result in dissatisfaction if not fulfilled. They can thus cause both satisfaction and dissatisfaction. Performance factors often refer to the quality of the services provided, such as how many sightseeing opportunities are provided on a package holiday and the quality of the shopping destinations, and can lead to both satisfaction and dissatisfaction.

Excitement factors increase customer satisfaction if they exist but do not cause dissatisfaction if they do not. Many major hotel chains now send follow-up questionnaires via e-mail to customers who have recently stayed with them. When a customer receives such an e-mail from the General or Customer Relationship Manager of a hotel, he or she normally feels that he or she is being treated as a valued customer, thereby enhancing satisfaction with the hotel's service. If the hotel does not send such an e-mail, the guest's satisfaction level is unlikely to decline as a result.

Figure 8.8 depicts the impact of these three types of factors on customer satisfaction. For performance attributes, the relationship between customer satisfaction and customer expectation fulfillment is leaner and symmetric, whereas it takes the form of a unilateral curve for both basic and excitement attributes. One influences only customer dissatisfaction, and the other only customer satisfaction.

It is very important that TSC members identify the nature of service attributes and their impact on the direction of change in customer satisfaction if they are to utilise resources appropriately to improve service quality.

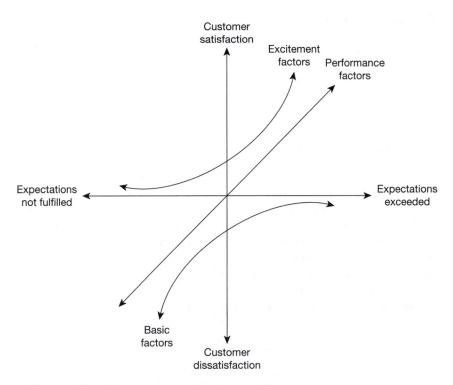

FIGURE 8.8 Three-factor structure of customer satisfaction

Source: adapted from Fuchs and Weiermair, 2003

8.5 e-CRM

The internet has developed into an important distribution channel for TSCs, providing TSC members with direct and effective means to communicate with their customers. It permits the following:

1. Direct connection between tourism suppliers and retailers.
2. Full information exchange among all TSC members.
3. Cost reduction in CRM as a result of savings in time and space.
4. Effective and efficient communication with TSC customers.
5. Real-time information updates.

TSC members can use the internet to build their customer knowledge base and implement effective CRM. e-CRM involves the improvement and application of existing techniques for customer value identification, segmentation, satisfaction enhancement and service management in an electronic environment (Constantelou, 2002).

Functions of e-CRM

A contemporary theme in CRM is to place customers within the context of a partnership rather than considering them as a marketing target (Stockdale, 2007). The emergence of e-commerce has propelled the realisation of customer-centric environments. The functions of CRM have also begun to change in response to the customer-centric CRM approach.

Identifying customers online

A key element of successful CRM strategies is customer identification. Before the emergence of the internet, travel agents learned their customers' needs through face-to-face consultations with them. Such interactions not only cost travel agents time and money, but also delayed customer information acquisition and processing. Internet use facilitates the identification of customers and their needs. More importantly, it allows customers to manage their own information by setting up profiles and modifying that information when they make online purchases. TSC members can collect and analyse customer information in a timely fashion and design appropriate promotional strategies based on customer needs.

Supporting customer information searches

A typical travel website offers more than a printed brochure, as it contains pictures, videos and other information about package holiday products and services. The provision of such websites saves on printing costs and reduces customer consultation time to allow tourism enterprises to spend more time on the design and improvement of their products/services. Moreover, it means that customers no longer need to acquire flight, accommodation and car rental information from the service providers, as they can check the availability of these services online and obtain answers to any questions they may have about their trips from the Frequently Asked Questions (FAQs) section or online help desk.

Booking and payment made easy

Online booking and payment options allow TSC members to speed up sales. Assume, for example, that Mr Johnson plans to travel from Hong Kong to Shanghai for business. He first checks the availability of flights and accommodation on a travel portal such as Ctrip.com, and then books his airline tickets and hotel room online. The entire process may take only ten to twenty minutes. If, in contrast, Mr Johnson chooses not to use an online booking service, then he may have to confirm his reservations and obtain his tickets and room confirmation a day after initially contacting a travel agent. Although online security issues have hindered the popularity of online booking and payment in some countries such as China, there is great potential for tourism businesses to further develop their online transaction systems.

Customer service

Customer care services in the e-CRM environment permit customers to comment on and lodge complaints about the products/services provided by TSC members, which helps tourism enterprises to improve their product/service offerings. e-CRM also provides a platform for TSC members to promote their products/services and offer special promotions through e-mail news and SMS.

Personalised communications with customers

Communication is also a central component of good relationships with customers. Although a many-to-many medium, the internet also serves as the best one-to-one communication tool between enterprises and customers (Stockdale, 2007). It provides an opportunity for TSC members to develop individual customer relationships by customising their products/services to fit each customer's needs. Such actions allow tourism businesses to maintain long-term relationships with their customers.

Impacts of e-CRM on TSCs

TSC members can build stronger, more personalised relationships with their customers through the use of e-CRM, although the implementation of e-CRM in a TSC may change its organisational structure. For example, each tourism business within the TSC may need to establish a special department to maintain its online services (e.g., online promotions, sales and enquiries). Its other departments or functions may also need to pay attention to these online services to support and cooperate with this unit. In a collaborative TSC, only one online service organisation may be required to service all TSC members with B2B and B2C relationships.

TSC members obtain greater profits by maintaining long-term relationships with their customers, and e-CRM can consolidate good customer relationships through personalised communications and customer services. Acquiring and retaining loyal customers is the key to competitive tourism businesses in the global marketplace.

8.6 Summary

CRM is the strategic utilisation of people, technologies and processes by TSC members to improve and sustain profitable relationships with customers and partners. In the TSC context, good CRM includes three critical concepts that interact with one another: the product concept, selling concept and marketing concept.

TSC members can attract the most valuable customers and establish stronger customer relationships through good CRM practice. The important components of CRM for TSCs include the identification of customer value requirements, the achievement of logistics leverage, resource re-allocation, customer segmentation, the prediction of customer behaviour, a determination of customer profitability and the personalisation of customer communications.

Customers may be unprofitable now, but profitable in future. TSC members thus need to recognise the lifetime value of their customers to distinguish those with the best potential for profitability over the long term. Lifetime value is calculated on the basis of a customer's current purchases, the average profit margin on the items purchased and the value of his or her purchasing lifetime. The present value of a customer's lifetime value can be formulated as follows:

$$NPV = a \left[\frac{(1+i)^n - 1}{(1+i)^n} \right],$$

where

α = average annual profit from this customer;
i = annual discount rate; and
n = expected lifetime in years.

CSM is also very important to TSCs, and involves ten critical elements: tangibles, reliability, responsiveness, competence, courtesy, credibility, security, access, communication and understanding of the customer. Customer satisfaction in the CSM context can help tourism enterprises to assess the gaps between the services provided by TSC members and customer expectations of those services. Service attributes can be divided into different categories (i.e., basic, performance and excitement factors) according to their impact on the direction of changes in customer satisfaction.

Contemporary businesses consider their customers to be partners rather than marketing targets. e-CRM focuses on this altered relationship between enterprises and customers to allow the realisation of customer-centric business strategies. e-CRM in a TSC enables tourism enterprises to contact their customers effectively and obtain feedback from them in a timely manner. It can also help them to sustain existing customers and attract potential future customers. Finally, it can also enhance TSC performance.

Discussion questions

1. What are the advantages of CRM strategies compared with traditional marketing approaches?
2. Explain the ways in which a customer's value requirement can be identified and managed.
3. Do you know how tourism enterprises segment their customers? Can you give some examples?

4. What do we mean by logistics leverage? How do we employ logistics leverage to enhance the customer relationships within a TSC?
5. Explain, with examples, the framework that describes the service gaps between TSC members.
6. How do we measure customer satisfaction based on the service gap model?
7. Can you give examples of the types of service attributes (factors) in a TSC that have different influences on customer satisfaction?
8. Please describe the functions of e-CRM and its impacts on TSC performance. What is your prediction for future e-CRM trends?

9

INFORMATION COMMUNICATION TECHNOLOGIES AND TSCM

Learning objectives

After reading this chapter you will be able to:

1. Describe the components of ICTs and their development stages of ICTs in the tourism industry.
2. Understand how ICTs influence individual tourism businesses and TSCs as a whole.
3. Be familiar with ICT applications in TSCs in China.
4. Understand the outlook for ICT-enabled tourism.

This chapter provides an introduction to the impact of ICTs on tourism through a review of their evolution over the past thirty years. The role of ICTs in enhancing TSC performance is discussed, and cases of ICT development and its influence on TSC development in China are presented. The chapter concludes with a consideration of possible new directions for ICTs and tourism developments.

9.1 Information communication technologies and tourism

The spectacular development of ICTs has changed the way in which consumers, businesses and governments behave. The largest impact these technologies have had on commerce has been the reduction in information asymmetry between consumers and business providers. Greater information symmetry has been brought about by modern ICTs through digitisation, interconnectivity and miniaturisation (Cosh, 2010). Digitisation refers to the process of converting information/data to binary form, which can be recognised by computers and other electronic devices. Because of digitisation, such industries as the software, music and film industries, whose products/services can be digitised, have greatly benefited in terms of added value to their products. Although tourism products/services, such as hotel rooms, attractions, airline seats, cruises and museum visits, cannot be digitised, information about them can be, and the tourism industry has accordingly been capitalising on the digitisation process with a view to enhancing its performance.

That performance has also been enhanced through increased interconnectivity, which has been facilitated through the digitisation of tourism product information. The main vehicles of such interconnectivity are the internet and wireless communication technologies, which together have enabled consumers to communicate more effectively and businesses to reach much wider markets. Governments and private businesses are increasingly developing the necessary ICT infrastructure to meet increased demand for interconnectivity. The past decade has seen the development of faster and more effective networks and rapid advances in communication technologies. Huge advances in data processing capabilities allow computers to handle ever more complex algorithms and have increased the speed of computation and communication. Moreover, computers and electronic devices in the past had to be attached to networks through cables, whereas wireless and mobile technologies have now rendered connection easier and more flexible. Tourists can stay connected while travelling, which has created new opportunities for the tourism industry.

Miniaturisation refers to the ongoing trend for the computing devices used for communication and data handling to become increasingly small. Processing capabilities that were formerly housed in fixed facilities are now portable, allowing tourists to remain connected while they travel.

As Buhalis and Law (2008, p. 609) note, 'technological progress and tourism have been going hand in hand for years'. Tourism is an increasingly ICT-intensive industry that is heavily dependent on innovations that enable the effective distribution of its products/services and the management of its customer relationships. All of the business functions of TSC partners, including marketing, product design and planning, demand management and forecasting, R&D, the management of physical, financial and information flows, CRM and human resource management (HRM), are closely linked to ICTs (see Figure 9.1). ICTs also propel the re-engineering of internal business processes, change the relationships amongst TSC partners and improve customer services.

As the barriers to entry and product differentiation for tourism products such as package holidays, tourism merchandise and accommodation are relatively low, many TSC members rely heavily on cost advantages to remain competitive. Tourists have become increasingly sophisticated, however, and are demanding high-quality products/services, thus forcing tourism businesses to seek alternative ways to reduce operational and distribution costs. The effective use of ICTs constitutes one such alternative method. For example, in 1999 American West, a medium-sized US airline, reduced its distribution cost from US$23 to US$6 per ticket through

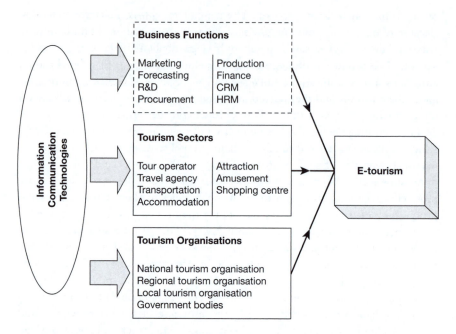

FIGURE 9.1 Links between ICTs and tourism

online sales (Schwartz and Zea, 1999), which allowed the firm to sell its products at a discount because of the savings it realised on commissions and distribution charges.

The management of customer relationships on a sustained and global basis is essential if TSC members are to achieve success in an increasingly competitive business environment. Customer information acquisition is critical for good CRM, and ICTs can help TSC members to capture customer profile/preference data directly for marketing research purposes and to improve their services with a view to enhancing customer loyalty. Most airlines today permit customers to purchase tickets online and offer personalised communications through various GDSs and the internet, thereby boosting customer satisfaction.

9.2 ICT-empowered tourism

ICTs comprise a wide range of electronic tools that facilitate the operational and strategic management of tourism organisations. For example, these organisations can employ ICTs to manage their internal and external information flows, organisational functions, and production processes and to communicate with customers to achieve organisational objectives (Buhalis, 2003).

Figure 9.2 illustrates the components of ICTs, which include hardware, software, telecommunications and networks. Hardware refers to the physical equipment used to store, process and transfer information, including computers, printers, telephones and mobile devices. Software controls the operation of the hardware components, and includes application programs and management systems such as databases, email systems, video playing programs and management information systems. Telecommunications and networks support the transmission and communication of information between different locations. The intranet provides a platform for information communication amongst the departments within a firm, whereas the extranet connects different suppliers within a TSC to allow them to share information conveniently. Firms can also reach customers directly through the internet.

ICTs enhance the ability of tourism businesses to manage their resources, communicate with customers and coordinate with their supply chain partners. In addition, they help public organisations to manage tourism businesses and activities. In fact, the tourism industry was a pioneer in the widespread use of ICTs, and it

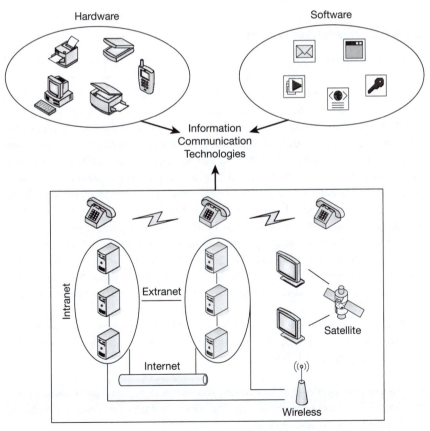

FIGURE 9.2 ICT components

FIGURE 9.3 Development phases of tourism–related ICTs

has a particular relationship with these technologies. On the one hand, ICTs have boosted the expansion and globalisation of tourism industries, but on the other the challenges brought about by tourism's geographic expansion need to be overcome through advanced technologies. Hence, tourism firms cannot operate their global businesses without utilising ICTs.

The development of ICTs in the tourism industry can be divided into three phases: the CRS phase, the GDS phase and the internet phase (see Figure 9.3).

Computer reservation systems

Airline operations require a phenomenal amount of information. Commercial airlines have to deal with thousands of flights, fares, seat inventories, crew members, passengers, cargoes and baggage due to the heavy demand for air travel (Sheldon, 1997). In the 1950s and 1960s, there were no standard platforms or solutions to handle information flows, and reservations were hand-coded, which was not only slow, but subject to human error. Airlines thus looked for ways to improve their operational management, although a number of challenges needed to be overcome. First, simultaneous access to information processing by many users required real-time interface amongst them. Second, information transmission amongst different service providers required larger and more reliable communication networks. Third, reliable business operations and information management became critical to survival in the increasingly competitive airline sector. Cooperation between American Airlines and IBM, which began in 1953, led to the development of the first CRS after years of research and US$40 million in investment (Sheldon, 1997). This CRS was called SABRE, which stands for 'semi–automated business research environment'.

Werthner and Klein (1999, p. 185) define CRSs as 'electronic airline reservation systems, used for managing flight and seat inventories for sales and operation purposes'. In general, a CRS:

- covers and handles flight schedules, seat inventories, availability and prices;
- provides information about other tourism products, e.g., package holidays, accommodation and car hire;
- enables reservations and ticketing;
- stores passenger name records;

- performs such management functions as reporting, accounting, planning and decision support.

In addition to being employed by airlines, CRSs were also adopted by such service providers as travel agents, tour operators, hotels and car hire firms in the mid-1970s to monitor, manage, and control their capacities and clients.

Global distribution systems

With increasing numbers of service providers adopting CRSs, demand for the expansion of these systems increased dramatically. Large CRS users began to open up their systems to other businesses, which led to the integration of different CRSs. These integrated systems are known as GDSs, which comprise a network of more than one CRS. They distribute different products/services and manage the functions of participating CRSs in different countries (Werthner and Klein, 1999).

Figure 9.4 depicts the structure of a GDS with many interconnected companies. A GDS contains all of the distribution information from suppliers and transmits that information to travel intermediaries. Such institutions and companies as the Official Airline Guide (OAG) and Airline Tariff Publishing Company (ATPCO)

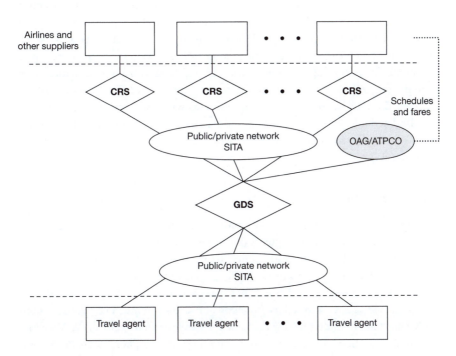

FIGURE 9.4 GDS structure

Source: adapted from Werthner and Klein, 1999

have built databases that include approximately forty million flight schedules and fares. Airlines and other suppliers file all of their schedules and fares with these institutions/companies once or twice a week. A GDS links the CRSs of airlines and other suppliers through public/private networks or the Société Internationale Télécommunications Aéronautiques (SITA). On the demand side, travel agents are also connected by similar types of communication networks.

Consumers can also access GDSs to obtain transparent and comparable information (e.g., on prices and availability) on a wide range of transport, accommodation and leisure services. They can also communicate with prospective suppliers and make immediate reservations through these systems. GDSs not only cost less than other distribution systems, but they also enable flexible pricing and capacity alterations when tourism businesses face uncertain demand (Buhalis, 2003). Suppliers can adjust prices and capacities according to the historical record, demand forecasts and the current sales situation via a GDS.

Internet

As previously noted, the development of the world wide web and the internet has had a significant impact on tourism. The internet is a communication platform that hosts many other ICT applications. Not only has it had a great impact on the way in which tourism businesses operate, but it has also changed consumer behaviour. Internet development has undergone the following stages: the initial stage, which mainly involved the display of as much information as possible on pre-designed web pages; the subsequent stage, which witnessed the enhancement of internet users' surfing experience through effective visual and structural web page design; and more recently, the increased popularity of Web 2.0 technology has seen the internet become more interactive, with users themselves supplying travel-related information on the web through various social media and networks. As a result, the amount of tourism information available online has grown enormously.

Mobile technologies

Thanks to the miniaturisation of communication devices, including laptop computers, tablet personal computers (PCs), Personal Digital Assistants (PDAs) and smart phones, and the ease with which they can be connected to the internet through wireless-radio connections (WiFi), people can travel with them very easily. The expansion of wireless and mobile networks and increased competition between service providers have also reduced the costs of access and use. The Global System for Mobile Communication (GSM) and Wireless Application Protocol (WAP) allow the communication of voice and other data over mobile phones and PDAs, and the development of third-generation (3G) mobile services has enabled the fast transmission of multimedia data (Buhalis and O'Connor, 2005).

Virtual travel communities

The introduction of Web 2.0 in recent years has also seen the emergence of Virtual Travel Communities (VTCs) that permit tourists to obtain information via social networks to assist their travel-related decision-making. VTCs have become very popular, as they allow users to share travel experiences and suggestions. They have also attracted the attention of tourism businesses, as the discussions and forums hosted on these sites facilitate a better understanding of travellers' behaviour and, in turn, improved marketing and distribution strategies. One of the most successful VTCs is Tripadvisor (www.tripadvisor.com), which provides reviews of hotels, restaurants, cruises and vacation homes in different destinations, thereby helping travellers and tourism businesses to make informed decisions (Buhalis and Law, 2008).

9.3 ICT impacts on TSCs

The rapid development of ICTs has had a profound effect on the operation and configuration of TSCs. Service providers can now sell their services (e.g., air tickets, hotel rooms, holidays and hire cars, etc.) directly to customers via the internet. They can also develop online CRM programmes with a view to interacting directly with customers. Such disintermediation[1] has helped service providers to reduce operational and distribution costs and also changed the way in which traditional travel agencies and tour operators do business. Many have had to switch from purely face-to-face interactions to online communication with customers and to undergo a transformation from traditional tour operator/travel agent to information consultant (Pan *et al.*, 2008). The emergence of re-intermediation[2] demonstrates the ability of innovative agencies to take advantage of ICTs to develop appropriate products and distribution strategies. All of the tourism businesses in a TSC need to adapt to the increased use of ITCs in tourism business operation to achieve sustainable growth.

Impact of ICTs on individual TSC members

The major players in TSCs, including airlines, accommodation providers, tour operators and travel agencies, have to sustain competitive advantage by adopting advanced technologies.

Airlines

Competition has been fierce amongst airlines due to the widespread establishment of open sky policies and bilateral agreements between countries, the emergence of low-cost carriers and continual rises in fuel prices. To stay in the game, many airlines have had to adopt new technologies. According to Doganis (2002), the airline industry has always been a pioneer in the adoption of new technologies.

As noted, airlines long ago began to employ CRSs and GDSs to manage sales in the supply chain. Many airlines also conduct direct sales through call centres and their own websites, thereby reducing the involvement of traditional travel intermediaries. The direct access to customers afforded by the internet has also allowed airlines to avoid paying commissions to travel intermediaries. All frontline airline employees today have access to passenger itineraries via the internet/intranet from initial bookings to check-in counters and boarding gates. ICTs also allow airlines to develop relationships with their customers and alliance partners.

As noted, many airlines have established their own websites through which travellers can purchase air tickets. E-ticketing programs save airlines printing and distribution costs. The use of ICTs and their application software also allows airlines to manage their revenues more effectively. The airline seats on a scheduled flight can be sold at different prices to maximise revenues, as revenue management systems permit ongoing fare adjustments during the sales process on the basis of the current sales situation and predictions of how many additional seats can be sold at a given price (European Commission, 2002).

Accommodation providers

Hotels were the first tourism businesses to adopt ICTs to manage their operations. According to Buhalis (2003), hotels have realised the following benefits from ICT use:

- improved capacity management and operational efficiency;
- enhanced room inventory control;
- ability to offer up-to-date room availability information;
- better database management;
- facilitation of marketing research and planning;
- ability to track frequent flyers and repeat hotel customers;
- enhanced travel agency tracking and commission payments.

Like the airlines, which have invested heavily in revenue management systems, hotels are also keen to maximise total operating revenues by minimising operating costs and maximising room occupancy and average room rates. Although many major hotel chains have developed their own revenue management systems, independent ICT providers have also established commercial revenue management systems, such as Rate Tiger (www.ratetiger.com), Travel Click (www.travelclick. net) and Amadeus Hospitality Solutions (www.amadeus.com/hotels/hotels.html). These systems are useful tools that afford hotels the ability to establish the most appropriate pricing strategies on the basis of demand forecasts and a great variety of inputs (e.g., previous experiences, anticipated events and existing customer information) and thereby achieve maximum occupancy rates and revenue.

Internet-based travel distribution channels such as Expedia (www.expedia.com), Hotels.com (www.hotels.com), Travelocity (www.travelocity.com), ctrip.com (www.ctrip.com) and eLong (www.elong.com) have revolutionised the way in which people book hotel rooms. Not only do they provide the best possible room rates, but they also provide additional information such as hotel locations and facilities and even customer evaluations. Hotels have also developed their own internet distribution channels with a view to reducing the sales costs associated with other channels. For example, seventy-five per cent of Marriott's hotel bookings are made through the company's own website (Cosh, 2010).

Intermediaries

Modern ICTs have changed the functions of tour operators significantly. In recent years, many tour operators have modernised their ICT-enabled operating systems either through system enhancement or replacement programs. Information on different elements of a tour can now be entered into a relational database, which allows tour operators to offer much more flexible and customised packages to tourists based on their individual needs. These product/service offerings are then made available for online booking, which has widened tour operators' distribution channels. Some tour operators also employ ICTs to enhance the travel experience. Real-time recommendations can be made to tourists on the basis of the preferences they enter into the system. Travel websites that incorporate intelligent software can also identify alternative products/services to online users, which renders travel decisions much easier.

As a result of the rapid increase in online bookings, traditional travel agents face substantial competition from internet-based travel product/service providers, forcing them to transform themselves from pure face-to-face sales agents into travel consultants in order to survive. Many travel agents have also gone online themselves, although doing so requires considerable investment in ICT infrastructure. One of the greatest hurdles to such transformation is ensuring the security of online transactions. Even when online transactions are completely secure, internet users may still consider it risky to supply their personal and credit card details, and some still prefer to contact service providers directly to make sure these transactions are secure and legitimate. For this reason, it is essential that internet-based travel agents maintain credibility in their tourism product offerings.

ICT impact on TSCs

Not only have ICTs affected the operations of individual tourism firms, but they have also had a major impact on the way in which TSCs operate. One of the most significant impacts that ICTs have had on TSCs is the disintermediation of the travel agents/tour operators within them. As previously discussed, the adoption of modern ICTs has led to a significant reduction in the commissions paid to travel agents/tour operators by airlines. Disintermediation has also affected the relationships amongst the suppliers within a TSC.

Figure 9.5 presents a flow chart showing the way in which TSC members are connected in providing and distributing tourism products/services. The material suppliers produce physical products as inputs for the service providers. These physical

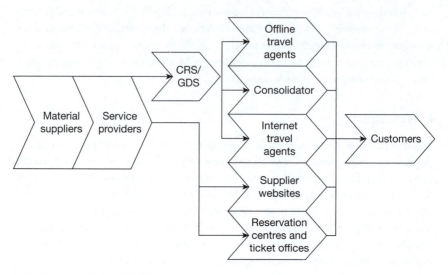

FIGURE 9.5 ICT-enabled TSC

products include, for example, the food products from farmers or catering companies for airlines, hotels, beds and tables from the furniture suppliers for hotels. Service providers include all the firms that supply tourism products/services, such as airlines, hotels, car rental companies, retail shops, restaurants and tourism operators. These suppliers could sell their products through their own internal distribution channels, such as a ticketing office or website, or through external channels, which are normally organised through a GDS or CRS. Both on- and off-line travel agents sell tourism products/services to customers directly. As Figure 9.5 suggests, customers can purchase these products/services from the TSC through a number of channels.

This figure also shows that suppliers' websites can offer alternative distribution channels by bypassing travel agents, thereby resulting in the latter's disintermediation. The introduction of modern ICTs has resulted in global enterprises that operate without the constraint of physical boundaries. For example, GDSs and CRSs have boosted the vertical integration of airlines and hotels with other suppliers and permitted them to sell their products/services directly to end customers. ICTs also enable connectivity amongst the suppliers within a TSC, thus creating virtual corporations and networked partnerships. Virtual corporations afford TSC members the ability to focus on their core competencies, be it flight scheduling, the supply of in-flight catering services or the provision of high-quality services to hotel guests.

ICTs promote the mass-customisation of tourism products, as they support the TSC in targeting niche markets in different locations. Hence, it is necessary for TSCs to re-engineer the entire process of producing and delivering tourism products, as well as to boost partnerships to satisfy the specific needs of individual customers

(Buhalis and Law, 2008). Tourism product suppliers have to rethink the distribution function in the electronic marketplace to develop value chains and exploit new distribution strategies, such as creating their own websites and introducing e-channels (by cooperating with online travel agencies and joining travel portals or search engines). In an ICT-enabled TSC, the distribution function is altered from the facilitation of information exchange and reservations to a more sophisticated mechanism with added value (Buhalis, 2003).

ICTs not only permit the customers of TSC members to purchase services and products online, but they also allow the handling of customer relations through online CRM systems. ICTs provide opportunities for TSC members to establish direct means of communication, and therefore to set up customer databases for marketing purposes. Effective websites usually include an area for product/service feedback, which serves as a useful channel for communication between TSC members and their customers. Service providers can then improve their services based on customer feedback, which is also crucial for the development of individual-oriented markets.

Although it is difficult to quantify the benefits of an interactive relationship amongst TSC partners in economic terms, open and trusting communication through ICTs has been shown to reduce the costs of business operations and to improve organisational efficiencies (Buhalis and O'Connor, 2005).

Figure 9.6 depicts the traditional tourism market as it looked before the widespread adoption of ICTs by TSC members. The traditional tourism market consisted primarily of three parties: suppliers, customers and intermediaries. The intermediaries on the right-hand side of the figure can be seen as the commercial and financial link between suppliers and customers, whereas those on the left-hand side are related to destination planning and administration. Inbound travel agents act on behalf of the tour operators within a destination. These tour operators produce new products by aggregating different services or products from suppliers (e.g., airlines and hotels). Travel agents can be viewed as the distribution channel for the tourism products/services provided by the tour operators, although tourists may also purchase these products/suppliers directly from the suppliers. National tourism organisations (NTOs), regional tourism organisations (RTOs) and local tourism organisations (LTOs), which can be seen on the left-hand side of the figure, play the role of managing the destination with a view to enhancing the tourist experience.

The emergence of ICTs has changed the traditional tourism market. Figure 9.7 shows that the introduction of these technologies (the internet in particular) has afforded suppliers direct access to consumers. The intranet has also improved internal information flows and cooperation between tourism suppliers. The new market structure illustrates the simultaneous nature of the intermediation, disintermediation and re-intermediation processes. In addition, the ICT-enabled market emphasises the role played by tourists in developing personalised products to meet their specific needs.

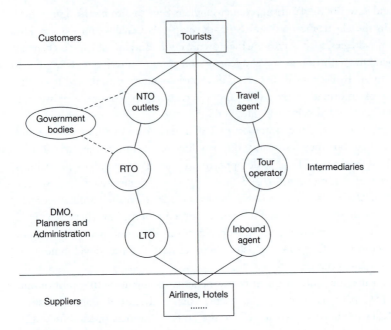

FIGURE 9.6 Traditional tourism market

Source: adapted from Werthner and Klein, 1999

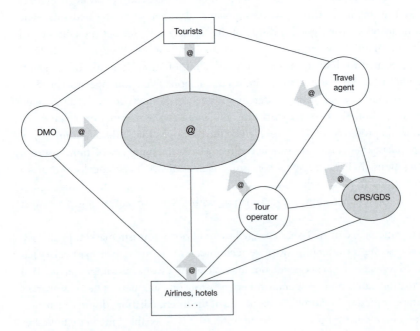

FIGURE 9.7 ICT-enabled tourism market

Source: adapted from Werthner and Klein, 1999

9.4 ICTs and tourism in China

China has become a major international tourism destination since the early 1980s, due to its historical and cultural attractiveness. In recent years, it has also become a key tourism source market due to the increased personal disposable income levels of its populace. The revolutionary development of ICTs, particularly that of the internet, over the past few decades has further propelled the country's tourism growth.

The development of online tourism services in China has gone through four main stages. The first stage began with the establishment of the HuaXia tourism website (www.ctn.com.cn) in 1996. At the time, tourism websites were simple in design and provided very limited information. Since 1997, increasing numbers of tourism organisations have developed websites that provide online services such as hotel and airline bookings and tourism product advertising. Since 2000, more professional and comprehensive tourism websites have been developed to compete with their international counterparts, and, since 2007, Web 2.0 or Travel 2.0 has become popular, pushing e-tourism in China to new frontiers. Table 9.1 summarises the four main stages of online tourism services in China.

TravelSky Technology Limited launched the first CRS in the Chinese airline industry in 1996, and it now handles almost all businesses within the industry, including ninety-seven per cent of domestic ticketing services and seventy-five per cent of overseas ticketing services. TravelSky's reservation system is the only CRS

TABLE 9.1 Four stages of online tourism services in China

Stage	Year	Features	Representative websites
1	1996–1997	Simple web pages. Few tourism web users. Slow connection speed.	HuaXia tourism web (www.ctn.com.cn); Chinaholiday.com
2	1997–2000	Combined online and physical tourism services. Commercial tourism websites beginning to realise real benefits.	Cytsonline.com; CITS (www.cits.cn)
3	2000–2007	Financial organisations become involved in tourism website development. Emergence of travel portals. Growing numbers of tourism web users.	Ctrip.com; eLong.com
4	2007–present	Online travel services penetrating deeply into society. Peer evaluation of tourism services emerging. Improved customer relationship management.	VTCs on travel portals (e.g., Ctrip.com) or portal sites (e.g., 163.com); travel search engines (e.g., Qunar.com)

Source: Lu and Lu (2004) and author's analysis

within China that allows ticket issuance with computer terminals that connect all ticketing agents. TravelSky is now linked up with all of the major GDSs in the world. Figure 9.8 shows the operation of the CRS in the Chinese airline industry.

Air China, the country's largest international airline, provides a good example of modern ICT adoption in the Chinese airline industry. The airline currently employs TravelSky for all of its domestic and international ticketing and has joined hands with major foreign GDSs to provide ticketing services for international routes.

International hotels used their own distribution systems when they began operations in China, and sales of domestic hotel rooms and food and beverage services still rely chiefly on sales personnel and word-of-mouth promotion, as no CRS has emerged in the Chinese hospitality industry to date. Most domestic hotels use the internet purely as a marketing tool, as a lack of trust of online reservation systems still prevails amongst Chinese consumers. Most hoteliers prefer telephone or fax bookings, although the recent emergence of travel portals (such as Ctrip.com and eLong.com) has speeded up the online reservation process.

Major hotel chains (both domestic and international) also employ ICTs to improve internal business operation efficiency, focusing on both front (e.g., reservations, reception, housekeeping, cashiers, marketing and CRM) and back office functions (e.g., procurement, accounting and security). The main systems within hotels include the Hotel Information System (HIS) and Property Management System (PMS).

Tourist attractions in China have been slow to adopt the latest ICTs. Very few employ e-ticketing systems to handle ticket sales, with most still selling admission tickets through traditional or online travel agents and travel portals.

Although the ICT applications of intermediaries in China have lagged behind those of the airlines, as in other parts of the world, the e-intermediaries in the country's TSCs can be classified into three types: the online services of traditional tour operators (e.g., CITS and Cytsonline.com), online travel agencies or travel portals (e.g., Ctrip.com, eLong.com and Byecity.com) and travel service

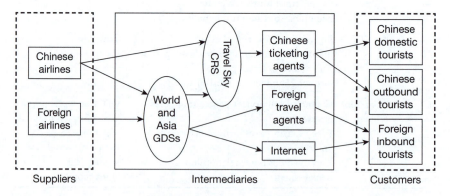

FIGURE 9.8 TravelSky CRS in the Chinese airline industry

information providers (e.g., the tourism division of Sina.com). Table 9.2 summarises the advantages and disadvantages of the three types of e-intermediaries.

Ctrip.com is a successful case of the use of modern ICTs to provide online tourism services. The site integrates service providers, tour operators/travel agencies and tourists on the same platform. Not only does it provide flight, hotel, car hire, corporate travel and package holiday reservation/booking services, it also provides sufficient information about these services to allow users to compare and contrast them with alternative services, thereby facilitating informed purchasing decisions. Potential travellers can also easily customise their package holidays once they have input their preferences, such as those for location, duration and other requirements.

The government-run China National Tourism Administration (CNTA) was established in the 1980s to manage, regulate and support tourism development at the national level. The CNTA has operated its own computer network system, which focuses on accounting, compiling statistics and publishing tourism-related information, since 1992. Local tourism boards have also been established at both the provincial and municipal levels under the leadership of the CNTA and local governments. Since 1993, the CNTA's computer system (see Figure 9.9) has been linked with those of local tourism boards to collect statistics on a monthly basis. The CNTA also set up an official tourism destination website (www.cnta.gov.cn)

TABLE 9.2 Comparative analysis of three types of e-intermediaries in China

	Online services of traditional tour operators	Online travel agencies or travel portals	Travel service information providers
Representatives	CITS (www.cits.cn)	Ctrip.com	Tourism division of Sina.com (tour.sina.com.cn)
Principal services	Air/train ticket reservations. Hotel reservations. Product promotion. Online consulting.	Third-party services for airlines, hotels and tour operators. Provision of tourism information. Integration of TSCs.	Platform for tourism information search and promotion. Creation of VCTs for travellers.
Advantages	Well-known brand. Professional consulting. Secure trading.	Huge databases of destinations, hotels and airlines. Personalised product packages.	Powerful search engines. Large tourism information databases.
Disadvantages	Poor customer coverage. High ratio of off-line businesses.	No provision of after-sales support services.	No support for online trading.

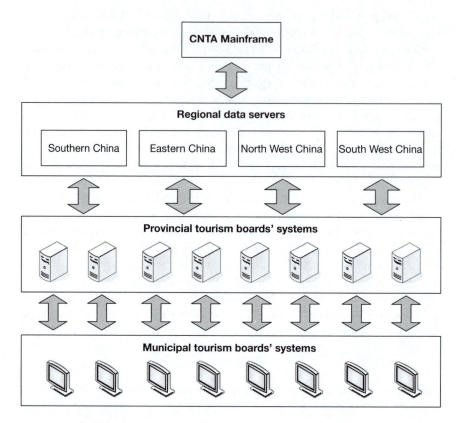

FIGURE 9.9 CNTA computer network system

Source: adapted from Ma *et al.*, 2003

in 1997 to provide information on accommodation, accessibility, attractions, culinary arts, local cuisine, shopping and entertainment in different destinations (Ma *et al.*, 2003).

9.5 Summary

This chapter discusses the impact that ICTs have had on the operations of TSCs and their members. The relevance of these technologies to the tourism industry is covered in Section 9.1, in which the three key drivers of ICT development – digitisation, interconnectivity and miniaturisation – are discussed and their impact on information symmetry highlighted. Section 9.2 presents the components of ICTs and their development paths, particularly those of CRSs, GDSs, the internet, mobile technologies and VTCs in the tourism context. Section 9.3 concentrates on a discussion of the impact of ICTs on individual tourism suppliers and the TSC as a whole. The final section describes ICT adoption by Chinese tourism organisations to assess the impact of ICTs on tourism in China.

Discussion questions

1. How can tourism businesses benefit from the use of ICTs?
2. Can you give an example of a CRS or GDS and describe its main functions?
3. Have you ever booked air tickets or hotel rooms through the internet? What benefits did online booking confer? How could the websites you used be improved (give one or two examples)?
4. What is a VTC? Have you ever joined one? If you have, then what were the benefits of doing so?
5. Do you think e-distribution channels will dominate the tourism marketplace in future? If so, why?
6. How can customers enjoy greater participation in the design of personalised tourism products?
7. What are the main challenges for China's tourism enterprises in future?

Notes

1 Electronic means allow customers direct access to suppliers and destinations, which leads to the elimination of intermediaries within the distribution channel.
2 New methods force existing intermediaries to re-engineer the tourism distribution channel, and ICTs are employed to develop new intermediaries.

10

CONCLUSIONS AND FUTURE RESEARCH DIRECTIONS

The emerging literature on TSCM has largely concentrated on tourism distribution channels, with a particular focus on the roles of intermediaries (Buhalis, 2001; Buhalis and Laws, 2001; Ujma, 2001; Pearce and Schott, 2005) rather than on the whole TSC, which consists of not only intermediaries but also various service providers including governments, tourists and the natural environment. Articles on TSC from an integrated perspective are currently very limited. Although rigorous development of TSCM research is underway, it is evident that more in-depth analysis is required, and further examination of the issues that are critical to TSCs is necessary. In this chapter we put forward some possible future research directions for TSCM based on the discussions of various chapters of this book. These research directions include collaborative TSC planning and forecasting, TSC coordination, TSC dynamics, and integrated product and TSC design. These directions are all in agreement with the TSCM philosophy towards coordination across organisations through a TSC.

10.1 Collaborative TSC planning and forecasting

Collaborative planning and forecasting is an approach facilitated by SCM concepts. It is based on cooperation and information sharing among the links in the chain. Existing non-tourism-related supply chain literature shows that collaborative supply chain planning and forecasting has become popular in supply chain demand management. For example, retailers have initiated collaborative agreements with their supply chain partners to establish collaborative planning and forecasting processes (Li, 2007). However, to the best of our knowledge, this topic has not yet been considered in the TSC literature.

Most studies of tourism demand forecasting have been based on statistical methods and rely on the availability and quality of historical data. Current knowledge about special events or information about marketing activities of TSC partners is difficult to include in statistical models. Two benefits that can be expected from collaborative TSC planning and forecasting are a reduced reliance on historical records and enhanced information sharing among TSC partners. The focus of collaborative TSC planning and forecasting is therefore not merely on the improvement of forecast accuracy but also on breaking down functional silos and smoothing the information flow along the TSC to benefit the entire TSC.

However, achieving collaborative TSC planning and forecasting is not an easy task. It requires a variety of participants from various echelons of the chain to work together. The first challenge is to establish a trusting relationship among TSC partners striving to help each other. The design of the forecasting process and the steps for effective implementation of the process constitute a challenging task. Last but not least is the technical side, such as the establishment of forecasting support systems to facilitate the forecasting process and information sharing among the players within a TSC.

10.2 TSC coordination

Coordination is the opposite of an arm's-length relationship in which both parties in a deal act in their own self interest and make their own decisions without any consideration of the impacts of the decisions on the other party. Coordination is also different from the fully integrated relationship in which both parties in a deal are integrated as one entity with common objectives. In general, coordination can be regarded as a decision-making strategy of firms that perform tasks to achieve supply chain goals (e.g., maximising supply chain profit) through contractual arrangements.

In the past two decades, various empirical tourism studies have been conducted to investigate the integration of businesses within a TSC (e.g., Lafferty and Fossen, 2001; Theuvsen, 2004). Leaving aside the issue that integration in a real TSC is not easy, full integration of tourism businesses leads to the problem of increased fixed costs and reduced flexibility (Gomez and Sinclair, 1991; Sinclair and Stabler, 1997). Moreover, TSC participants are often autonomous, while independent enterprises frequently have conflicting objectives. Coordination taking the form of contractual relationships among individual firms in a TSC provides a new opportunity for further research.

TSC coordination can take a variety of forms, ranging from full or partial integration of business processes to contractual arrangements between or among individual firms, either horizontally or vertically. Therefore, various studies can be conducted to investigate different programmes of TSC coordination. When we look at studies of supply chains in the manufacturing industry, it is found that coordination schemes have been extensively studied. It would also be very interesting and practical to investigate how different types of coordination schemes can help improve the performance of individual enterprises and the entire TSC in different market situations.

10.3 TSC dynamics

Supply chains are dynamic systems that evolve over time. One well-known phenomenon is the fluctuation and amplification of demand from the downstream to the upstream channel of a supply chain (Forrester, 1961), which is called the bullwhip effect (Lee *et al.*, 1997). It is mainly due to the lack of information sharing among enterprises (Sterman, 1989; Simchi-Levi *et al.*, 2003). Information sharing can improve interactions among enterprises in supply chains and therefore facilitate successful coordination among supply chain participants. Given that tourism businesses are dynamic activities characterised by changing customer demand, and tour operators have a far greater power to influence the activities throughout the TSC and direct demand than their counterparts in other industries, the bullwhip effect may be more severe in TSCs. Therefore, the strategy of information sharing in TSCs is worthy of investigation.

TSC dynamics can also be caused by evolving TSC relationships, which are a very important phenomenon in the tourism industry. A better understanding of such relationships in TSCs would be very helpful for tourism decision makers to achieve efficient and effective TSCM. The research reviewed in Chapter 1 (i.e., Accinelli *et al.*, 2006b; Bimonte and Punzo, 2007) has already investigated the evolution passes of the interactions between tourists and residents in a destination. More in-depth analysis of TSC dynamics is necessary in the future.

10.4 Integrated product and TSC design

In today's buyers' market, many industries face the challenges of providing sufficient product variety to meet diverse customer requirements and responding quickly to dynamic customer needs while maintaining economies of scale and scope within the service provision process. This new paradigm was termed by Stan Davis 'mass customisation' in his book entitled *Future Perfect* (Davis, 1987).

To shorten product delivery times and achieve a balance between product customisation and an economy of scale, many firms are pursuing specific product design strategies. The most popular product design strategy in the manufacturing industry has been the utilisation of the product family and modular product architecture. A product family is a range of products that share a collection of common elements and architecture. The positive impacts of product commonality have been widely demonstrated in a number of studies. For example, it has led to simplified planning and scheduling (Berry *et al.*, 1992), lower setup and holding costs (Collier, 1982), lower safety-stock levels (Baker, 1985), and order quantity economies (Gerchak and Henig, 1989). However, utilising commonality often requires the company to bear the additional costs involved in substitutions and thus reduces profitability (Krishnan and Gupta, 2001), or reduces the range of customer choices (Robertson and Ulrich, 1998). Modular product architecture, however, retains an optimum number of options for a module in configuring the necessary product variety without leading to such problems as increased supply chain complexity and high inventory levels, which are often associated with product proliferation. In terms of TSCs, the products normally consist of different service components, and the concepts of product families and modular product design are suitable for tourism product development.

Extensive research has shown that coordination among supply chain partners in the early stage of product development benefits the successful development of new products in the era of mass customisation (Monczka *et al.*, 1997; Ragatz *et al.*, 1997, 2002; Petersen *et al.*, 2005). Recent research also shows the advantages of optimising the product design, process design, and supply decisions in an integrated and simultaneous manner (Rungtusanatham and Forza, 2005; Huang *et al.*, 2005). Supplier integration has been well documented in the manufacturing industry. In today's competitive environment, the sheer number of tourism service suppliers provides abundant input possibilities for tour operators to assemble tour packages, and it is believed that effective integration of suppliers with tourism product development processes could increase the competitive edge of tour operators as well as the TSC as a whole.

10.5 ICT-empowered TSCM

The rapid development of ICTs has had a profound effect on the operation and configuration of TSCs. Service providers can now sell their services (e.g., air tickets, hotel rooms, holidays, hire cars, etc.) directly to final customers via the internet. They can also develop online CRM programmes with a view to interacting directly with customers. Such disintermediation has helped service providers to reduce operational and distribution costs and also changed the way in which traditional travel agencies and tour operators do business. Many have had to switch from purely face-to-face interactions to online communication with customers and to undergo a transformation from traditional tour operator/travel agent to information consultant (Pan *et al.*, 2008). The emergence of re-intermediation demonstrates the ability of innovative agencies to take advantage of ICTs to develop appropriate products and distribution strategies. All of the tourism businesses in a TSC need to adapt to the increased use of ITCs in tourism business operation to achieve sustainable growth. Researchers need to pay increasing attention to the impacts of ICTs on the individual TSC members as well as on the whole TSC.

REFERENCES

Accinelli, E., Brida, J. G. and Carrera, E. (2006a). A good policy of sustainable tourism. Retrieved August 2, 2007, from http://ssrn.com/abstract=901205.

Accinelli, E., Brida, J. G., Carrera, E. and Punzo, L. F. (2006b). Emergence of long run behaviours in a game theoretic setting with host and guest populations: Residents and tourists. International Tourism Conference, November 20–26, 2006, Antalya, Turkey.

Adams, B. (2000). Maxing out. Hotel and Motel Management, 215 (4), 38–39.

Agarwal, S., Ball, R., Shaw, G. and Williams, A. M. (2000). The geography of tourism production: Uneven disciplinary development? Tourism Geographies, 2 (3), 241–63.

Akal, M. (2004). Forecasting Turkey's tourism revenues by ARMAX model. Tourism Management, 25, 565–80.

Alamdari, F. (2002). Regional development in airlines and travel agents relationship. Journal of Air Transport Management, 8 (5), 339–48.

Alegre, J. and Cladera, M. (2006). Repeat visitation in mature sun and sand holiday destinations. Journal of Travel Research, 44 (1), 288–97.

Alford, P. (2005). A framework for mapping and evaluating business process costs in the tourism industry supply chain. In A. J. Frew (ed.), Information and communication technologies in tourism 2005. Vienna: Springer Verlag.

Appelman, J. and Go, F. (2001). Transforming relationships between airlines and travel agencies: Challenges for distribution and the regulatory framework. In D. Buhalis and E. Laws (eds.), Tourism distribution channels: Practices, issues and transformations (pp. 202–12). London: Continuum International Publishing Group.

Armstrong, J. S. (1985). Long-range forecasting (2nd ed.). New York: John Wiley & Sons.

Athanasopoulos, G. and Hyndman, R. J. (2008). Modelling and forecasting Australian domestic tourism. Tourism Management, 29, 19–31.

Au, N. and Law, R. (2000). The application of rough sets to sightseeing expenditures. Journal of Travel Research, 39, 70–77.

Au, N. and Law, R. (2002). Categorical classification of tourism dining. Annals of Tourism Research, 29, 819–33.

Bahaire, T. and Elliott-White, M. (1999). The application of geographical information system (GIS) in sustainable tourism planning: A review. Journal of Sustainable Tourism, 7 (2), 159–74.

Baker, K. R. (1985). Safety stocks and commonality. *Journal of Operations Management*, 6 (1), 13–22.

Baker, K. and Collier, D. (1999). A comprehensive revenue analysis of hotel yield management heuristics. *Decision Sciences*, 30 (1), 239–63.

Baloglu, S. and Mangaloglu, M. (2001). Tourism destination images of Turkey, Egypt, Greece, and Italy as perceived by US-based tour operators and travel agents. *Tourism Management*, 22 (1), 1–9.

Band, W. A. (1991). *Creating value for customers: Designing and implementing a total corporate strategy*. New York: John Wiley & Sons.

Bastakis, C., Buhalis, D. and Butler, R. (2004). The perception of small and medium sized tourism accommodation providers on the impacts of the tour operators' power in Eastern Mediterranean. *Tourism Management*, 25 (2), 151–70.

Baum, T. and Mudambi, R. (1994). A Ricardian analysis of the fully inclusive tour industry. *Service Industries Journal*, 14 (1), 85–93.

Belobaba, P. P. (1987). Airline yield management: An overview of seat inventory control. *Operations Research*, 21 (2), 63–73.

Belobaba, P. P. (1989). Application of a probabilistic decision model to airline seat inventory control. *Operations Research*, 37 (2), 183–97.

Bennett, M. M. (1993). Information technology and travel agency: A customer service perspective. *Tourism Management*, 14 (4), 259–66.

Berry, W. L., Tallon, W. J. and Boe, W. J. (1992). Product structure analysis for the master scheduling of assemble-to-order products. *International Journal of Operations and Production Management*, 12 (11), 24–41.

Bimonte, S. and Punzo, L. F. (2007). The evolutionary game between tourist and resident populations and tourism carrying capacity. *International Journal of Technology and Globalisation*, 3 (1), 73–87.

Bitran, G. R. and Mondschein, S. V. (1995). An application of yield management to the hotel industry considering multiple days stays. *Operations Research*, 43 (3), 427–43.

Blank, D. (2002). Extended-stay segment struggles to achieve ideal yield management. *Hotel and Motel Management*, 217 (10), 52–55.

Box, G. and Jenkins, G. (1970). *Time series analysis: Forecasting and control*. San Francisco: Holden Day.

Bramwell, B. (1998). User satisfaction and product development in urban tourism. *Tourism Management*, 19 (1), 35–47.

Braun, B. M. and Soskin, M. (1999). Theme park competitive strategies. *Annals of Tourism Research*, 26 (2), 438–42.

Braun, B. M., Soskin, M. and Cernicky, M. (1992). Central Florida theme park pricing: Following the Mouse. *Annals of Tourism Research*, 19, 131–36.

Buhalis, D. (1998). Strategic use of information technologies in the tourism industry. *Tourism Management*, 19 (5), 409–21.

Buhalis, D. (2000). Relationships in the distribution channel of tourism: Conflicts between hoteliers and tour operators in the Mediterranean region. *International Journal of Hospitality and Tourism Administration*, 1 (1), 113–39.

Buhalis, D. (2001). Tourism distribution channels: Practices and processes. In D. Buhalis and E. Laws (eds.), *Tourism distribution channels: Practices, issues and transformations*. London: Continuum International Publishing Group.

Buhalis, D. (2003). *eTourism: Information technology for strategic tourism management*. London: Pearson (Financial Times/Prentice-Hall).

Buhalis, D. and Law, R. (2008). Progress in information technology and tourism management: 20 years on and 10 years after the Internet – The state of eTourism research. *Tourism Management*, 29 (4), 609–23.

Buhalis, D. and Laws, E. (eds.) (2001). *Tourism distribution channels: Practices, issues and transformations*. London: Continuum International Publishing Group.

Buhalis, D. and Main, H. (1998). Information technology in peripheral small and medium hospitality enterprises: Strategic analysis and critical factors. *International Journal of Contemporary Hospitality Management*, 10 (5), 198–202.

Buhalis, D. and O'Connor, P. (2005). Information communication technology revolutionizing tourism. *Tourism Recreation Research*, 30 (3), 7–16.

Caccomo, J.-L. and Solonandrasana, B. (2001). Tourism activities and price differences: Imperfect information and asymmetric competition. The 28th Annual Conference of the European Association for Research in Industrial Economics, August 30-September 2, 2001, Dublin, Ireland.

Cachon, G. and Netessine, S. (2004). Game theory in supply chain analysis. In D. Simchi-Levi, S. D. Wu and M. Shen (eds.), *Supply chain analysis in the e-business era*. Boston: Kluwer Academic Publishers.

Campo, S. and Yagüe, M. J. (2009). Exploring non-linear effects of determinants on tourists' satisfaction. *International Journal of Culture, Tourism and Hospitality Research*, 3 (2), 127–38.

Candela, G. and Cellini, R. (2006). Investment in tourism market: A dynamic model of differentiated oligopoly. *Environmental and Resource Economics*, 35, 41–58.

Carey, S., Gountas, Y. and Gilbert, D. (1997). Tour operators and destination sustainability. *Tourism Management*, 18 (7), 425–31.

Chadee, D. and Mattsson, J. (1996). An empirical assessment of customer satisfaction in tourism. *Service Industries Journal*, 16 (3), 305–20.

Chen, F. R. (2003). Information sharing and supply chain coordination. In A. G. de Kok and S. C. Graves (eds.), *Handbooks in operations research and management science* (Vol. 11, pp. 341–421). Amsterdam: Elsevier.

Chen, F., Federgruen, A. and Zheng, Y. (2001). Coordination mechanisms for a distribution system with one supplier and multiple retailers. *Management Science*, 47 (5), 693–708.

Chen, I. J. and Paulraj, A. (2004). Understanding supply chain management: Critical research and a theoretical framework. *International Journal of Production Research*, 42 (1), 131–63.

Christopher, M. (1992). *Logistics and supply chain management*. London: Pitman.

Chung, K. Y. (2000). Hotel room rate pricing strategy for market share in oligopolistic competition: Eight-year longitudinal study of super deluxe hotels in Seoul. *Tourism Management*, 21 (2), 135–45.

Clark, T. H., Croson, D. C. and Schiano, W. T. (2001). A hierarchical model of supply-chain integration: Information sharing and operational interdependence in the US grocery channel. *Information Technology and Management*, 2 (3), 261–88.

Clemmer, E. C. and Schneider, B. (1989). Toward understanding and controlling customer dissatisfaction with waiting during peak demand times. In M. J. Bitner and L. A. Crosby (eds.), *Designing a winning service strategy* (pp. 87–91). Chicago: American Marketing Association.

Cobanoglu, C., Corbaci, K., Moreo, P. J. and Ekinci, K. (2003). A comparative study of the importance of hotel selection components by Turkish business travelers. *International Journal of Hospitality and Tourism Administration*, 4 (1), 1–22.

Collier, D. A. (1982). Aggregate safety stock levels and component part commonality. *Management Science*, 28 (11), 1296–1303.

Connolly, D., Olsen, M. and Moore, R. (1998). The Internet as a distribution channel. *Cornell Hotel and Restaurant Administration Quarterly*, 39 (4), 42–54.

Constantelou, A. (2002). Emerging trends in customer relation management using ICT: The travel industry, STAR Issue Report, No. 22. Athens, Greece: National Technical University of Athens.

Cooper, M. C., Lambert, D. M. and Pagh, J. D. (1997). Supply chain management: More than a new name for logistics. *International Journal of Logistics Management*, 8, 1–13.

Corbett, C. and de Groote, X. (2000). A supplier's optimal quantity discount policy under asymmetric information. *Management Science*, 46 (3), 444–50.

Cosh, K. (2010). The introduction of ITC's into the tourism industry. Retrieved February 1, 2011, from http://cis.payap.ac.th/wp-content/uploads/2010/06/The-Introduction-of-ICTs-into-the-Tourism-Industry-Dr.-Ken-Cosh.pdf.

Cox, A. (1997). *Business success*. Midsomer Norton: Earlsgate.

Cross, R. G. (1997). *Revenue management: Hard-core tactics for market domination*. New York: Broadway Books.

Curtin, S. and Busby, G. (1999). Sustainable destination development: The tour operator perspective. *International Journal of Tourism Research*, 1 (2), 135–47.

Davidson, J., Hendry, D. F., Saba, F. and Yeo, S. (1978). Econometric modelling of the aggregate time series relationships between consumer's expenditure and income in the United Kingdom. *Economic Journal*, 88, 661–92.

Davis, S. M. (1987). *Future perfect*. Reading, MA: Addison-Wesley.

Day, G. S. and Van den Bulte, C. (2002), Superiority in customer relationship management: Consequences for competitive advantage and performance. Unpublished manuscript, The Wharton School, Philadelphia, PA.

Day, G. S. and Wensley, R. (1988). Assessing advantage: A framework for diagnosing competitive superiority. *Journal of Marketing*, 52, 1–19.

De Mello, M. M. and Nell, K. S. (2005). The forecasting ability of a cointegrated VAR system of the UK tourism demand for France, Spain and Portugal. *Empirical Economics*, 30, 277–308.

Deaton, A. and Muellbauer, J. (1980). An almost ideal demand system. *American Economic Review*, 70, 312–26.

Doganis, R. (2002). *Flying off course – The economics of international airlines*. London: Routledge.

Donaghy, K., McMahon, U. and McDowell, D. (1995). Yield management: An overview. *International Journal of Hospitality Management*, 14 (2), 139–50.

Dorfman, P. W. (1979). Measurement and meaning of recreation satisfaction: A case study in camping. *Environment and Behavior*, 11, 483–510.

Duffy, R. and Fearne, A. (2004). Partnerships and alliances in UK supermarket supply networks. In M. A. Bourlakis and P. W. Weightman (eds.), *Food supply chain management*. Oxford: Blackwell.

Duliba, K. A., Kauffman, R. J. and Lucas, H. C. (2001). Appropriating value from computerized reservation system ownership in the airline industry. *Organization Science*, 12 (6), 702–28.

Eadington, W. R. and Redman, M. (1991). Economics and tourism. *Annals of Tourism Research*, 18, 41–56.

Ellram, L. M., LaLonde, B. J. and Weber, M. M. (1989). Retail logistics. *International Journal of Distribution and Materials Management*, 19 (12), 29–39.

Emmer, R. M., Tauck, C., Wilkinson, S. and Moore, R. G. (1993). Marketing hotels using global distribution systems. *Cornell Hotel and Restaurant Administration Quarterly*, 34 (6), 80–89.

Engle, R. F. and Granger, C. W. J. (1987). Co-integration and error correction: Representation, estimation, and testing. *Econometrica*, 55, 251–76.

European Commission (2002). ICT and e-Business in the tourism sector, The European e-Business Market Watch, Sector Report, No. 13.

Farmer, D. (1997). Purchasing myopia – Revisited. *European Journal of Purchasing and Supply Management*, 3 (1), 1–8.

Fearne, A. (2000). Building effective partnerships in the meat supply chain: Lessons from the UK. *Canadian Journal of Agricultural Economics*, 46 (4), 491–518.

Fernie, J. (1995). International comparisons of supply chain management in grocery retailing. *The Service Industries Journal*, 15 (4), 134–47.

Fisher, M. L. (1997). What is the right supply chain for your product? *Harvard Business Review*, 75, 105–16.

Forrester, J. W. (1961). *Industrial dynamics*. Cambridge, MA: Massachusetts Institute of Technology Press.

Frechtling, D. C. (2001). *Forecasting tourism demand: Methods and strategies*. Oxford: Butterworth-Heinemann.

Frew, A. J. (2000). Information and communications technology research in the travel and tourism domain: Perspective and direction. *Journal of Travel Research*, 39 (2), 136–45.

Fuchs, M. and Weiermair, K. (2003). New perspectives of satisfaction research in tourism destinations. *Tourism Review*. Retrieved from October 24, 2008, from http://www. etourism-austria.at/portal/destinometer/documents/new_perspectives.pdf.

Fujii, E. T., Khaled, M. and Mak, J. (1985). An almost ideal demand system for visitor expenditures. *Journal of Transport Economics and Policy*, 19, 161–71.

Ganeshan, R., Jack, E., Magazine, M. J. and Stephens, P. (1999). A taxonomic review of supply chain management research. In S. Tayur, R. Ganeshan and M. Magazine (eds.), *Quantitative models for supply chain management* (pp. 840–79). Boston: Kluwer Academic Publishers.

García, D. and Tugores, M. (2006). Optimal choice of quality in hotel services. *Annals of Tourism Research*, 33 (2), 456–69.

García-Falcón, J. M., and Medina-Muñoz, D. (1999). The relationship between hotel companies and travel agencies: An empirical assessment of the United States market. *Service Industries Journal*, 19 (4), 102–22.

Gee, C. Y., Boberg, K. B., Choy, D. J. L. and Markens, J. C. (1990). *Professional travel agency management*. London: Prentice Hall.

Gerchak, Y. and Henig, M. (1989). Component commonality in assemble-to-order systems: Models and properties. *Naval Research Logistics*, 36, 61–68.

Gimenez, C. and Ventura, E. (2003). Supply chain management as a competitive advantage in the Spanish grocery sector. *International Journal of Logistics Management*, 14 (1), 77–88.

Go, F. M. and Williams, A. P. (1993). Competing and cooperating in the changing tourism channel system. *Journal of Travel and Tourism Marketing*, 2 (2–3), 229–48.

Goh, C. and Law, R. (2002). Modeling and forecasting tourism demand for arrivals with stochastic nonstationary seasonality and intervention. *Tourism Management*, 23, 499–510.

Gomez, V. B. and Sinclair, M. T. (1991). Integration in the tourism industry: A case study approach. In M. T. Sinclair and M. J. Stabler (eds.), *The tourism industry: An international analysis* (pp. 67–90). Wallingford, UK: CAB International.

Goodwin, P. and Wright, G. (1994). Heuristics, biases and improvement strategies in judgmental time-series forecasting. *Omega-International Journal of Management Science*, 22 (6), 553–68.

Greenberg, P. (2001). *CRM at the speed of light: Capturing and keeping customers in Internet real time*. Emeryville, CA: McGraw-Hill.

Hadjinicola, G. C. and Panayi, C. (1997). The overbooking problem in hotels with multiple tour-operators. *International Journal of Operations and Production Management*, 17 (9), 874–85.

Hakansson, H. and Snehota, I. (1995). *Developing relationships in business networks*. London: Routledge.

Han, D., Kwon, I.-W. G., Bae, M. and Sung, H. (2002). Supply chain integration in developing countries for foreign retailers in Korea: Wal-Mart experience. *Computers and Industrial Engineering*, 43 (1–2), 111–21.

Han, Q., Dellaert, B. G. C., Van Raaij, W. F. and Timmermans, H. J. P. (2004). Supporting tourist activity planning decisions from an urban tourism management perspective. *Tourism Analysis*, 8, 153–57.

Hanks, R. D., Cross, R. G. and Noland, R. P. (1992). Discounting in the hotel industry: A new approach. *Cornell Hotel and Restaurant Administration Quarterly*, 33 (2), 40–45.

Harland, C. M., Lamming, R. C. and Cousins, P. D. (1999). Developing the concept of supply strategy. *International Journal of Operations and Production Management*, 19, 650–73.

Helper, S. R. (1991). How much has really changed between US automakers and their suppliers. *Sloan Management Review*, 3, 15–28.

Hendry, D. F. (1986). Empirical modeling in dynamic econometrics. *Applied Mathematics and Computation*, 20, 201–36.

Hill, C. A. and Scudder, G. D. (2002). The use of electronic data interchange for supply chain coordination in the food industry. *Journal of Operations Management*, 20, 375–87.

Hines, P. (1994). *Creating world class suppliers: Unlocking mutual competitive advantage.* London: Pitman.

Hogendorn, C. (2005). Tacit collusion in capacity investment: The role of capacity exchange. Working paper. Department of Economics, Wesleyan University.

Holder, J. S. (1991). Tourism, the world and the Caribbean. *Tourism Management*, 12 (4), 291–300.

Hornibrook, S. A. and Fearne, A. (2002). Vertical co-ordination as risk management strategy – A case study of a retail chain in the UK beef industry. *Journal of Farm Management*, 11 (6), 194–207.

Houlihan, J. B. (1985). International supply chain management. *International Journal of Physical Distribution and Materials Management*, 15, 22–38.

Huang, G. Q., Zhang, X. Y. and Liang, L. (2005). Towards integrated optimal configuration of platform products, manufacturing processes, and supply chains. *Journal of Operations Management*, 23, 267–90.

Hugos, M. and Thomas, C. (2006). *Supply chain management in the retail industry.* Hoboken, NJ: John Wiley & Sons.

Humphreys, B. K. (1994). *Yield management: Applications to air transport and other service industries.* Paris: Institut du Transport Aérien.

Jagels, M. and Coltman, M. (2004). *Hospitality management accounting.* Hoboken, NJ: John Wiley & Sons.

James, A. T. and Dale, H. (2004). *The supply chain handbook.* Orlando, FL: Tompkins Press.

Jeuland, A. P. and Shugan, S. M. (1983). Managing channel profits. *Marketing Science*, 2, 239–72.

Jespersen, B. D. and Skjøtt-Larsen, T. (2005). *Supply chain management in theory and practice.* Copenhagen: Copenhagen Business School Press.

Jobber, D. (2001). *Principles and practices of marketing.* New York: McGraw-Hill.

Kalman, R. E. (1960). A new approach to linear filtering and prediction problem. *Transaction ASME Journal of Basic Engineering*, 17, 17–24.

Kämäräinen, V. and Punakivi, M. (2002). Developing cost-effective operations for the e-grocery supply chain. *International Journal of Logistics: Research and Applications*, 5 (3), 285–98.

Karamustafa, K. (2000). Marketing-channel relationships: Turkey's resort purveyors' interactions with international tour operators. *Cornell Hotel and Restaurant Administration Quarterly*, 41 (4), 21–31.

Karoway, C. (1997). Superior supply chains pack plenty of byte. *Purchasing Technology*, 8, 32–35.

Kaukal, M., Höpken, W. and Werthner, H. (2000). An approach to enable interoperability in electronic tourism markets. *Proceedings of the 8th European Conference on Information System* (ECIS 2000), 1104–11.

Kaynak, E. and Macaulay, J. (1984). The Delphi technique in the measurement of tourism marketing potential: The case of Nova Scotia. *Tourism Management*, 5 (2), 87–101.

Kimes, S. E. (1989). Yield management: A tool for capacity-constrained service firms. *Journal of Operations Management*, 8 (4), 348–63.

Kimes, S. E. (2000). A strategic approach to yield management. In A. Ingold, U. McMahon-Beattie and I. Yeoman (eds.), *Yield management: Strategies for the service industries* (2nd Ed., pp. 3–14). London: Continuum.

Kimes, S. E. (2001). Revenue management on the links. *Cornell Hotel and Restaurant Administration Quarterly*, 41 (1), 120–27.

Klein, S. (2002). Web impact on the distribution structure for flight tickets. In K. W. Wöber, A. J. Frew and M. Hitz (eds.), *Information and communication technologies in tourism 2002* (pp. 219–28). New York: Springer.

Klemm, M. and Parkinson, L. (2001). UK tour operator strategies: Causes and consequences. *International Journal of Tourism Research*, 3 (5), 367–75.

Kon, S. C. and Turner, W. L. (2005). Neural network forecasting of tourism demand. *Tourism Economics*, 11 (3), 301–28.

Koss-Feder, L. (1994). Yield management software needs to be refined. *Hotel and Motel Management*, 209 (11), 30–35.

Kozak, M. (2001a). Comparative assessment of tourist satisfaction with destinations across two nationalities. *Tourism Management*, 22 (4), 391–401.

Kozak, M. (2001b). Repeaters' behaviour at two distinct destinations. *Annals of Tourism Research*, 28 (3), 784–807.

Krishnan, V. and Gupta, S. (2001). Appropriateness and impact of platform-based product development. *Management Science*, 47 (1), 52–68.

La Londe, B. J., Cooper, M. C. and Noordewier, T. G. (1988). *Customer service: A management perspective*. Chicago: Council of Logistics Management.

Lafferty, G. and Fossen, A. V. (2001). Integrating the tourism industry: Problems and strategies. *Tourism Management*, 22 (1), 11–19.

Lambert, C. U., Lambert, J. M. and Cullen, T. P. (1989). The overbooking question: A simulation. *Cornell Hotel and Restaurant Administration Quarterly*, 29, 15–20.

Lambert, D., Stock, J. and Ellram, L. (1998). *Fundamentals of logistics management*. Boston: Irwin/McGraw-Hill.

Law, R. and Au, N. (1999). A neural network model to forecast Japanese demand for travel to Hong Kong. *Tourism Management*, 20, 89–97.

Lawrence, M., Goodwin, P., O'Connor, M. and Onkal, D. (2006). Judgmental forecasting: A review of progress over the last 25 years. *International Journal of Forecasting*, 22 (3), 493–518.

Laws, E. (2000). Perspectives on pricing decision in the inclusive holiday industry. In A. Ingold, U. McMahon-Beattie and I. Yeoman (eds.), *Yield management: Strategies for the service industries* (2nd Ed., pp. 69–83). London: Continuum.

LeBlanc, G. (1992). Factors affecting customer evaluation of service quality in travel agencies: An investigation of customer perceptions. *Journal of Travel Research*, 30 (4), 10–16.

Lee, H., Padmanabhan, V. and Whang, S. (1997). Information distortion in a supply chain: The bullwhip effect. *Management Science*, 43 (4), 546–58.

Leenders, M. R., Fearson, H. E., Flynn, A. E. and Johnson, P. F. (2002). *Purchasing and supply management*. New York: McGraw-Hill/Irwin.

Li, G., Song, H. and Witt, S. F. (2004). Modelling tourism demand: A dynamic linear AIDS approach. *Journal of Travel Research*, 42, 141–50.

Li, G., Song, H. and Witt, S. F. (2005a). Time varying parameter and fixed parameter linear AIDS: An application to tourism demand. *International Journal of Forecasting*, 21 (1), 27–71.

Li, G., Song, H. and Witt, S. F. (2005b). Recent developments in economic modelling and forecasting. *Journal of Travel Research*, 44, 82–99.

Li, G., Wong, K. F., Song, H. and Witt, S. F. (2006). Time varying parameter ECM model for tourism forecasting. *Journal of Travel Research*, 45 (3), 175–85.

Li, L. (2007). *Supply chain management: Concepts, techniques and practices enhancing value through collaboration*. Singapore: World Scientific.

Liang, H., Corbitt, B. and Peszynski, K. (2009). Impact of logistics service performance through IT on overall tourist satisfaction and loyalty. Retrieved from http://is2.lse.ac.uk/asp/aspecis/20080191.pdf.

Liberman, V. and Yechiali, U. (1978). On the hotel overbooking problem – An inventory system with stochastic cancellations. *Management Science*, 24 (11), 1117–26.

Lieberman, W. H. (1993). Debunking the myths of yield management. *Cornell Hotel and Restaurant Administration Quarterly*, 34 (1), 34–41.

Lovelock, H. C. (1980). Why marketing management needs to be different for services. In J. H. Donnelly and W. R. George (eds.), *Marketing of services* (pp. 5–9). Chicago: American Marketing Association.

Lovelock, H. C. (1983). Classifying services to gain strategic marketing insights. *Journal of Marketing*, 47 (2), 9–20.

Lu, J. and Lu, Z. (2004). Development, distribution and evaluation of online tourism services in China. *Electronic Commerce Research*, 4 (3), 221–39.

Ma, J. X., Buhalis, D. and Song, H. (2003). ICTs and Internet adoption in China's tourism industry. *International Journal of Information Management*, 23 (6), 451–67.

Malone, T. W. (1987). Modeling coordination in organizations and markets. *Management Science*, 33 (10), 1317–32.

March, R. (1997). An exploratory study of buyer-supplier relationships in international tourism: The case of Japanese wholesales and Australian suppliers. *Journal of Travel and Tourism Marketing*, 6 (1), 55–68.

March, R. (2000). Buyer decision-making behavior in international tourism channels. *International Journal of Hospitality and Tourism Administration*, 1 (1), 11–25.

Mazzeo, M. (2002). Product choice and oligopoly market structure. *Rand Journal of Economics*, 33, 221–42.

McDaniel, C. D., Lamb, C. W. and Hair, J. F. (2006). *Introduction to marketing*. Mason, OH: Thomson South-Western.

Medina-Muñoz, D. and García-Falcón, J. M. (2000). Successful relationships between hotels and agencies. *Annals of Tourism Research*, 27 (3), 737–62.

Medina-Muñoz, D. R., García-Falcón, J. M. and Medina-Muñoz, R. D. (2002). Building the valuable connection: Hotels and travel agents. *Cornell Hotel and Restaurant Administration Quarterly*, 43 (3), 46–52.

Medina-Muñoz, R. D., Medina-Muñoz, D. R. and García-Falcón, J. M. (2003). Understanding European tour operators' control on accommodation companies: An empirical evidence. *Tourism Management*, 24 (2), 135–47.

Medlik, S. and Middleton, V. T. C. (1973). Product formulation in tourism. *Tourism and Marketing*, 13.

Mentzer, J. T. (2004). *Fundamentals of supply chain management*. Thousand Oaks, CA: Sage Publications.

Mentzer, J. T. and Williams, L. R. (2001). The role of logistic leverage in marketing strategy. *Journal of Marketing Channels*, 8 (3/4), 29–47.

Middleton, V. T. C. and Clarke, J. (2001). *Marketing in travel and tourism*. Oxford: Elsevier.

Min, H. and Zhou, G. (2002). Supply chain modeling: Past, present and future. *Computers and Industrial Engineering*, 43, 231–49.

Monczka, R. M., Ragartz, G. L. and Handfield, R. B. (1997). Supplier integration into new product development: Preliminary results. *Advances in the Management of Organizational Quality*, 2, 87–138.

Morgan, J. and Monczka, R. M. (1996). Supplier integration: A new level of supply chain management. *Purchasing*, 120, 110–13.

Narus, J. A. and Anderson, J. C. (1995). Using teams to manage collaborative relationships in business markets. *Journal of Business-to-Business Marketing*, 2, 17–47.

Nash, J. F. (1950). The bargaining problem. *Econometrica*, 18, 155–62.

Nykamp, M. and McEachern, C. (1999). The CRM business cycle. *DM Review Magazine*, November 1999.

O'Connor, P. (1999). *Electronic information distribution in tourism and hospitality*. Wallingford, UK: CAB International.

O'Connor, P. and Murphy, J. (2004). Research on information technology in the hospitality industry. *International Journal of Hospitality Management*, 23 (5), 473–84.

O'Connor, P., Buhalis, D. and Frew, A. J. (2001). The transformation of tourism distribution channels through information technology. In D. Buhalis and E. Laws (eds.), *Tourism distribution channels: Practices, issues and transformations* (pp. 332–50). London: Continuum International Publishing Group.

Owen, G. (1995). *Game theory*. London: Academic Press.

Özgener, Ş. and İraz, R. (2006). Customer relationship management in small-medium enterprises: The case of Turkish tourism industry. *Tourism Management*, 27 (6), 1356–63.

Page, S. J. (2003). *Tourism management: Managing for change*. Oxford: Butterworth-Heinemann.

Page, S. J. (2006). *Tourism management: Managing for change* (2nd Ed.). Oxford: Butterworth-Heinemann.

Pan, S., Chon, K. and Song, H. (2008). Visualizing tourism trends: A combination of ATLAS.ti and BiPlot. *Journal of Travel Research*, 46, 339–48.

Parasuraman, A., Zeithaml, V. A. and Berry, L. L. (1988). SERVQUAL: A multiple-item scale for measuring consumer perceptions of service quality. *Journal of Retailing*, 64 (1), 12–40.

Parlar, M. and Wang, Q. (1994). Discounting decisions in a supplier–buyer relationship with a linear buyer's demand. *IIE Transactions*, 26 (2), 34–41.

Pearce, D. G. (2007). Supplier selection in the New Zealand inbound tourism industry. *Journal of Travel and Tourism Marketing*, 23 (1), 57–69.

Pearce, D. G. and Schott, C. (2005). Tourism distribution channels: The visitors' perspective. *Journal of Travel Research*, 44, 50–63.

Pearce, D. G. and Tan, R. (2004). Distribution channels for heritage and culture tourism in New Zealand. *Asia Pacific Journal of Tourism Research*, 9 (3), 225–37.

Pearce, D. G., Tan, R. and Schott, C. (2007). Distribution channels in international markets: A comparative analysis of the distribution of New Zealand tourism in Australia, Great Britain and the USA. *Current Issues in Tourism*, 10 (1), 33–60.

Petersen, K. J., Handfield, R. B. and Ragatz, G. L. (2005). Supplier integration into new product development: Coordinating product, process and supply chain design. *Journal of Operations Management*, 23 (3–4), 371–88.

Piga, C. A. G. (1999). Pigouvian taxation and sustainable development in tourism. Working paper 99/1, Christel DeHaan Tourism and Travel Research Institute, Nottingham University Business School.

Piga, C. A. G. (2003a). Pigouvian taxation in tourism. *Environmental and Resource Economics*, 26, 343–59.

Piga, C. A. G. (2003b). Territorial planning and tourism development tax. *Annals of Tourism Research*, 30 (4), 886–905.

Pizam, A. and Milman, A. (1993). Predicting satisfaction among first time visitors to a destination by using the expectancy disconfirmation theory. *International Journal of Hospitality Management*, 12 (2), 197–209.

Porter, M. (1980). *Competitive strategy: Techniques for analyzing industries and competitors*. New York: Free Press.

Porter, M. E. (1985). *Competitive advantage: Creating and sustaining superior performance*. New York: Free Press.

Porter, M. E. (1998). *On competition*. Boston: Harvard Business School.

Porter, M. E. and Millar, V. (1985). How information gives you competitive advantage. *Harvard Business Review*, 63 (4), 149–60.

Prater, E., Frazier, G. V. and Reyes, P. M. (2005). Future impacts of RFID on e-supply chains in grocery retailing. *Supply Chain Management: An International Journal*, 10 (2), 134–42.

Prideaux, B. (2001). Airline distribution systems: The challenge and opportunity of the Internet. In D. Buhalis and E. Laws (eds.), *Tourism distribution channels: Practices, issues and transformations* (pp. 213–30). London: Continuum International Publishing Group.

Radstaak, B. G. and Ketelaar, M. H. (1998). *Worldwide logistics: The future of supply chain services*. The Hague: Holland International Distribution Council.

Ragatz, G. L., Handfield, R. B. and Petersen, K. (2002). Benefits associated with supplier integration into new product development under conditions of technology uncertainty. *Journal of Business Research*, 55 (5), 389–400.

Ragatz, G. L., Handfield, R. B. and Scannell, T. V. (1997). Success factors for integrating suppliers into new product development. *Journal of Production Innovation Management*, 14, 190–202.

Reisinger, Y. and Turner, L. W. (2002). The determination of shopping satisfaction of Japanese tourists visiting Hawaii and the Gold Coast compared. *Journal of Travel Research*, 41, 167–76.

Robertson, D. and Ulrich, K. (1998). Planning for product platforms. *MIT Sloan Management Review*, 39 (4), 19–31.

Ross, D. F. (2004). *Distribution: Planning and control: Managing in the era of supply chain management*. Boston: Kluwer Academic Publishers.

Rothstein, M. (1971). An airline overbooking model. *Transportation Science*, 5 (2), 180–92.

Rothstein, M. (1974). Hotel overbooking as a Markovian sequential decision process. *Decision Sciences*, 5, 389–404.

Rothstein, M. (1985). OR and the airline overbooking problem. *Operations Research*, 33 (2), 237–48.

Rowe, G. and Wright, G. (1999). The Delphi technique as a forecasting tool: Issues and analysis. *International Journal of Forecasting*, 15, 351–81.

Rowe, G. and Wright, G. (2001). Expert opinions in forecasting: The role of the Delphi technique. In J. S. Armstrong (ed.), *Principles of forecasting: A handbook for researchers and practitioners*. Boston: Kluwer Academic.

Rungtusanatham, M. J. and Forza, C. (2005). Special issue on 'Coordinating product design, process design, and supply chain design decisions'. *Journal of Operations Management*, 23 (3–4), 257–65.

Saleh, F. and Ryan, C. (1992). Client perceptions of hotels: A multi-attribute approach. *Tourism Management*, 13 (2), 163–68.

Scavarda, A. J., Lustosa, L. J. and Scavarda, L. F. (2001). The tourism industry chain. Proceedings of the Twelfth Annual Conference of the Operations Management Society (POM 2001), March 30–April 2, 2001, Orlando, FL.

Schwartz, N. and Zea, M. (1999). Surfing for value. *Airline Business*, July, 68–70.

Sheldon, P. (1994). Information technology and computer systems. In S. Witt and L. Moutinho (eds.), *Tourism marketing and management handbook* (2nd Ed., pp. 126–30). London: Prentice Hall.

Sheldon, P. J. (1997). *Tourism information technology*. Oxford: CAB International.

Shin, H. and Benton, W. C. (2007). A quantity discount approach to supply chain coordination. *European Journal of Operational Research*, 180, 601–16.

Shlifer, E. and Vardi, Y. (1975). An airline overbooking policy. *Transportation Science*, 9 (2), 101–14.

Simchi-Levi, D., Kaminsky, P. and Simchi-Levi, E. (2003). *Designing and managing the supply chain*. Boston: Irwin McGraw-Hill.

Sims, C. A. (1980). Macroeconomics and reality. *Econometrica*, 48, 1–48.

Sinclair, M. T. and Stabler, M. (1997). *The economics of tourism*. London: Routledge.

Småros, J. (2007). Forecasting collaboration in the European grocery sector: Observations from a case study. *Journal of Operations Management*, 25 (3), 702–16.

Smeral, E. and Wüger, M. (2005). Does complexity matter? Methods for improving forecasting accuracy in tourism: The case of Australia. *Journal of Travel Research*, 44, 100–110.

Smith, B. C., Leimkuhler, J. F. and Darrow, R. M. (1992). Yield management at American airlines. *Interfaces*, 22 (1), 8–31.

Smith, S. L. J. (1994). The tourism product. *Annals of Tourism Research*, 21 (3), 582–95.

Smith, S. L. J. and Xiao, H. (2008). Culinary tourism supply chains: A preliminary examination. *Journal of Travel Research*, 46, 289–99.

Song, H. and Li, G. (2008). Tourism demand modelling and forecasting – A review of recent research. *Tourism Management*, 29 (2), 203–20.

Song, H. and Turner, L. (2006). Tourism demand forecasting. In L. Dwyer and P. Forsyth (eds.), *International handbook on the economics of tourism*. Cheltenham, UK: Edward Elgar.

Song, H. and Witt, S. F. (2003). General-to-specific modelling to international tourism demand forecasting. *Journal of Travel Research*, 42 (1), 65–74.

Song, H. and Witt, S. F. (2006). Forecasting tourist flows to Macau. *Tourism Management*, 27 (2), 214–24.

Song, H., Li, G. and Witt, S. F. (2009). Forecasting tourism demand using time-varying parameter structural time-series models. 29th International Symposium on Forecasting, July 21–24, 2009, Hong Kong.

Song, H., Witt, S. F. and Jensen, T. C. (2003). Tourism forecasting: Accuracy of alternative econometric models. *International Journal of Forecasting*, 19, 123–41.

Song, H., Witt, S. F. and Li, G. (2003). Modelling and forecasting demand for Thai tourism. *Tourism Economics*, 9 (4), 363–87.

Song, H., Witt, S. F. and Li, G. (2009). *The advanced econometrics of tourism demand*. London: Routledge.

Song, H., Yang, Y. and Huang, G. (2009). Price interaction between theme park and tour operator. *Tourism Economics*, 15 (4), 813–24.

Song, H., Zhang, X. and Witt, S. F. (2008). Collaborative forecasting for tourism supply chain via the Internet. Paper presented at the 18th International Symposium on Forecasting, June 22–25, 2008, Nice, France.

Sterman, J. D. (1989). Modeling managerial behavior: Misperceptions of feedback in a dynamic decision making experiment. *Management Science*, 35 (3), 321–39.

Stockdale, R. (2007). Managing customer relationships in the self-service environment of e-tourism. *Journal of Vacation Marketing*, 13 (3), 205–19.

Stuart, P., Pearce, D. and Weaver, A. (2005). Tourism distribution channels in peripheral regions: The case of Southland, New Zealand. *Tourism Geographies*, 7 (3), 235–56.

Tan, K. C. (2001). A framework of supply chain management literature. *European Journal of Purchasing and Supply Management*, 7, 39–48.

Tapper, R. and Font, X. (2004). *Tourism supply chains: Report of a desk research project for the travel foundation*. Retrieved September 11, 2006, from Leeds Metropolitan University, Environment Business and Development Group, http://www.lmu.ac.uk/lsif/the/Tourism-Supply-Chains.pdf.

Taylor, P. (1996). Oligopoly or contestable markets in the UK package tour industry? *Service Industry Journal*, 16 (3), 379–88.

Taylor, P. (1998). Mixed strategy pricing behaviour in the UK package tour industry. *International Journal of the Economics of Business*, 5 (1), 29–46.

Tepelus, C. M. (2005). Aiming for sustainability in the tour operating business. *Journal of Cleaner Production*, 13, 99–107.

Theuvsen, L. (2004). Vertical integration in the European package tour business. *Annals of Tourism Research*, 31 (2), 475–78.

Thorelli, H. (1986). Networks: Between markets and hierarchies. *Strategic Management Journal*, 7, 37–51.

Tian-Cole, S. and Crompton, J. L. (2003). A conceptualization of the relationships between service quality and visitor satisfaction, and their links to destination selection. *Leisure Studies*, 22 (1), 65–80.

Tsaur, S.-H., Yung, C.-Y. and Lin, J.-H. (2006). The relational behavior between wholesaler and retailer travel agencies: Evidence from Taiwan. *Journal of Hospitality and Tourism Research*, 30 (3), 333–53.

Tse, A. C.-B. (2003). Disintermediation of travel agents in the hotel industry. *International Journal of Hospitality Management*, 22 (4), 453–60.

Ujma, D. (2001). Distribution channels for tourism: Theory and issues. In D. Buhalis and E. Laws (eds.), *Tourism distribution channels: Practices, issues and transformations* (pp. 33–52). London: Continuum International Publishing Group.

UNCTAD (2001). *E-commerce and Development Report 2001*. New York and Geneva: United Nations.

UNWTO (1975). *Distribution channels*. Madrid: World Tourism Organization.

UNWTO (1994). *Global distribution systems in the tourism industry*. Madrid: World Tourism Organization.

Uysal, M. and Roubi, M. S. E. (1999). Artificial neural networks versus multiple regression in tourism demand analysis. *Journal of Travel Research*, 38, 111–18.

Vogel, H. (2006). *Travel industry economics – A guide for financial analysis*. Oxford: Oxford University Press.

Waller, M., Johnson, M. E. and Davis, T. (1999). Vendor-managed inventory in the retail supply chain. *Journal of Business Logistics*, 20 (1), 183–203.

Weatherford, L. R. and Bodily, S. E. (1992). A taxonomy and research overview of perishable asset-revenue management: Yield management, overbooking, and pricing. *Operations Research*, 40 (5), 831–44.

Webby, R. and O'Connor, M. (1996). Judgemental and statistical time series forecasting: A review of the literature. *International Journal of Forecasting*, 12 (1), 91–118.

Weng, Z. K. (1995). Channel coordination and quantity discounts. *Management Science*, 41, 1509–22.

Werthner, H. and Klein, S. (1999). *Information technology and tourism: A challenging relationship.* New York: Springer.

Wie, B.-W. (2004). Open-loop and closed-loop models of dynamic oligopoly in the cruise line industry. *Asia-Pacific Journal of Operational Research*, 21 (4), 517–41.

Wie, B.-W. (2005). A dynamic game model of strategic capacity investment in the cruise line industry. *Tourism Management*, 26 (2), 203–17.

Williams, P. W. and Richter, C. (2002). Developing and supporting European tour operator distribution channels for Canadian aboriginal tourism development. *Journal of Travel Research*, 40, 404–15.

Winters, P. R. (1960). Forecasting sales by exponentially weighted moving average. *Management Science*, 6, 324–42.

Wisner, J. D., Tan, K. C. and Leong, G. K. (2008). *Principles of supply chain management: A balanced approach.* Mason, OH: South-Western Cengage Learning.

Witt, S. F. and Witt, C. A. (1995). Forecasting tourism demand: A review of empirical research. *International Journal of Forecasting*, 11, 447–75.

Witt, S. F., Song, H. and Louvieris, P. (2003). Statistical testing in forecasting model selection. *Journal of Travel Research*, 42, 151–58.

Wong, W. Y. C., Heng, Michael S. H. and Chau, P. Y. K. (2007). *Supply chain management: Issues in the new era of collaboration and competition.* Hershey, PA: Idea Group Publishing.

Woodruff, R. B. and Gardial, S. F. (1996). *Know your customer: New approaches to understanding customer value and satisfaction.* Cambridge, MA: Blackwell Business.

Wu, C., Li, G. and Song, H. (2011). Analyzing tourist consumption: A dynamic system-of-equations approach. *Journal of Travel Research*, 50 (1), 46–56.

Wynee, C., Berthon, P., Pitt, L., Ewing, N. and Napoli, J. (2001). The impact of the internet on the distribution value chain – The case of the South African tourism industry. *International Marketing Review*, 18 (4), 420–31.

Yang, S., Huang, G. Q. and Song, H. (2009). Game-theoretic approach to competition dynamics in tourism supply chains. *Journal of Travel Research*, 47 (4), 425–39.

Yang, S., Huang, G. Q., Song, H. and Liang, L. (2008). A game-theoretic approach to choice of profit and revenue maximization strategies in tourism supply chains for package holidays. *Journal of China Tourism Research*, 4 (1), 45–60.

Yilmaz, Y. and Bititci, U. S. (2006). Performance measurement in tourism: A value chain model. *International Journal of Contemporary Hospitality Management*, 18 (4), 341–49.

Yu, L. and Goulden, M. (2006). A comparative analysis of international tourists' satisfaction in Mongolia. *Tourism Management*, 27 (6), 1331–42.

Zeithaml, V. A., Bitner, M. J. and Gremler, D. D. (2006). *Service marketing: Integrating customer focus across the firm* (4th Ed.). New York: McGraw-Hill Education.

Zeithaml, V. A., Parasuraman, A. and Berry, L. L. (1990). *Delivering quality service: Balancing customer perceptions and expectations.* London: Collier Macmillan.

Zhang, X., Song, H. and Huang, G. Q. (2009). Tourism supply chain management: A new research agenda. *Tourism Management*, 30 (3), 345–58.

INDEX